The Mobilities Paradigm

Over the last two decades, the conceptualisation and empirical analysis of mobilities of people, objects and symbols has become an important strand of social science. Yet, the increasing importance of mobilities in all parts of the social does not only happen as observable practices in the material world but also takes place against the background of changing discourses, scientific theories and conceptualisations and knowledge. Within the formation of these mobilities discourses, the social sciences constitute a relevant actor. Focussing on mobility as an object of knowledge from a Foucauldian perspective rather than a given entity within the historical contingency of movement, this book asks: How do discourses and ideologies structure the normative substance, social meanings, and the lived reality of mobilities? What are the real world effects of/on the will and the ability to be mobile? And, how do these lived realities, in turn, invigorate or interfere with certain discourses and ideologies of mobility?

Marcel Endres is a PhD Candidate at Darmstadt University of Technology, Germany.

Katharina Manderscheid is Lecturer at the University of Lucerne, Switzerland.

Christophe Mincke is Operational Head Criminology at the National Institute for Forensic Sciences and Criminology and Professor at the Saint-Louis University in Brussels, Belgium.

The Mobilities Paradigm

Discourses and ideologies

**Edited by Marcel Endres,
Katharina Manderscheid and
Christophe Mincke**

Routledge
Taylor & Francis Group

LONDON AND NEW YORK

First published 2016
by Routledge
2 Park Square, Milton Park, Abingdon, Oxon OX14 4RN

and by Routledge
711 Third Avenue, New York, NY 10017

First issued in paperback 2018

Routledge is an imprint of the Taylor & Francis Group, an informa busines

British Library Cataloguing in Publication Data
A catalogue record for this book is available from the British Library

Library of Congress Cataloging-in-Publication Data
Names: Endres, Marcel, author. | Manderscheid, Katharina, author. |
    Mincke, Christophe, author.
Title: The mobilities paradigm: discourses and ideologies / by Marcel
    Endres, Katharina Manderscheid and Christophe Mincke. Other titles:
    Transport and society.
Description: Burlington, VT: Ashgate, [2016] | Series: Transport and
    society | Includes bibliographical references and index.
Identifiers: LCCN 2015033033 | ISBN 9781472429346 (hardback: alk. paper)
Subjects: LCSH: Transportation–Social aspects. | Population geography. |
    Communication–Social aspects.
Classification: LCC HE151 .E53 2016 | DDC 303.48/32–dc23
LC record available at http://lccn.loc.gov/2015033033

ISBN 13: 978-1-138-54672-1 (pbk)
ISBN 13: 978-1-4722-2934-6 (hbk)

Typeset in Times New Roman
by Apex CoVantage, LLC

for John

Contents

Notes on contributors

Ander Audikana is Research Fellow at the Urban Sociology Laboratory (LaSUR), Ecole Polytechnique Fédérale de Lausanne, and Research Associate at the Institute of European Studies, University of Deusto. Ander received a PhD in Sociology from Paris-Est University with a dissertation on the politics of high-speed rail in Spain. He was a Fulbright-Schuman scholar at George Mason University and University of California, Berkeley. He holds a master's in City and Regional Planning from University Paris 12 and Sociology degrees both from École normale supérieure de Paris and University of Deusto.

Camelia Beciu is Professor at the University of Bucharest, Faculty of Journalism and Communication Studies, and a researcher at the Institute of Sociology of the Romanian Academy. Her areas of interest are the media construction of public issues, media discourse and the public sphere, identity and discourse on Europe. She currently leads a research programme on the media construction of diasporic identities within the Communication, Discourse, Public Issues laboratory (CODIPO). She has authored several books, including most recently *A Sociology of Communication and the Public Sphere* (Polirom, 2011), *Europe in Context. Identities and Discursive Practices* (Ars docendi, 2010), *Communication and Media Discourse* (Comunicare.ro, 2009).

Thomas Birtchnell is a Lecturer in Geography and Sustainable Communities at the University of Wollongong, Australia. His books include *3D Printing for Development in the Global South: The 3D4D Challenge*, co-authored with William Hoyle (Palgrave Macmillan, 2014), *Indovation: Innovation and a Global Knowledge Economy in India* (Palgrave Macmillan, 2013), *Elite Mobilities*, co-edited with Javier Caletrío (Routledge, 2014) and *Cargomobilities: Moving Materials in a Global Age*, co-edited with John Urry and Satya Savitzky (Routledge, 2015). In 2014 he was awarded the Wiley-Blackwell Publishers prize for New Research in Geography for the journal area (Royal Geographical Society with the Institute of British Geographers).

Zenhua Chen received his PhD in Public Policy at George Mason University. He is currently a Postdoctoral Research Associate at the Sol Price School of Public Policy, University of Southern California. His research interest includes economic geography, regional science, transportation planning and policy, and public finance. His recent book is *Chinese Railways in the Era of High Speed*, co-authored with Kingsley Haynes (Emerald, 2015).

Marcel Endres holds an MA in Sociology, Geography and Cultural Anthropology. He is a PhD candidate and Coordinating Assistant in the graduate programme Topology of Technology at Technische Universität Darmstadt, His doctoral thesis focuses on sociospatial relations of highly mobile lifestyles. His main research interests are social theories of space, sociology of technology, cultures of mobility and dwelling, life-style studies, and social phenomenology.

Birgitta Frello holds an MA in Cultural Sociology and a PhD in European Studies. She is an Associate Professor in the Cultural Encounters programme at Roskilde University, Denmark. She has published broadly on constructions of cultural identity and on representations of Otherness and various forms of transgression of cultural, racial and geographical boundaries. Recent publications include 'On Legitimate and Illegitimate Blendings. Towards an Analytics of Hybridity'. In *Researching Identity and Interculturality*, edited by Fred Dervin and Karen Risager (Routledge 2015) and 'Celebrity Witnessing: Shifting the Emotional Address in Narratives of Development Aid', with Lene Bull Christiansen (*European Journal of Cultural Studies*, forthcoming 2015).

Mirela Lazar currently works as a Professor at the University of Bucharest (Romania). Her areas of research are discourse analysis, media discourse, European journalism and diasporic identity. She has authored, among others, *The Newspaper in the Likeness of Television* (Editura Universitatii din Bucuresti, 2005), *Neo-Television and the Journalism Show* (Polirom, 2008), as well as co-authoring chapters of *Reporting and Managing European News* (Bochum/ Freiburg Projekt, 2007) and Understanding the Logic of EU Reporting from Brussels (Bochum/Freiburg Projekt, 2007), and she edited *Romania and the European Integration – Journalistic Logic and Routines* (Ars Docendi, 2008). She is a board member of the Centre for Research in Communication on Public Space, Reception and News Technologies (SPARTA–FJSC).

Laura Bang Lindegaard is an Assistant Professor in the Department of Culture and Global Studies and a core member of the Centre for Discourses in Transition (C-DiT), at Aalborg University, Denmark. She has published within the fields of the philosophy of language and critical discourse analysis and, most recently, in conversation analysis and membership categorisation analysis. Topically, her current research interests include the interactional accomplishment of the governing of climate change and the moral ordering of everyday transportation practices.

Katharina Manderscheid holds a PhD in sociology and completed her habilitation on mobilities and social inequality. She is a Senior Lecturer and Researcher at the University of Lucerne, Switzerland. Her research interests include methods and methodologies of spatial and mobilities research, subjectivities, discourse and dispositive analysis, international comparisons of mobility patterns and future trends of automobility.

Christophe Mincke is Head of the Criminology Department of the National Institute for Forensic Science and Criminology (NICC-INCC–Belgium) and Professor at Université Saint-Louis (Brussels). As a sociologist and criminologist, he has studied the Belgian prosecution services, and his PhD thesis was on victim–offender mediation. He is now working on mobilitarian ideology and the place of the mobility theme in contemporary legitimation discourses. He has applied it to management (of justice), victim–offender mediation, prison, insecurity, among other areas. He recently published, with Anne Lemonne, "Prison and (Im)mobility. What about Foucault?" (*Mobilities*, 2014).

Frank Neubert works as an Assistant Professor in the study of religions at the University of Bern, Switzerland. His research focuses on discursive approaches to the study of religion, the sociology of religion, globalised Hindu traditions and religions in the contemporary world.

John Urry is Distinguished Professor of Sociology at Lancaster University. His latest books include *Societies beyond Oil* (Zed Books 2013), *Offshoring* (Polity 2014) and *Cargomobilities* (Taylor & Francis 2015). He is a founding co-editor of *Mobilities* and Co-Director of the new Institute for Social Futures at Lancaster.

Pauline Wolff is a PhD candidate and Lecturer at the Faculty of Environmental Design at the University of Montreal, Canada. Her research focuses on the history of urban planning and its link to transport planning while using an epistemological approach. Originally from Strasbourg, France (located at the border with Germany), she lived in Oklahoma as a teenager, and this experience definitely shaped her interests in understanding how, why and when different cultures look at similar objects or actions and adapt their environment to them. She did an undergraduate degree in Architecture and another in Geography at the University of Strasbourg, and she focused on transport and mobility issues while pursuing a master's degree in Urban Planning at the University of Montreal.

Discourses and ideologies of mobility

An introduction

Marcel Endres, Katharina Manderscheid and Christophe Mincke

About 10 years ago, the 'mobilities paradigm' or 'mobility turn' (Hannam et al. 2006; Sheller and Urry 2006) was officially and prominently declared and announced: issues of movement, of too little movement or too much, or of the wrong sort or at the wrong time, are central to many lives and many organisations. From SARS to train crashes, from airport expansion controversies to SMS texting on the move, from congestion charging to global terrorism, from obesity caused by 'fast food' to oil wars in the Middle East, issues of 'mobility' are centre stage. And partly as an effect, a 'mobility turn' is spreading into and transforming the social sciences, transcending the dichotomy between transport research and social research, putting social relations into travel and connecting different forms of transport with complex patterns of social experience conducted through communications at a distance. (Sheller and Urry 2006, 208)

This turn was prefigured by a range of contributions from anthropology, cultural studies, geography, migration studies, science and technology studies, tourism and transport studies and sociology (e.g. Amin 2002; Appadurai 1990; Augé 1994; Bauman 2000; Castells 2005; Clifford 1989, 1992; Graham 2002; Kaplan 1996; Moland Law 1994; Urry 2000; Virilio 1998), which had argued for a perspective that takes movement and mobility rather than static structures, sedentarism or territorial borders as the central fact of modern or postmodern life (Cresswell 2011, 551; Sheller and Urry 2006, 208).

Since then, it seems, mobilities research – the tracing and tracking of moving people, objects and symbols – has become a recognised and institutionalised strand in social sciences – at least in the English and Scandinavian academia. As an indicator for its establishment, one may take the setting up of journals on the topic (e.g. *Mobilities, Transfers*) and several book series (Transport and Society at Ashgate, Changing Mobilities at Routledge, Studien zur Mobilitäts und Verkehrsforschung at Springer), the appearance of academic introductory textbooks (Adey 2010) and research field reports (Cresswell 2011, 2012, 2014; Merriman 2015), the ongoing institutionalisation of mobilities research into universities [to name a few: Centre for Mobilities Research (CEMORE) at Lancaster University, UK; Centre for Mobilities and Urban Studies (CMUS) at Aalborg University, DK; Center for Mobilities Research and Policy (MCenter) at Drexel University, Philadelphia, USA; Cultural Mobilities Research (CuMoRe) at Leuven University,

BE; Observatoire bruxellois de la mobilité at Saint-Louis University, BE] and study programmes, internal discussions on standards and methods (Bissell 2010; Büscher and Urry 2009; Büscher et al. 2011; Fay 2007; Fincham et al. 2010; Freudendal-Pedersen et al. 2010; Huete et al. 2013; Manderscheid 2014) and, last but not least, the representation within the scholarly literature.

The cause and reason of the institutionalisation and establishment of mobilities research in social sciences are commonly identified as the rapid increase of movement, technology-based acceleration and the diversification of space-transgressing connections. These developments on the social and technological levels are often seen as key indicators of an epochal change in relation to the spatial dimension of societies. For example, Ulrich Beck diagnosed a change from the nationally framed class society to a reflexive world risk society (Beck 2007); Zygmunt Bauman observed the 'liquefaction' of the formerly 'heavy modernity' (Bauman 2000); and Manuel Castells described an increasing hegemony of the 'space of flows' in relation to the 'space of places' (Castells 2005). Yet this claim of the 'newness' of mobilities is at times contested (Cresswell 2010) as well as accused of co-constituting the very mobility regime it draws its legitimation on. Thus, whereas the increasing importance of mobilities in all parts of the social figures as the cause and origin of the establishment of this new paradigm, we would like to take a different perspective by focusing on the discursive constitution of mobilities as an object of knowledge through (social) scientific theories and the constitution of social knowledge about movement and mobilities. Rather than distinguishing in a positivist fashion between existing realities 'outside' and their adequate representation through empirical research and resulting theories, we adopt a Foucauldian view of a co-evolvement of discourses and their objects (Foucault 1972). This perspective stands in contrast to a differentiation of mobility made by Cresswell (2006a, 3f.) by three relational moments. First, mobility as a brute fact – something that is potentially observable, a thing in the world, an empirical reality. Second, there are ideas about mobility that are conveyed through a diverse array of representational strategies ranging from film to law, medicine to photography, literature to philosophy. These representations of mobility capture and make sense of it through the production of meanings that are frequently ideological. Third, mobility is practised, it is experienced, it is embodied. Mobility is a way of being in the world.

As a powerful rejection of this differentiation, Frello (2008, 29f.) argued in her influential paper that 'movement cannot be grasped in a strictly "empirical" sense outside, above or below the meaning that is ascribed to it'. Rather, applying the terminology of Foucault's archaeological approach to discourse analysis, the *rules of discourse formation* 'determine both, what can appear as "movement", and the subject positions according to which one can move meaningfully and legitimately and according to which one can claim agency and insight in relation to movement' (Frello 2008, 30).

Frello concludes that the resulting questions for mobilities research should go beyond the empirical analyses of mobilities to encompass, ' "How do movement and mobility become something that we can know something about in the first place?" That is, how do they become objects of knowledge?' (Frello 2008, 30). In this view, the increased social importance and scientific focus on mobility also reflects and, in part, affirms a changed way of contemplating and ordering the world (ibid.). This means that the increasing importance of mobilities in all parts of the social does not only happen as observable practices in a given material world but should be seen as part and parcel of changing discourses, scientific theories and conceptualisations and knowledge.

By this token, Mimi Sheller and John Urry argue that the 'new mobilities paradigm' should not be 'a question of privileging a "mobile subjectivity", but rather of tracking the power of discourses and practices of mobility' (Sheller and Urry 2006, 211). Along these lines, scholars have argued that discourses and practices of mobility are part and parcel of certain 'social relations that involve the production and distribution of power' and 'the ways in which mobilities are both productive of such social relations and produced by them' (Cresswell 2010, 14). This also entails analyses of the constitution of immobilities as well as the differentiated forms and hierarchised meanings of movements that seem to be highly dependent on the perceived agents or authors of these practices (cf. Frello 2008).

However, the contribution of social sciences, social theory and thus mobilities research as relevant speakers within the formation of these mobilities discourses has not yet gained sufficient attention. In this sense, this book pursues the goal of conceptualising mobility as an ever-changing *object of knowledge* co-shaped and co-constituted by social sciences as well as other scientific discourses. By approaching mobility this way, change gains a peculiar duality of significance: firstly, as a transformation of 'real-world' entities, dimensions and practices of mobility and secondly, as a changing mode of understanding, systematising and ordering the world. By this token, discourses and knowledge cannot be reduced to representations of 'empirical realities'; rather, they constitute necessary preconditions for the very practices they claim to observe as well as for the sociopolitical ordering and governing of movement. Analysing the historic emergence of car traffic and its hegemony in public space, Bonham (2006) argues that transport and movement had to be constituted as objects of knowledge first in order to hierarchise and govern movements and traffic. It is this formation of 'movement-cum-knowledge' – discourses, ideologies, classifications, prioritisations and obscurings – that engenders mobilities as objects of government, power struggles and scientific truth regimes. This approach transcends some common differentiations by shedding light on the constitution and various discursive strategies deployed to distinguish between licit and illicit 'movers', free and forced mobility, good and bad movements, namely, illegal migrants, high-status expatriates, Gypsies, leisure travellers, creative nomads, and so on (Cresswell 2006b; Urry 2007). Within these knowledge formations, social sciences can no longer claim a neutral standpoint of unconcerned observation and description but are to be seen as active co-constructors, e.g. in regards to new differentiations and terms of mobilities, like transnationalism, cosmopolitanism, global diasporas or network sociality, whose impact is not limited to internal debates but has long since radiated into and from everyday practices and broader discourses as well.

Following Michel Foucault, we regard discourses and ideologies on mobility as systems of thought, which 'systematically constitute the objects of which they speak' (Foucault 1972, 54). In a sense, both discourses and ideologies permanently build connections 'from matters of fact to matters of concern' (Latour 2004, 225), which are far from 'exclusive from science' (Foucault 1972). Mobilities, as Peter Adey puts it, 'are underpinned by specific ideological and discursive meanings, which are not limited to any boundary between both academic and real social worlds' (Adey 2010, 14). Thus, social scientists can critically engage with the construction of these changing discourses by de- and reconstructing them, for instance in the concept of automobility, in debates on the right to mobility, in ideas of cosmopolitanism and sustainable mobility, and, not least, in general equations of mobility with modernity and freedom.

Put in a nutshell, the book's topic is on mobility as a *knowledge object* rather than as an *identified subject* within the historical contingency of movement. How do discourses and ideologies structure the normative substance, social meanings, and the lived reality of mobilities? What are the real-world affects of/on the *will and the ability to be mobile*? And, how do these lived realities, in turn, invigorate or interfere with certain discourses and ideologies of mobility?

Based on this framework, the book will address these changing discourses of mobility on three interrelated levels, set up in the following outline. The first part, 'Mobility and Normativity', highlights the normative power of current mobility discourses, reaching from the discursive impact of mobility as an overgeneralised social norm and its current instrumentalisation in politics and media, to the persistency of certain rationalities for or against various forms of mobility. Dealing with the central term of mobilities research, *Christophe Mincke* in Chapter 1 focuses on the concept of mobility itself as an articulation between description and prescription, as a specific form of representing the social world. The theoretical construction of the discursive use of mobility is then confronted with the empirical discourse around the legitimisation of the prison in Belgium. Moving beyond the simple dualism of movement and stasis, Mincke illustrates four imperatives – activity, activation, participation and adaptation – that illustrate what he calls the mobilitarian ideology, the mandatory character of practices labelled mobility.

Analysing contemporary reports on pilgrim walks on the Way of St James and the so-called Hippie trail, *Frank Neubert* in Chapter 2 focuses on the combination of ideas of mobility with the construction of self-image. In both cases, it seems that the journey itself as corporeal travel in co-presence with similar others, rather than the endpoint, is the aim of the endeavour. Furthermore, these defined and discursively policed forms of travel are interwoven with a continual process of individual transformation. Both forms of travel can be interpreted as more or less explicit critics of everyday hyper-mobility and their meaninglessness.

In Chapter 3, *Camelia Beciu* and *Mirela Lazar* highlight the relation of social meanings and normative patterns of mobility in the Romanian public media. Based on a discourse analysis of media reports about transnational migrants, they point out that hegemonic discourses mainly led by the countries of destination are reproduced in the Romanian national news by the construction of a moral context between symbolic ownership, anti-migration rhetorics and arguments of economic competition.

In the last contribution in this part, *Laura Bang Lindegaard* in Chapter 4 shows how different components are mobilised to justify a personal status quo through the analysis of the discourses of inhabitants of a Danish village engaged in a process of promoting the reduction of automobility. From an ethnomethodological perspective, she shows how the reduction of automobility is resisted through discursive skills and the ability of citizens to protect their freedom (as autonomy) and, to this end, their car.

The second part, 'Mobile Subjects', assembles chapters dealing with different delineations and constructions of mobile subjectivity and the specific connotations attributed to certain mobile subjects, from isolation, solitude and social detachment to activeness, liberation and savoir vivre. *Katharina Manderscheid* in Chapter 5 highlights the role of automobility for the idea of a rational autonomous subject. Against this background, she understands the claims of the mobility turn also as a critique of this subject conception, since it abstracts from the social embedding and its relationality. Yet, by exposing an apparent gap between theoretical claims and methodological concepts, she argues that current mobility research runs the risk, once again, of affirming and reproducing the concept of the solitary rationale subject. In Chapter 6 *Marcel Endres* addresses the question of the mobile self: the appropriation and internalisation of mobility at the individual level. On the basis of an empirical study, he shows how the discourse about neo-nomadism and hypermobility hides the fact that spatial bounds and life consistencies are necessary to the people described as disembedded selves. Thus, even hypermobile subjects are rather individuals in permanent negotiation between drift and anchorage. In the last chapter of this part, *Birgitta Frello* addresses the question of the position of Roma people in the European context of valorisation of free movement. Though they are commonly – and wrongly – identified as nomads, they are not recognised as ideal Europeans. Through the example of a small group of Romas in Copenhagen, she shows how cultural conventions and discourses regulate norms of mobility, rendering some forms of mobility recognisable and legitimate, while others are rendered dubious if not downright threatening.

The third part of this volume, 'Mobilised Infrastructures', focuses on various discourses of infrastructural and mobile technology systems and on the impacts originating from certain dispositives on which such systems are legitimated and established, like concepts of circulation, speed, ubiquity or miniaturisation. In their contribution, Chapter 8, *Ander Audikana* and *Zenhua Chen* analyse the ideologies of mobility that underlie the promotion and criticism of high-speed rail (HSR). HSR has become a political object, a topic that has been mobilised by many actors to support their political options. The authors propose three types of political use of the HSR and of the mobility ideologies attached to it. In Chapter 9 *Thomas Birtchnell* and *John Urry* explore multiple 'small' technologies wrapped up in the ideologies of complex mobility systems. They show that movement depends on non-transport technologies that embody 'incumbents' to ensure access and that, at the same time, affect the capability and transition of mobility systems.

By emphasising these ambivalent qualities to run – or even disrupt – systems, they discuss their transformative role as small but integral elements within the future scenario of a post-car system.

By scrutinising the adoption of the mobility turn in planning science, *Pauline Wolff* in Chapter 10 unfolds an epistemological perspective on the history of urban planning by considering the *dispositif* of *circulation* as a key concept and intentional dimension. Following Foucault's works on 'rationality fields', she shows how the historical reconstruction of the circulation *dispositif* could be helpful to better understand how the field of urban planning is informed by a specific way of thinking, describing and managing mobility, and to disclose the paradoxical relationship between valuations of mobility and certain ideas of spatial development.

References

Adey, P. 2010. *Mobility*. London, New York: Routledge.

Amin, A. 2002. Spatialities of globalisation. *Environment and Planning A* 34(3): 385–399.

Appadurai, A. 1990. Disjuncture and Difference in the Global Cultural Economy. In *Global Culture: Nationalism, Globalization and Modernity*, edited by M. Featherstone, 295–310. London, Thousand Oaks, CA, New Delhi: Sage.

Augé, M. 1994. *Orte und Nicht-Orte: Vorüberlegungen zu einer Ethnologie der Einsamkeit*. Frankfurt am Main: Fischer Taschenbuch Verlag.

Bauman, Z. 2000. *Liquid Modernity*. Cambridge: Polity.

Beck, U. 2007. *Weltrisikogesellschaft: Auf der Suche nach der verlorenen Sicherheit*. Frankfurt am Main: Suhrkamp.

Bissell, D. 2010. Narrating Mobile Methodologies: Active and Passive Empiricisms. In *Mobile Methodologies*, edited by B. Fincham, M. McGuinness and L. Murray, 53–68. New York: Palgrave Macmillan.

Bonham, J. 2006. Transport: Disciplining the Body That Travels. In *Against Automobility*, edited by S. Böhm, J. Campbell, C. Land and M. Paterson, 57–74. Malden, MA, Oxford: Blackwell.

Büscher, M., and J. Urry. 2009. Mobile methods and the empirical. *European Journal of Social Theory* 12: 99–116.

Büscher, M., J. Urry and K. Witchger. 2011. *Mobile Methods*. London, New York: Routledge.

Castells, M. 2005. Space of Flows, Space of Places: Materials for a Theory of Urbanism in the Information Age. In *Comparative Planning Cultures*, edited by B. Sanyal, 45–63. New York: Routledge.

Clifford, J. 1989. Notes on travel and theory. *Inscriptions* 5: 177–188.

———. 1992. Travelling Cultures. In *Cultural Studies*, edited by L. Grossberg, C. Nelson and P. Treichler, 96–116. New York: Routledge.

Cresswell, T. 2006a. *On the Move: Mobility in the Modern Western World*. New York, London: Routledge.

———. 2006b. The right to mobility: The production of mobility in the courtroom. *Antipode* 38: 735–754.

———. 2010. Towards a politics of mobility. *Environment and Planning D: Society and Space* 28: 17–31.

———. 2011. Mobilities I: Catching up. *Progress in Human Geography* 35: 550–558.

———. 2012. Mobilities II: Still. *Progress in Human Geography* 36: 645–653.

————. 2014. Mobilities III: Moving on. *Progress in Human Geography* 38: 712–721.

Fay, M. 2007. Mobile subjects, mobile methods: Doing virtual ethnography in a feminist online network. *Forum Qualitative Sozialforschung/Forum: Qualitative Social Research* 8(3): Art. 14 [64 paragraphs].

Fincham, B., M. McGuinness and L. Murray. 2010. *Mobile Methodologies*. London: Palgrave Macmillan.

Foucault, M. 1972. *Archeology of Knowledge and the Discourse on Language*. New York: Pantheon.

Frello, B. 2008. Towards a discursive analytics of movement: On the making and unmaking of movement as an object of knowledge. *Mobilities* 3: 25–50.

Freudendal-Pedersen, M., K. Hartmann-Petersen and L. Drewes. 2010. Mixing Methods in Search for Mobile Complexity. In *Mobile Methodologies*, edited by B. Fincham, M. McGuinness and L. Murray, 25–43. Basingstoke: Palgrave Macmillan.

Graham, S. 2002. FlowCity: Networked mobilities and the contemporary metropolis. *Journal of Urban Technology* 9: 1–20.

Hannam, K., M. Sheller and J. Urry. 2006. Editorial: Mobilities, immobilities and moorings. *Mobilities* 1: 1–22.

Huete, R., A. Mantecón and J. Estévez. 2013. Challenges in lifestyle migration research: Reflections and findings about the Spanish crisis. *Mobilities* 8: 331–348.

Kaplan, C. 1996. *Questions of Travel: Postmodern Discourses of Displacement*. Durham, NC: Duke University Press.

Latour, B. 2004. Why has critique run out of steam? From matters of fact to matters of concern. *Critical Inquiry* 30: 225–248.

Manderscheid, K. 2014. Criticising the solitary mobile subject: Researching relational mobilities and reflecting on mobile methods. *Mobilities* 9: 188–219.

Merriman, P. 2015. Mobilities I: Departures. *Progress in Human Geography* 39: 87–95.

Mol, A., and J. Law. 1994. Regions, networks and fluids: Anaemia and social topology. *Social Studies of Science* 24: 641–671.

Sheller, M., and J. Urry. 2006. The new mobilities paradigm. *Environment and Planning A* 38: 207–226.

Urry, J. 2000. *Sociology beyond Societies: Mobilities for the Twenty-First Century*. New York: Routledge.

————. 2007. *Mobilities*. Cambridge: Polity.

Virilio, P. 1998. *Rasender Stillstand*. Frankfurt am Main: Fischer Taschenbuch Verlag.

Part I
Mobility and normativity

1 From mobility to its ideology

When mobility becomes an imperative

Christophe Mincke

The springboard for this work was the observation, often repeated, that a 'mobility turn' has placed mobility at the heart of our social practices, both concretely and in discourses (Sheller and Urry 2006). We are said to be on the verge of a transition towards new relationships with mobility, expressed by geographic mobility behaviours as yet unseen, but also by the evolution of our collective relation with mobility. Indeed, the social constructions of what mobility is – of the meaning it should hold and the value it confers on mobile entities – is undergoing considerable evolution.

Nonetheless, we should not lose sight of the central concept – mobility itself – if we are to attempt to understand, on the one hand, the phenomena it embodies and, on the other, what it says about the way we relate to the world. This is our first question in this chapter.

Furthermore, the articulation between description and prescription – what is and what should be – must be examined more closely. The accent is most often placed on changes in practices and less frequently on the social representations linked to mobility. Yet the social normativities that emerge from this new relationship with mobility need to be studied. Although it is true that we are developing new representations, what are their effects on social prescriptions? In short, what social norms are linked to mobility's central role in the way we relate to the world? This will be the second focus of our discussion.

In this chapter, the distinction between description and prescription will be crucial. On the one hand, description is an attempt to produce a discourse that can tell what reality is. Description, of course, is a social construction: a collectively created discourse that is collectively thought to be a 'true' description of reality. Description is, thus, about social representations (Berger and Luckmann 2006). On the other hand, prescription is about telling what must be. A prescription is an imperative, telling how reality should be considered and how one should act in relation to it. A coherent set of prescriptions constitutes an ideology: a system of prescriptions, related to practices, founded on an enforced 'truth' and exclusive from other systems. Description and prescription need to be conceptually distinguished, even if they are not independent one from the other.[1] A specific description of reality limits the scope of possible prescription. In the same way, particular prescriptions need specific descriptions of reality to be sustainable. For instance, if you describe the world as fundamentally mobile, immobility will be a non-natural pattern. Immobility could then be prescribed as a way for mankind to abstract from nature or proscribed as a counterproductive behaviour in a mobile context.

The work we propose here is part of a theoretical reflection that aims to distinguish the general issue of mobility from the more limited context of studying physical movements. More precisely, this involves giving serious consideration to the hypothesis of mobility as a representational and ideological paradigm that is capable of shedding new light on several aspects of our society, in particular the significant mutations we are presently undergoing.

Such an endeavour obviously implies taking the risk of advancing a particular theoretical elaboration. The reader can already note that our work refers to hypotheses that cannot demonstrate their fecundity until they are confronted in the field by empirical studies that are much broader than those undertaken up to now. This is what we are already endeavouring through studies of contemporary discourses on the prison system (Mincke 2010, 2012a, 2012b; Mincke and Lemonne 2013a, 2013b), on (justice) management (Mincke 2013) and on alternative dispute resolutions (Mincke 2014a).

The approach we have chosen is based on a study of social representations and the discourses and practices that illustrate them. It is thus less a question of reporting on concrete mobility practices than it is to analyse the representational relation to mobility, in other words, how it is socially constructed not only as an object (Frello 2008) but also as a collective value, conveying ideological developments. Our central question will thus be that of the universe of meaning linked to mobility.

We shall confront our theoretical construction of the discursive use of mobility to a special field: the legitimisation of the prison in the parliamentary documents of the Belgian Prison Act of 2005. Our hypothesis is that, if mobility is such a value in itself, it can be successfully used to legitimise an institution that once was the symbol of immobilisation; it indicates the current thrust of these ideas.

An approach that is both inductive and deductive

The theoretical construction that we will present follows the example of Boltanski and Chiapello, who theorised on the basis of a corpus of observation of (managerial) discourses (Boltanski and Chiapello 1999). It has been built by induction derived from the observation of a wide range of discourses and practices. It is thus an attempt to rationalise, in a coherent model, a series of features we could trace through various texts and contexts.

We then apply our model deductively to analyse new objects. Although each confrontation with the empiric challenge risks breaking the model, it also works to improve it, especially by refining our understanding of its limits. For as crucial as it is to understand what a model can explain, we learn more when it fails. Thus, in the same process, we induced a model from a large set of observations and then deduced from our model an analysis of specific objects, in particular contemporary discourses on prisons (Mincke and Lemonne 2014).

More specifically, we undertook the study of a discourse that was 'serious' in the Foucauldian sense of the term. Our tool was the preparatory work leading to the recent (Belgian) law of 12 January 2005 on principles governing the administration of prison establishments and the legal position of detainees, the so-called Prison Act. One particular text was the report of a study commission of experts to prepare draft legislation. Our aim when we studied these works was to discover the characteristics of this contemporary discourse justifying prisons and, more specifically, those aspects relating to the notion of mobility.

The fact that prisons are a priori the epitome of an immobilising institution clearly entered into our choice of subject. Our initial idea was that if we could even find a usage we call mobilitarian ideology in justifications for incarceration, then we could reasonably conclude that it was a particularly powerful notion.

Mobility, space, time

The simplest definition of mobility is a movement in space over time.[2] It will thus be no surprise when we affirm that mobility is intrinsically linked to these two dimensions and that, even more, the mutations that affect the space–time relation would result in corresponding changes in the relation to mobility. And vice versa. Mobility, space and time are thus interdependent notions, and we must think of all three together.

A further point is that, rather than space and time, we will concern ourselves more with space–time. For as we shall see, space and time, as social constructs, are intrinsically linked in particular morphologies. All notions of space do not fit well with all notions of time and vice versa. Corresponding forms of time and space are thus associated in what, together with Bertrand Montulet, we call morphologies (Montulet 1998).

We still need to define the space that will interest us (we'll come back to time a bit later). To do so, we will start with something self-evident: sociologists are interested in space and time not as objective dimensions – we are not physicists[3] – but as social constructions (Mincke 2014b). In all logic, we are looking at the way, in today's world, our societies construct time and space.

Our understanding of space will be based on a sociology approach, in other words one that considers space as a dimension that structures realities.[4] In this perspective, spatiality is the result of a spatialising process. Regardless of the reality to which this spatialisation applies, it leads to spaces being created. Nothing forces sociologists to restrict their understanding to processes that only spatialise physical realities.

This is why we see as spaces all the results of social spatialisation processes, whether they apply to material reality or not. As sociologists, we do not consider space to be a dimension solely of the physical world. Social, conceptual, religious, family and relational spaces are, in our minds, just as much spaces as their geographical counterpart. They are not metaphors but the product of a bona fide process of spatialisation.[5]

Sociology is familiar with the notion of non-physical space and has used it for years to describe a number of phenomena. Social space (and the related social mobility), field (Bourdieu), uncertainty zone (Crozier) and experience framework (Goffman) are notions that clearly imply a spatialisation. Our proposal thus seems to be directly in line with a long tradition in sociology.

In a very classical way, we shall also consider time as a social construction and not as an objective measure of the fourth dimension in which objects develop their interactions.

It follows that, for the sociologist, mobility concerns more than mere physical spaces and objective time. In the following pages, we will thus often refer to the notions of space and mobility and apply them to non-physical realities. We will defend the idea that our contemporary situation can be explained by a tip of the balance between two spatial–temporal morphologies (the limit-form and the flow-form), which has modified our social representations of space–time and thus influenced our conceptions of mobility.

Limit-form

The limit-form is grounded in a representation of space as an indistinct stretch that is structured by its circumscription (Montulet 1998). The borders traced are what make it possible to define an inside and an outside and thereby order the space. Borders are determined by applying a distinguishing criterion that renders uniform what it encloses and distinguishes it from what is stranger to the circumscription thus constituted. A border is obviously not easy to cross and, with a few exceptions, must remain closed.[6] Everything inside state borders thus equally belongs to the national territory. The border itself is one-dimensional and has no 'thickness', like a razor's edge. On the other side is the stranger, uniformly foreign. Multiple circumscriptions can, of course, exist side by side, structuring the space 'horizontally' in a collection of territories at the same hierarchical level, for example other nation states. Each circumscription in turn can be divided into lower-level circumscriptions. Provinces, regions, *départements*, towns are territories that fit into other territories, producing a vertical structuring of sorts broken into different hierarchical levels. The nation states of the late 19th century, in their interrelations and internal structures, are perfect examples of how space is structured in a limit-form. The interplay of physical borders just described corresponds, trait by trait, with other non-physical borders: the national territory reflects the delimitation of a national community formed by the inclusion of some members in the state's political community, by the attribution of certain rights and obligations (military service, diplomatic protection, tax obligations, etc.) or by the inclusion in a collective national narrative. Likewise, the structuring of a national territory corresponds to an equivalent legal spatialisation that delimits the competences of various authorities through *ratione loci* (i.e. depending on administrative circumscriptions, legal districts, etc.) but also through *ratione materiae* (in reference to specific jurisdictions: federal, regional, provincial or local, the attributes of various districts, and so on).

Nonetheless, the border – the key element of this spatial–temporal morphology – can be fathomed only in a context of relative stability allowing it to continue over time. This corresponds to a particular construction of time in a cadence of stases and ruptures. Time is socially constructed through a strict periodisation: periods are clearly distinct and follow from one to another, separated by sudden ruptures that Michon has called '[Foucault's] time in blocks of archaeology' (Michon 2002). Although obviously time does not stop, socially it is perceived as if it were made of periods of stability dotted by moments of revolution that spark the brutal entry into a new era. Conquests, revolutions, federations and the reconstitution of the national territory are all pivotal elements leading into new eras through changes to a border. A large part of a national state's energy is thus devoted to protecting its borders and to stabilising them through lines of defence, territorial treaties, boundary markers, customs offices, anti-smuggling measures, controlling entry to and exit from the country, and so on. Several power technologies – in the Foucauldian sense of the term – are thus mobilised in order to stabilise the territorial construction.

Areas and eras are the foundation for this spatial–temporal morphology that we call the limit-form. In this context, mobility is conceived in a special way. As space is structured by a system of borders that enclose standardised spaces, spatial anchoring is thus primary. One must first belong to a set of territories before considering any movement. We are born in the territory of a state, are citizens of a state, are male or female, are members of one or another social class, etc. Mobility occurs when one is taken from a space of belonging to cross a border and attain a new anchoring. Crossing borders and substituted anchorings are thus two essential characteristics of mobility in the context of the limit-form. Mobility is experienced brutally when the border is crossed, inaugurating a new era of belonging. Rather than gradual movement, it is primarily a switch 'to the other side'. Mobility thus requires an effort, an investment in the means – symbolic, practical, financial, etc. – that make it possible to cross over. [7] There are, for sure, borders harder to cross than others: the one between blue and white collars is much more closed than the one between unqualified and qualified workers, for instance. Some borders have also long been considered as impossible to cross, like the one that separates the sexes.

The limit-form is typical of Western modernity. One striking example of this is the evolution of the state, its territory, the corresponding population, culture, language and legal organisation. The modern nation state is the perfect incarnation of limit-form as it is largely built on a set of strict borders defining internally uniform territory, national population and culture, language practices and legal order. Although, even if this model may seem natural, it could not remain eternally unchallenged.

Flow-form

We maintain that although the limit-form prevailed for years and years, it has been challenged since the sixties and, in Western countries at least, by an emerging model: the flow-form. This morphology is based on time being represented not as a dimension in which humans can impose pauses but as a constant flow that erodes everything. There is no longer a question of brutal ruptures but of continual changes, of an ever-present past, a future already with us, and a present enriched by what came before and what is to come. There are no more sudden ruptures, but this does not necessarily bring more stability. In this context, the history of revolutions and conquests gives way to that of mentalities, ideas and social practices. It is no longer a question of pinpointing exactly when the Roman Empire fell but rather to understand the phenomenon throughout its duration: what led to the fall and then what survived it. It is no longer a question of determining which great individual left an imprint on the world of knowledge but rather understanding the genesis of ideas and how, progressively and collectively, they reached the formalisation that assumed a person's name and entered into history. Not at all like Archimedes's 'Eureka'. The vision of time is no longer made of cadences but of progressive sliding.

We can find this feature in an interpretation of the ages of life, which are no longer clearly defined periods, separated by ruptures marked by special rituals and conferring specific statuses. The passage from childhood to adulthood no longer entails being hired at the factory, doing one's military service or getting married. It is a continual evolution which, through an ever expanding adolescence leads from one period to another via a considerable zone of interpenetration that also allows some childhood traits to survive into adulthood.[8]

One can imagine that this vision of time may pose a problem when it comes to borders. Without duration, a border cannot claim to have the fixed nature consubstantial to its very idea. Space subject to this temporal regime can no longer be perceived in terms of limits, even if these limits were never tangible but merely lasting. As a result, the border loses its credibility. In a world in movement, it is either itself moving or is constantly transgressed. In any case, it can no longer stand as the structuring reference it was in the limit-form context. It now appears as a counterfeit, like an artifice imposed on what is real or else an illusion. National borders in the Schengen Area are a perfect example: on one side, border controls are no longer allowed yet on the other they no longer bar police forces from legally entering the territory of the neighbouring country for pursuits or surveillance.[9] Although the border has not exactly disappeared, it no longer gives a univocal meaning to the area.

Yet this does not mean that space has become an unstructured area. New ways to organise space are emerging, conferring meaning through relational systems organised around points of attraction. No longer partitioned, space becomes punctuated: it is dotted with points of attraction that appear irregularly. And location in space is no longer determined by borders and whether one is on the inside or out but by the relations maintained with the various points. It is no longer a question of being on the territory of one state *or* another but of determining the relations between one *and* another, from one moment or subject to the next. Cities, for example, are seen less as coherent (administrative, topographical, morphological, etc.) circumscriptions in relation to the suburb or outskirts or from the vantage of inside or beyond city walls. They are now perceived through the category of hinterland – zones of economic, cultural, logistic and professional influence – creating a manifold extension of the city. In this representation of space, we move gradually from one point to draw closer to another, without jumping from one area into another. The areas of attraction are thus combinable.

In the context of the flow-form, a particular representation of mobility develops.[10] Indeed, if the spatially situated elements no longer belong to a closed space surrounded by borders and uniform on the inside, mobility can no longer be seen as transgressing a border. In a punctuated space, mobility is rather seen as a change in locality in relation to a set of points that structure the spatial area. In this view, mobility can affect the relation with some elements and not others, just as it depends on the movements of the two nodes in relation: the entity under consideration and also the point with which it is in relation. For instance, professional mobility is not about climbing the ladder of functions, through promotions, exams and formal changes of function, but about the ability to take on (increasingly) various types of tasks, to be multifunctional, to multitask – in a word, to be flexible. Similarly, in this particular way of conceiving mobility, the prototype for international mobility will not be migration – leaving for good one's country and settling somewhere else – but rather, the Erasmus way of travelling: accumulating experiences and contacts through travels, becoming a 'citizen of the world', mixing identities and always being on the move. It is more about the abolition of borders than about authorisations to cross them.

At the same time, when time is experienced as a continuous, constantly eroding flow, mobility can no longer be conceived as characterised by a stability occasionally broken by clearly identified movements. Rather than being something infrequent and brutal, mobility is permanent. The definition of one situation in relation to a set of reference points can thus be modified at each instant, on the one hand, because of the constant adjustment of the entity considered but also, on the other hand, because the positions of the points themselves have evolved. For they are also capable of continuous movement. Their position is not set by a perfectly stable spatial background but arises solely from their own relations with other reference elements. Thus a relationship with the prison, for instance, is also capable of evolving not only because of a prisoner's individual prison career but also through the constant reform of the prison system both within and outside the penitentiary. It is no longer possible to clearly distinguish the inside from the out, nor can someone be considered to pass from prison to freedom simply by crossing the threshold of the prison gate.

The mobility is irrepressible in the flow-form. The very principle of relational localisation and the constant evolution of the position of each point[11] along this spatialisation system renders it impossible to maintain a fixed position or even have a representation of what a fixed position might be. The idea of position thus loses all connotation of fixedness, just as space has lost the limit-form's notion of border.

Space–time in prison

We now have two ideal types – in the Weberian sense – offering two different ways to consider space–time and mobility. We definitely do not think that sociologists can choose between them or say which one could be the more accurate to describe 'reality'. They are ways to shape discourses and social representations, and we think that they can help us to analyse fields where the relation to space–time and mobility is crucial. Moreover, the transition from one spatial–temporal morphology to another and the non-physical meaning of space makes it possible to understand phenomena that would normally not be discussed through the prism of spatial–temporality. This is especially the case for a discourse to legitimise prison, such as the one adopted in the framework of works to prepare the Prison Act previously mentioned, which, in the coming pages, will be our main example. We shall try, through its analysis, to show how a broad conception of mobility opens new perspectives to understand recent social, political or penal reforms. This confrontation with a precise empirical material will also be the occasion to test the interest of our specific theoretical construction.

The classic prison (Mincke and Lemonne 2014) reflects the limit-form: a building whose overriding feature is its outer walls but that is also partitioned on the inside. It is a social space fragmented by rules that prohibit the inmates from communicating among themselves or with the prison staff.[12] The prison population itself is partitioned into different categories of inmates at the same time as they are physically and symbolically isolated from ordinary citizens, and so on. The whole institution is thus dependent on an interplay of borders. The prison is also a legally exceptional territory where some of its occupants have been deprived of most of their basic rights. So we can see that physically, socially and legally, the classic prison space is founded on the notion of borders.

This view is quite contrary to the one developed by the experts who drafted the Prison Act. They present prison as ideally open, both socially and physically. It is seen in a continuity with space beyond the prison.

> [F]ulfilling the basic principles for the 'limitation of the adverse affects of confinement, reparation, rehabilitation and reintegration' implies that the implementation modes other than confinement in a prison environment must be made possible, that the transition between confinement and life in society occur earlier, gradually, and that contacts with the outside world be a key component to the normal regime the penitentiary administration offers each prisoner.
>
> (Decroly and Van Parys, *Final report of the Commission on the 'Law of Principles Concerning Penitentiary Administration and the Legal Status of Prisoners'. Final Report on Behalf of the Justice Commission 2001*, 376; hereafter *Final Report* 2001)[13]

Similar remarks are found on several instances, which is logical, because one of the law's main objectives is to normalise prison and limit the harmful effects of confinement, which are clearly related to the very characteristics of the prison as a social and physical space.

> The adverse affects of confinement are primarily imputable to the fact that the penalty of deprivation of liberty is carried out in a prison, the prototype of

what E. Goffman described as a 'total' institution, that is, an institution that manages all the aspects of peoples' lives.

(*Final Report* 2001, 66)

When the prison is deprived of a wall that serves as an uncrossable border, it loses a significant part of its specificities in relation to free society, in which a penalty depriving one of liberty may also be carried out, clearly indicating a dilution of the prison throughout the rest of society.

The detention phase must be placed in the context of a gradual extension in the freedom to come and go. In this perspective, the prison may no longer be considered as the sole place to serve a sentence of deprivation of liberty.

(*Final Report* 2001, 121)

In this context, 'prisoners' are not necessarily confined in the strict sense of the term, but they maintain a particular – and variable – relationship with the prison institution, including services outside the prison like parole surveillance, electronic monitoring, automatic localisation devices and so on.

This concept of physical and social prison space clearly reflects the flow-form. Does this mean, then, that time itself is seen as a continual flow? In the classic view of the prison as a limit-form, time is extremely cadenced and repetitive. Not only does the internal compartmentalisation lend itself to a certain type of mobility and only through strict respect of daily rhythms (exercise time, office hours, visitors schedule, etc.), but furthermore the impermeability of the wall is also tied to a clear distinction between time in prison and time out of it, articulated by the lock-up (entering) and the release (exit). The classical prison is not familiar with the notion of organising the time of confinement, so it relies on a particularly strong cadencing of time (Mincke and Lemonne 2014). Lastly, the time sliced from the life of a prisoner during detention was an empty, useless time, as the sentence was served perfectly simply by being deprived of this time.

Quite the contrary, in the preparatory work for the Prison Act, confinement was seen as a time of preparation and progressive restoring of liberty. The extreme modulation of confinement gave way to the notion of a continuum between total liberty and confinement, passing through several measures of freedom, conditional or not, using geolocation devices or not, short or long term. Much more, confinement is placed in the direct prospect of being freed, and its meaning is largely derived from leading to this end.

Preventing or limiting the adverse affects of confinement . . . implies the suppression as far as possible of the prison as a 'total institution', the maximal normalisation of daily life in the prison, an opening as broad as possible to the outside world and the definition of a carceral trajectory placed in the perspective of early release.

(*Final Report* 2001, 69)

Furthermore, in general release from prison no longer signals the end of the sentence but rather the entry into a new period of control – parole – which is both a time of confinement (parole is one way to serve a liberty-depriving sentence) and a time of freedom. This is even more striking when parole is coupled with an electronic monitoring measure, whose main effect is to partially extend to the outside world the prison's temporal regulation by imposing periods when the person must be at home. We can see here that prison time is no longer seen as a period completely distinct from liberty time but as part of a time continuum that organises progressive transitions and temporal interpenetrations.

Likewise, time in confinement is no longer seen as unchangeable but as a period to be adapted to the prisoner's personal career.

> Considering, in particular, the importance given in the draft law to the individual sentence plan, which can be considered as a means to individualise the way the liberty deprivation penalty is served, as a necessary condition to render it more human, there must be possibilities for differentiation in the programming and in the form to be given to the prison career, where organizing confinement in phases must reflect aims to gradually increase the freedom to come and go.
>
> (*Final Report* 2001, 418)

Obviously the preparatory work for the Prison Act still contains elements entrenched in the limit-form. Nonetheless, there emerges a sharply drawn vision of a liberty-depriving penalty served both inside and beyond prison walls, a view of a prison that is open socially and physically, of a period of confinement seen in continuity with the time before and after a prison term and of a penalty intended to lead individuals to change their personal life paths (see the 'prison career' mentioned in the preceding extract). The prison is thus conceived as a space–time that flows and the prison project as a mobility effort. We are far from the limit-form prison, the site of immobilisation (Mincke and Lemonne 2014).

Description and prescription

The passage from the limit-form to the flow-form provides the opportunity to characterise the nature of the mutations in our descriptive relation to space–time: the way we conceive and conceptualise it. It would nevertheless be quite strange for this evolution to relate solely to our description of the world around us. Indeed, if the notion of border becomes a powerless basis for a system to structure space, it appears as counterfeit. If collectively it seems to be permanently eroded by the constant flow of time, then it is logical to reject it. It is hard to justify founding a relationship to the world on a category perceived as inappropriate. Attempting to trace borders, maintaining strict time cadences, and promoting anchoring to mobility are options that will seem absurd, unacceptable, in a world that adheres to the flow-form representation of space–time.

As we have seen, it is a mere step from description to prescription, and this is what we shall now discuss.

It is therefore perfectly logical for this new description of the world, as a flow-form, to give rise to a new prescription for the social realm. We also seem to detect, in the discourses around us, the emergence of a new ideology, a so-called mobilitarian ideology that turns mobility itself into a value. Regardless of the space, one has to keep moving, and immobility in turn is presented as inevitably problematic.[14] Affirming the obligatory nature of mobility is not enough, however. The form it takes remains to be defined. This is what we will attempt to do through four imperatives that we see as vectors to impose a generalised mobility: activity, activation, participation and adaptation. They are a theoretical attempts to qualify the characteristics of the mobility that is required today, without focusing on physical mobility.

Activity

The first imperative concerns activity. It is important in our days to be constantly in motion, like those organisations and individuals held up as role models whose normal operational mode is overdrive. One must be super busy, not have a moment free, never leave a stone unturned, appear to be overwhelmed, overbooked, on the verge of total exhaustion. Obviously in this scenario, the inactive person is stigmatised as lazy, and anyone who can't keep up the pace as delicate, incapable, inadequate. In this context, it is not legitimate to find the easier solution, to be content with the minimum required, or to hide behind a safe routine to limit one's activity. The optimum is not to do what has to be done and with the least amount of energy but to expend as much energy as possible and strive for maximum yield.

Any kind of activity goes, as long as it is non-stop.[15] And it is no longer, as before, a question of alternating periods of action when activity is required with periods of rest, leaving things be. For example, when people retire, they are no longer urged to slow down and go fishing or do some gardening; they are urged to become active senior citizens, constantly on the ball, taking up new challenges to ward off the pitfall of inactivity, much more dangerous than old age. For inactivity, not time, is the source of decline and dependency. In the same way, workers are invited to be proactive, to not settle for doing the work assigned to them but to continually search for new tasks, which will become new accomplishments. It is no longer enough simply to do one's 'nine to five'. Our world praises constant activity and the acceleration of rhythms, not in the name of progress, but for the sake of stabilisation. We should constantly be struggling to do more, in order to prevent a crisis (Rosa 2012).

> This constant activity can of course lead to exhaustion when individuals are incited to use their last drop of energy in pursuit of self-realization, that indefinite and infinite imperative.
>
> (Bauman 2000, 32; Ehrenberg 1998; Rosa 2012, 10)

The preparatory work for the Prison Act is clearly marked by this activity imperative. For instance, when restorative approaches are discussed, they are promoted in reference to activity.

> The draft law highlights the fact that reparation is not something the prison administration can accomplish itself, or by itself, but it is par excellence the field of action for the perpetrator and the victim.
>
> *(Final Report* 2001, 78)

Likewise, although the report recalls that the prisoner has the right to conserve the benefits of a respectable social position, it is not solely in virtue of their basic rights.

> [T]he prisoner, both in relation to himself and to others, must be considered . . . as someone who deserves to enjoy the basic rights inherent to active citizenship.
>
> *(Final Report* 2001, 82)

And neither do the prison staff escape this call to action:

> Extending and enriching their tasks, maximising human potential thanks to training . . . these are the elements considered as essential in all the literature on [work] organisation which the prison administration cannot neglect.
>
> *(Final Report* 2001, 125)

Activation

The second mobility imperative expects individuals to be the ones launching their own movement. No longer a question of waiting for instructions, an order or signs. No one else is in the same exact position; no one else can know the most appropriate action. As we no longer belong to a large uniform group, we alone can discover what is relevant to the situation. It is thus useless to wait for someone else. Here again we see the injunction to be oneself, described by Alain Ehrenberg (1998). This is the obligation to start off spontaneously in search of oneself, even if this 'oneself' is not described or there is no explanation for the way to define it (Bauman 2000, 62).

If the activity imperative imposed movement, that of activation defines its modes: it must be 'spontaneous'. This is obligatory. The entity concerned must be the one to start this movement. We are now oceans away from the heteronomy of heavy capitalism, the subject so dear to Bauman (2000, 63), this world of individuals instructed by others to pursue objectives set by others.

It is thus impossible to receive close guidance. At the most, we may be coached, advised in the exercise of our self-determination (thus at the process level).[16] And there is less certainty as to whether one is doing enough and on the right tract. There are no general norms to reassure social actors that they are not mistaken.

The framework for individual action can thus become unsettling because it is unpredictable. In a context of strict norms, where people are asked to conform to a pre-established script, it is easy to determine the right thing to do. If needed, they can cite scrupulous respect of the norms to indicate that they are irreproachable. This is harder to do, however, in a mobility context. How can an employee know if she is sufficiently motivated, proactive or flexible? How can a spouse be certain he can measure up to his partner's expectations for their relationship? How can welfare recipients sufficiently prove their search for a job or social integration? How to know if one is a good prisoner when it's no longer a matter of sitting quietly in one's cell but rather of defining a sentence plan whose contents and outline are anything but clear-cut (Mincke and Lemonne 2014)?

In the framework of the Prison Act, the virtues of reparation are stressed. It must come from the prisoner's initiative, in particular by drawing up a sentence plan.

> [A]ll effort must be expended during the time in prison time in order to . . . make available [to the inmate] an offer – with no imperative nature – of activities and services as varied as possible, corresponding as closely as possible to his necessities and needs, particularly in view of his future reintegration into free society. More concretely, the draft law on [prison] principles calls for an individual sentence plan drawn up together with the inmate. This plan identifies the obstacles to reintegration and elaborates strategies to overcome them. In agreement with the inmate, it also includes a programme of activities of which he can take advantage in the prospect of his release.
>
> (*Final Report* 2001, 74)

Along similar lines, assistance to the inmates is redefined, according to the Minister of Justice himself, as reflecting a logic of activation rather than assistance.

> In the framework of the sentence being served, the task of the social workers and the social activation they attempt to achieve is highly important. It is not that easy to shift from an assistance point of view to implementing a principle of action.
>
> (*Final Report* 2001, 13)

Likewise, problems specific to the prison system, like exclusion from social security benefits, are defined as barriers to assuming responsibility, meaning that they keep the inmates from active efforts towards their reintegration or making amends for damage caused.

> [T]he (partial) exclusion from the social security system, in a way, is an (unintentional) additional penalty; it is the source of an avoidable adverse effect of incarceration; it is contrary to the principle of normalisation and limits an inmate's right to assume personal and social responsibilities.
>
> (*Final Report* 2001, 148–149)

Participation

The perpetual and spontaneous movement imposed on individuals takes place in a special social context. In the punctuated flow-form space, localisation requires establishing relationships with the entities that punctuate the space. This implies both the idea that the activity is developed through the social relationship, rather than attachment to predefined territories, and also the idea that relations thus forged are in constant evolution. As a result, the projective logic prevails, founded on successive and simultaneous contributions to temporary collective projects (Boltanski and Chiapello 1999, 141–142). There is no longer question of a lasting membership to collectivities or to an area, or of subordination to categories or incorporation in productive structures (regardless of the nature of the production),[17] or even of a stable assignment to a task or role (Bauman 2000, 7). On the contrary, it is a question of establishing relationships that are limited in time, at the service of a temporary activity – in other words a question of participating in projects.

This projective logic is omnipresent. For example, it is the base of integration policies that do not attempt to turn an unemployed into a worker but to restore the potentials of the unemployable in order to attract the interest of the working world, especially by installing a *habitus* focused on the projective logic of individual life paths (Mauger 2001, 13). Thus finding employment evolves from providing a job for someone who is 'jobless' to becoming a collective reintegration project focusing on a 'job seeker' and instilling the participation logic. Social assistance, for example, increasingly comes with the question, 'What is your plan, your project?' (Lacourt 2007). In a similar manner, contemporary management tends to present the situation of working not as the employer hiring a worker but as a personal involvement in a collective project in which each actor is merely a participant among others, regardless of the hierarchical level.

A large number of human activities can thus be analysed through the lens of participation in projects. The result of promoting a constant mobility makes any action the occasion for forming relationships but also turns any relationship into a temporary bond whose purpose is to undertake a project, with its continuation afterwards having no justification. Life itself is a series of participations in temporary projects.

The opposite of participation is dependency, an attitude that, rather than helping to start or continue a project, consists in being led along, a deadweight that holds the others back (and hampers their mobility). This dependency is stigmatised through the criticism of being assisted, fear of dependency among the elderly or handicapped, or even denunciation of inmates who allow themselves to be infantilised rather than take responsibility for their lives via a 'sentence plan'. Thus the preparatory work for the Prison Act redefines the 'prison problem'[18] as relating to the loss of autonomy, being assisted, as the incapability – learned in prison – to assume responsibility, in other words to accomplish projects that each one must accomplish. Respect for human dignity, becoming responsible and participation are clearly associated.

The principle of becoming responsible covers responsibility for one's own life, for those who are close, for harm caused to victims and suffering inflicted on the victims' families. If we wish people to become responsible, they must be respected and associated with the decisions that concern them.

(Final Report 2001, 8)

Similarly, when work in prison is discussed, the issue of employability is cited, in other words the individual's ability to attract and potential to become integrated in a professional project (Boltanski and Chiapello 1999, 145).

It is a question of finding or fostering . . . a job that enables . . . the inmate to maintain the ability to make a living for himself after he is released.

(Final Report 2001, 158)

Prison itself must cease to be the institution that seized individuals to govern every aspect of their life. It must become a collective and participative project.

All these elements make up the "dialectic of control": the inmates are not purely passive beings who merely undergo control, but rather they are "actors" who react to situations and attitudes. 'Order' is thus not a static given element but rather a dynamic that arises from social interactions in the [prison]establishment.

(Final Report 2001, 177)

This evolution concerns inmates and prison staff alike.

Participation by the staff, concertation and work in teams – have these methods been sufficiently developed? Are the staff able to work to the best of their capacity? It is not simply a question of adapting administrative measures, but rather one of acknowledging that the staff is a key element in truly applying a prison policy.

(Final Report 2001, 125)

Adaptation

The fourth mobility imperative concerns adaptation. An entity expected to become integrated in a multitude of projects – to link them up or accumulate them – must have excellent faculties of adaptation. In the same way, life in a constantly changing environment requires constant adaptation. As such in today's world, terms like adaptability, flexibility or even reconversion hold positive connotations, indicating a healthy capacity to seize each opportunity without bias, constraints or prerequisites.[19] This adaptation is a form of mobility that enables a person, by working on oneself, to see an evolution in relations to the environment and thus establish relations with it more easily. It is both a response to a movement and a movement to re-form the entity itself.

The model individual (just like the model organisation) is able to move from one project to another, one register to another, one field of activity to another or one type of relationship to another, quickly and without hesitating. It is no longer possible to establish oneself socially; individuals are summoned to be in constant movement, without ever finding a stable state they can consider as acquired (Bauman 2000, 33–34). What we call the posture is the concrete result of this requirement, replacing the social role as the expression of a stable status (Goffman 1973). If in the framework of the limit-form, people were given a social status, that is, a fixed social position expressed by a particular role one had to play consistently, the flow-form imposes new requirements. The individual must now assume, temporarily yet effectively, an attitude that corresponds to the needs of the moment, to be able to combine this with other ways of behaving and to be able to slough them off as quickly and thoroughly as they were adopted. This is what we mean by the posture of the role.

In this context, any geographical, philosophical, religious, material or intellectual anchoring can become a barrier. A person must renounce all rigidity in order to freely develop one's actions.[20] Henceforth, it is no longer a question of leaving one anchor to move on to another [what Bauman (2000, 33), after Giddens, calls re-embedding], but rather of pulling all anchors, regardless of their form. The person valorised by mobilitarian ideology – the ideology that values mobility for itself – is free of all chains and perfectly ready for any adaptation.

This relation to adaptation leads to a view of individual relations to space arising from the trajectory – always personal and never finished. Mobility is thus at the very heart of the way one's relation to the social realm is conceived. Rather than individuals being stabilised in the place they 'deserve', they now must claim rights to the mobile dimension of life. 'Each one in his place' is now replaced by 'to each his own path'. Adaptation is a cardinal virtue that makes it possible to maintain a harmonious relationship to the context. Assigned places gave way to implementation of a personal ecology, constantly evolving, where stability comes from moving around rather than remaining fixed in place.

Thus time and again incarceration is presented neither as a state nor as a period of immobility but instead as a moment along a career and also, in itself, a career within a prison system that stretches beyond the penitentiary walls. The inmate's readaptation to a free life in view of his reintegration – where prison is seen as a place aiming to change a personal trajectory marked by deviation – corresponds to the prison trajectory's adaptation to his personal characteristics. Being a prisoner is no longer a state but a path.

> [T]here must be broad possibilities to establish differentiations in the programming and models of the prison career, where the detention phase must be considered as a gradual progress towards the freedom to come and go.
>
> (*Final Report* 2001, 121)

The principle of equivalence is closely related to the principle of continuity set down in article 87, according to which the inmate has the right during his prison career to continue health care treatments equivalent to those before he entered prison.

(Final Report 2001, 167)

At the start [of the sentence plan] the detention career is summarised. . . . Consequently, establishing the detention career largely takes into account the legal possibilities for individualisation and progressive reintegration of the convict in free society.

(Final Report 2001, 221)

All things considered, it is the overall system, the prison and its actors, that is invited to invest in a process of permanent mutual adaptation.

Different principles found in the draft law, such as the principles of respect, normalisation and participation, by analogy are applicable to the staff. In principle the draft law not only recommends investing in the adaptation of structures, but also in strategies for change, especially as concerns the penitentiary culture.

(Final Report 2001, 125)

Mobilitarian ideology

The four imperatives we have just described give shape to an imperative relationship with a particular mobility. The question is indeed that of shaping a specific mobility, as the notion of mobility is not a given but a social construct that reflects a particular representation of space–time and the ways we may relate to it. The mobility in question is not episodic or punctuated by occasional border crossings. It is constant and must remain so. The activity imperative thus requires abandoning all rest, all security. There is no longer a question of choosing not to move. In the social, family, conceptual or physical space, the actor cannot afford to rest. Furthermore, this constant mobility must arise from the actor's own initiative (activation). There is no longer a question of being acted on or of faithfully following instructions. The mobilitarian subject is self-referenced (Rosa 2012, 12–13). Deciding individually to revise family or professional ambitions, individuals tally up their own successes or failures in terms of professional mobility or set out alone to discover the world. The projects initiated are for the most part collective, and the actor's mobility thus reflects a participatory logic. Even personal development, setting oneself in motion, which Vranken calls 'work on oneself' (Vranken 2006; Vranken and Macquet 2006) stems from a growing potential for participation, the ability to respond favourably to solicitations from one's environment and ignoring any obstacles or blocks. Participation is thus an extra quality of mobility as consecrated by mobilitarian ideology. This leads to the imperative for adaptation, so that the various participants will be able to adjust to a project and the context of an action. Mobility cannot be constant if people are willing to sit and wait for predefined conditions to converge. Examining all options means turning each situation into an opportunity, thus being adaptable.

The mobilitarian ideology, therefore, is not just about placing value on mobility in itself. It is about imposing a specific relationship to a specific mobility. Other social practices, previously considered as forms of mobility – such as patiently advancing along a pre-traced career path – are henceforth seen as belonging to a logic of immobility. The mobilitarian ideology thus constructs a certain type of mobility at the same time as it makes it mandatory, thereby constructing a universe that is coherent with the representations of space–time that underpin it.

Should we understand from all this that we are on the verge of a world entirely devoted to mobility, one that would attempt to banish all immobility? Certainly not. What we are interested in here is highlighting different universes of meaning, models of discourses relating to space, time and mobility. Yet we are all aware that the relation between directly discursive and non-discursive practices is quite complex and that the emergence of a discourse – even if it is the dominant one – does not necessarily – not to say never – accompany the installation of concrete practices that would be the perfect application of this discourse.

In the first place, our approach does not aim at sustaining the idea of an undivided reign for mobilitarian ideology. Indeed, the typical ideological *dispositifs* of the limit-form, which for lack of a better term we call the anchoring ideology, still persist in many areas.

The parliamentary works we analysed still contain numerous elements grounded in this anchoring ideology. The project itself was to establish a strict legal framework, seen as drawing a clear line between legal and illegal, between admissible and inadmissible, to end the legal vagueness and arbitrary nature of Belgian prison administration. The heart of the draft law was based on the will to trace borders; nothing could be closer to the limit-form. This said, the fact that a legislative project can be colonised to such extent by a discourse reflecting the flow-form and mobilitarian ideology clearly indicates the current thrust of these ideas. From there to affirming that it has the field to itself is a step we do not take.

There is nothing surprising in this. No system of thought has ever been able to rule without rivals, just as, as Foucault reminds us, social evolution is made less of replacements than of shifts in balance and parallel existence of different mechanisms (Foucault 2004, 10).

Another important element is the fact that an ideology is not a direct relation to the world but a set of concepts and normative categories to be mobilised in the context of social relations. This means that beyond the ideological discourse, specific uses of the normative resources are developed. These will or will not be mobilised to govern highly diverse situations.

As such, certain mobilities will be recognised while others will not. The non-contractual worker who accepts a long bus commute or sets aside her qualifications to adapt to the market and accept any work available is showing perfect respect for the mobility imperative; yet no one will congratulate her. She has merely done the least that can be expected: she has avoided dependence on welfare and the social demotion it implies.

On the other hand, the young manager on an upward professional path, who travels abroad in agreeable and comfortable conditions or who changes positions in his company to take on a more interesting and motivating job, will be praised, held up as an example of the joy of being mobile.[21] People like him are models even though nothing indicates that they made a greater sacrifice in what Boltanski and Thévenot call the 'investment formula' (Boltanski and Thévenot 1991); this sacrifice to obtain social recognition, which in our day consists of abandoning all anchoring (Boltanski and Chiapello 1999). The present value placed on mobility thus does not imply that all mobilities are recognised as equal, independently of their intensity and the cost for those who practice them.

In the same way, at the very time a discourse on the prison is formulated by those who promote opening, normalisation, temporal continuity and mobility for prisoners – to the point that one may well wonder whether the perfect realisation of this programme would be abolishing prisons altogether – Belgium is in the midst of building new penitentiaries, largely oriented towards an objective of security and maximum confinement, where is it hard to find traces of mobility discourses. In parallel to a mobility discourse attempting to justify the prison system looms a heady rival who preaches confinement without any adjustments, intensive use of prison, the strictest regime in applying the prison constraint, impermeability of prison walls and so on.

It thus clearly emerges that mobilitarian ideology does not permit affirmation that mobility is systematically prized, no more than it denounces immobility. The construction of social practices in mobilities and immobilities, collectively seen as such (Frello 2008), is a condition for mobilising this ideology. Social practices thus cannot be automatically classified as either mobility or immobility but are formed by facets of one and the other.

Therefore, in our view, one issue at stake in the research to come must be to understand the cases where mobilitarian ideology is mobilised and how this comes about. Other cases for study are those where behaviours may be seen as mobilities even if they aren't and, conversely, immobilities that go unnoticed or are legitimatised, and so on. The issue, indeed, is to use mobilitarian ideology as an instrument to understand uses of the theme of mobility in order to establish relations of power (Frello 2008, 47).

Conclusion

In this brief *tour d'horizon*, our objective was to trace the perspective for one development in mobility studies whereby mobility is no longer considered as mere physical movement and became a tool to analyse contemporary social mutations and power relationships.

What seems to foster this evolution is linking up studies on mutations in relationships to (physical) space with a set of phenomena traditionally described by various means: responsibilisation, deinstitutionalisation, contractualisation, flexibilisation, activation and so on – phenomena that are too rarely linked together. The advantage of this approach appears obvious not only for social practices that are now described as non-physical mobilities and finding a common interpretation but also for mobilities based on physical movement that find new potentials as explanations grounded in the social context, in collective representations or cross-cutting social imperatives that avoid seeing the relationship to physical space as arising solely from a relation with its materiality.

We see no need to stretch any points to achieve this approach. It is enough to accept that space is a dimension that structures more than just our relation to the physical world. It's a small step, but one that goes a long way. It implies that sociologists acknowledge the wealth of approaches to the human geography of physical movements but also that geographers accept seeing their prized concept – space – used and partially redefined by sociologists. And then it will be possible to examine mobilities in a broader manner and to elicit a whole set of practices and discourses, traces of an ideology that we see as deeply structuring the social realm.

This may lead us to see in a new light subjects that have already been extensively studied in the social sciences. This was our own experience, for example, with the perspective we were able to give to the 'prison problem'. For so long this question was built around the idea that prisoners were submitted to a regime that derogated from common *rights* (deprived of liberty, inroads on privacy, restrictions to therapeutic freedom, exceptions to the right to work, etc.). Today a radical reformulation is coming about: prison poses a problem because it deprives the inmate of autonomy. By submitting the individual to a regime that takes away responsibility, by frustrating any attempt at initiative or the ability to make one's own plans, it diminishes this autonomy and self-determination that are intrinsic to human dignity.

This observation may lead one to conclude that prison management has turned a corner, evoking responsibilisation for inmates or holding the individual up as the entrepreneur of the self. As rich as they may seem, these approaches nonetheless limit understanding of the phenomena to relations with sectors working in roughly the same terrain. For example, although it may indeed be true that a managerial logic has been imported, this says nothing about the reasons that led a commission of renowned experts to use this discourse as a basis for defining society's relation to the prison institution.

Our proposal seems to open a new innovating perspective that, obviously, does not claim to shed light on the whole phenomenon but bring a new way of seeing this object already the subject of so many studies. In the discursive framework of mobilitarian ideology, being deprived of autonomy is the worst thing that could happen. A heteronomous being cannot be submitted to injunctions regarding activity, activation, participation and adaptation as they have been just defined. It is therefore important for the prison to make the conditions for its legitimation by becoming compliant with mobility imperatives. The first step is to create a context where it is possible to claim the widest possible application of the four previously cited principles, as they open the way towards tests for legitimation or de-legitimation. In a way, the possibility of maintaining a discourse on preserving the capacity for autonomy among people in prison is the first mobility test imposed on the system. And it will or will not emerge legitimised. In the first case, the mobility-legitimate prison can claim to be an instrument that imposes mobility criteria on inmates and, more generally, in all its stakeholders. In such a context, questions of management, responsibilisation or self-entrepreneurship are no more than paths through which mobilitarian ideology can enter the prison. And this illustrates our view of how mobility issues can be summoned to lend us a new way of looking at particularly diverse social phenomena.

Notes

1 As shown in the contribution of Marcel Endres.
2 We prefer this open-ended definition to others that refer explicitly to geographic space or to an intention by a social actor, for instance as in Kaufman's definition: "In a broad perspective, mobility can be defined as the intention, then realisation of crossing a geographic space which implies a social change" (Kaufmann 2012).
3 Even though there are serious doubts as to whether physics is concerned about the relation to an 'objective' space, considering how relations between physics and reality evolved over the 20th century.
4 We shall consider as 'realities' entities socially constructed as effectively existing, whether they are material (cities, landscapes, national territories, etc.) or not (law, ideas, political ideologies, etc.).
5 For a development of this thesis, see our working paper (Mincke 2014b) on a presentation recently made at a colloquium called Thinking Space in Sociology (Mincke 2014c).
6 On this subject we can cite "heavy capitalism", as described by Bauman, which endeavours to keep tightly closed the borders that structured the world of solid modernity (Bauman 2000, 58).
7 On this subject, see Vincent Kaufman's notion of motility (Kaufmann 2004).
8 For example, the fondness for playing games, once considered as inappropriate but now perfectly acceptable to the extent that the phenomenon has been coined 'kidults': adults who are nostalgic for the TV series, computer games, comic strips or cartoons of their childhood and practice activities in relation to this universe.
9 Art. 40 and 41, Convention implementing the Schengen agreement (Valynseele 2007).
10 We stress the fact that, what we are discussing here is not the way mobility concretely occurs but the characteristics of the social representations surrounding mobility.
11 What Bauman calls 'a world that refuses to stand still' (Bauman 2000, 58).
12 The rule of silence remained applicable in France until the 1970s (Demonchy 2004, 280, 290).
13 *Rapport final de la commission 'loi de principes concernant l'administration pénitentiaire et le statut juridique des détenus'. Rapport fait au nom de la commission de la Justice par Vincent Decroly et Tony Van Parys.* Translations of extracts are the author's.
14 Even though it had been demonstrated that immobilities were necessary for the development of mobilities.
15 For Boltanski and Chiapello, activity is the common superior principle of the projective (Boltanski and Chiapello 1999, 165).
16 Bauman distinguishes advisors from leaders (Bauman 2000, 64).
17 On this question, see the importance of identifying and constituting populations to which individuals are incorporated in Foucault's bio-power (Andrieu 2004, 12; Blanchette 2006, 7). We have discussed the question of incorporating populations in the prison system in other works (Deleuze 1992, 5; Mincke and Lemonne 2014).
18 This is the term we use for the questioning that, from its very origins, the prison system has always posed for democracies: that of its legitimate nature.
19 It is along these lines, we think, that Gérard Mauger speaks of installing a flexible *habitus* corresponding to expectations of the business world (Mauger 2001).

20 This is what Boltanski and Chiapello describe as rejection of attachments in the projective city (Boltanski and Chiapello 1999, 179).
21 Unless the fact that, frequently, the positive depiction of their experience of mobility belies the reality of the way they actually live it.

References

Andrieu, Bernard. 2004. La fin de la biopolitique chez Michel Foucault: Le troisième déplacement. *Le Portique* 13–14 (June). Accessed 11 January 2016. http://leportique.revues.org/index627.html.

Bauman, Zygmunt. 2000. *Liquid Modernity*. Cambridge, Malden, MA: Polity, Blackwell.

Berger, Peter L., and Thomas Luckmann. 2006. *La construction sociale de la réalité*. Paris: Armand Colin.

Blanchette, Louis-Philippe. 2006. Michel Foucault: Genesé du biopouvoir et dispositifs de sécurité. *Lex Electronica* 11(2): 1–11.

Boltanski, Luc, and Eve Chiapello. 1999. *Le nouvel esprit du capitalisme*. NRF Essais. Paris: Gallimard. [2005. *The New Spirit of Capitalism*, translated by G. Elliott. London, New York: Verso.]

Boltanski, Luc, and Laurent Thévenot. 1991. *De la justification: Les économies de la grandeur*. Paris: Gallimard.

Decroly, Vincent, and Tony Van Parys. 2001. Rapport final de la commission loi de principes concernant l'administration pénitentiaire et le statut juridique des détenus. *Rapport fait au nom de la commission de la Justice*. Documents parlementaires.

Deleuze, Gilles. 1992. Postscript on the societies of control. *October* 59(October): 3–7.

Demonchy, Christian. 2004. L'architecture des prisons modèles françaises. In *Gouverner, enfermer: La prison, un modèle indépassable?*, edited by Pierre Artières and Pierre Lascoumes, 269–293. Paris: Presses de Science Po.

Ehrenberg, Alain. 1998. *La fatigue d'être soi: Dépression et société*. Paris: Odile Jacob.

Foucault, Michel. 2004. *Sécurité, territoire, population*. Paris: Seuil.

Frello, Birgitta. 2008. Towards a discursive analytics of movement: On the making and unmaking of movement as an object of knowledge. *Mobilities* 3(1): 25–50. doi:10.1080/17450100701797299.

Goffman, Erving. 1973. *La mise en scène de la vie quotidienne*. Paris: Les Editions de Minuit.

Kaufmann, Vincent. 2004. La mobilité comme capital? In *Mobilités, fluidités . . . libertés?*, edited by Bertrand Montulet, 25–41. Brussels: Publications des Facultés universitaires Saint-Louis.

———. 2012. Mobilité. *Forum Vies Mobiles*. Accessed 11 January 2016. http://fr.forum viesmobiles.org/reperes/mobilite-446.

Lacourt, Isabelle. 2007. "Quel est votre projet?" L'insertion socioprofessionnelle des usagers dans les CPAS bruxellois. *Brussels Studies* 5(March). www.brusselsstudies.be/publications/index/file/id/36/type/pdf/lang/fr.

Mauger, Gérard. 2001. Les politiques d'insertion. *Actes de la recherche en sciences sociales* 136(1): 5–14. doi:10.3406/arss.2001.2706.

Michon, Pascal. 2002. Strata, blocks, pieces, spirals, elastics and verticals: Six figures of time in Michel Foucault. *Time & Society* 11(2–3): 163–192. doi:10.1177/0961463X02011002001.

Mincke, Christophe. 2010. *Prison et mobilités: Des immobilités pénibles aux mobilités éprouvantes*. Paper presented to the colloquium Les mobilités éprouvantes. (Re) connaître les pénibilités des déplacements ordinaires, Université libre de Bruxelles, 26 March.

———. 2012a. *Moving Fixed People. Prison and Mobility*. Presented at the Mobile & the Immobile, University of Technology Dortmund, School of Spatial Planning, 10 February. Accessed 11 January 2016. http://mincke.be/Christophe_Mincke/Blog_-_activites_scientifiques/Entrees/2012/2/10_Prison_and_mobility.html.

———. 2012b. *Mobility, a New Paradigm for Prison?* Presented to Social Justice & Democratization. 2nd ISA Forum of Sociology, Buenos Aires, 4 August.

———. 2013. Mobilité et justice pénale: L'idéologie mobilitaire comme soubassement du managérialisme. *Droit et Société* 84: 359–389.

———. 2014a. La médiation pénale, contre-culture ou nouveau lieu-commun? Médiation et idéologie mobilitaire. In *Médiation pénale. La diversité en débat. Bemiddeling in strafzaken. En wispelturig debat*, edited by Carl Beckers, Dieter Burssens, Alexia Jonckheere and Anne Vauthier, 85–110. Antwerp, Apeldoorn: Maklu.

———. 2014b. *L'espace est-il une dimension physique? Sociologie de l'espace ou spatialisation de la sociologie?*. Louvain-la-Neuve: Dépôt institutionnel de l'Académie Louvain. Accessed 11 January 2016. http://hdl.handle.net/2078.3/144668.

———. 2014c. *L'espace est-il une dimension physique? Sociologie de l'espace ou spatialisation de la sociologie?*. Presented at Penser l'espace en sociologie, Université de Tours (France), 3 July.

Mincke, Christophe, and Anne Lemonne. 2013a. *Prison and (Im)mobility: A Foucaldian Inspiration*. Intervention symposium presented at Foucault and mobilities research, Luzern Universität, 7 January.

———. 2013b. Prison et mobilité: Et Foucault? In *HAL archives ouvertes*. Accessed 11 January 2016. http://hal.archives-ouvertes.fr/docs/00/85/97/13/PDF/Mincke_Lemonne_2013_Foucault_et_mobilitA_.pdf.

———. 2014. Prison and (im)mobility: What about Foucault? *Mobilities* 9(4): 528–549.

Montulet, Bertrand. 1998. *Les enjeux spatio-temporels du social: mobilités*. Volume collection: Cities and Companies. Paris: Harmattan.

Rosa, Hartmut. 2012. Accélération et dépression: Réflexions sur le rapport au temps de notre époque. *Les cahiers du Rhizome* 43(January): 4–13.

Sheller, Mimi, and John Urry. 2006. The new mobilities paradigm. *Environment and Planning A* 38: 207–226. doi:10.1068/a37268.

Valynseele, Jean-François. 2007. L'Union européenne à 27: Vers une dégradation de l'espace Schengen? *Institutions: La revue géolpolitique* (June). Accessed 11 January, 2016. www.diploweb.com/L-Union-europeenne-a-27-vers-une.html.

Vranken, Didier. 2006. Psychologisation ou transformation des modes de traitement social de la "question sociale"? In *Psychologisation de l'intervention sociale: mythes et réalités*, edited by Maryse Bresson, 25–34. Paris: L'Harmattan.

Vranken, Didier, and C. Macquet. 2006. *Le travail sur Soi*. Paris: Belin.

2 Identity construction and mobility in pilgrims' and travelers' writings

Contemporary reports about the Way of St James and the Hippie Trail

Frank Neubert

Please note: All English renderings of quotations from German language sources throughout the text are the author's.

Introduction

Pilgrimaging booms in Europe. Since the late 1990s, more and more people walk the Way of St James, hailing from all over Europe, and lately also from all over the world. They are not only Catholics but also describe themselves as Protestants, Non-Believers, Evangelicals, New Agers, or in one case even 'Buddhist with a Christian superstructure' (Kerkeling 2006). It may be that part of pilgrimages' new attractiveness derives from its increasing detachment from church or even religious structuring (Schützeichel 2012, 19). New forms of social structuring and institutionalisation transform or replace the old ones (Puschmann 2012). The individual quest for personal, spiritual or religious meaning is one of the most common social features that characterise the discourse on present-day pilgrimage. Even though pilgrimage has probably always been a highly individual affair, the variety of meanings to be searched for and found has been increasingly detached from official church doctrines in favour of a postmodern variety of meaningfulness. 'The emphasis on personal autonomy, separate from any religious affiliations, is rarely, if ever, found in earlier times' (Reader 2007, 224). This enhanced individuality of pilgrimage is demonstrated by the many texts that modern-day pilgrims produce about their journeys. They report extensively on their experiences along the way. They write books, edit series of photographs, and post daily blogs, tweets and other messages about 'their route'. It seems that with new forms of mediatised presentation and reflection of one's travel, individualised aspects gain in prominence and are newly interpreted. If, as Turner and Turner (1978) have stated, pilgrimage constitutes a liminal state where *communitas* is formed, then we might say that in present pilgrimage along the Way of St James, *communitas* becomes a virtualised form of communion of individual seekers who seek to authenticate their individual experiences by publishing their reports and reading those of other pilgrims (Hervieu-Léger 2004, 109–139). The reports as 'articulations . . . of an external pilgrimage' may then be read fruitfully 'as an exteriorised expression of an internal spiritual journey' (Reader 2007, 215).

The same holds true for a rather new genre of literature about past travelling along the so-called Hippie Trail in the 1960s and 1970s. Diaries written then and memories of the travels have rather recently started to crystallise in books and on websites about the Hippie Trail. Authors (predominantly men, as far as I can see) describe their travels from back then in terms of self-realisation, individual search for meaning and an experience between belonging to small groups and lone travelling along the route.

This chapter, however, is not about travels, or about routes, but rather about the texts in which the writers report and reflect on their travels. These texts are presented in books and online, and they are in their great mass a recent phenomenon. Life stories and transforming events have long been described by using the metaphor of the journey; however, the new emergence of reporting on travels in various media formats is unprecedented. The combination of specific forms of travel (such as pilgrimage or backpacking) with writing has even been institutionalised in courses such as one advertised in 2014 on a leaflet in Switzerland entitled 'Pilgrimage and Writing on the Way of St James', wherein the teacher stresses the individual experience and its transformation into text this way: 'Follow your longing, find clarity, research the space within you, be open for what the route keeps ready for you.' Students are expected to 'follow their inner voices in writing' (all from a leaflet by course teacher Susanne Wallimann 2014).

My aim in this chapter is to describe and analyse a current discourse of reporting on and writing about 'pilgrimage', taken as a term of self-identification used by travellers to Santiago and on the Hippie Trail. I do not analyse practices of mobility and pilgrimaging *en route*; I do not come up with new findings about the Way of St James or the Hippie Trail. In other words, I start from the assumption that *reporting about* religious, or spiritual, or individualising experiences during a specifically individual journey full of willingly endured hardships has become a new trend. This trend reflects new discursive entanglements of individual search for meaning, identity construction and what may be called *decelerated mobility*. Indeed, pilgrimage can be taken to represent 'a paradigmatic form of slow travel' (Howard 2012, 17). To move on foot along an old or otherwise meaningful route for many appears as a mode of temporary escape from the stressful mobility of everyday life. 'Amidst the increasingly fast tempo of life in late modernity, contemporary pilgrims and other "slow travellers' express needs and desires for alternative forms of temporality, while subverting the dominant "cult of speed"' (Howard 2012, 11). Pilgrims take the time to 'find themselves' and their spiritual paths in a way that Winfried Gebhardt (2013) has described as 'a self-empowerment of religious subjects'. Self-empowered subjects stress their autonomy, sovereignty and self-competence; they share a strong anti-institutional affect and the hope for enhanced sociality due to the transformations brought about by their individual quests (Gebhardt 2013, 92). This trend is often associated with pilgrimage, when travellers positively classify themselves as pilgrims. In doing so, they also use, perpetuate and reshape the old literary trope of life as a journey or even a pilgrimage.

In the texts under consideration, the term pilgrimage has come to be more and more used as a metaphor to circumscribe forms of modern spirituality (Puschmann 2012). It has also become a positive classifier in terms of mobility as opposed to more negatively connoted classifications such as 'tourism' (Frello 2008, 34). However, the usage of the category itself varies, depending on the perspectives and related interests of both observers and travellers: '[t]he kinds of behaviours that make anthropologists (and travellers themselves) regard people as pilgrims will inevitably change over time as systems of transport, articulations of spiritualities, secular ideologies, forms of syncretism and so on are transformed' (Coleman 2008, 362). Therefore, and in line with Coleman's passionate statement against (too narrowly) defining pilgrimage in order to keep theorising fruitful instead of dogmatically dominated, I shall here refrain from defining pilgrimage myself, but will rather stick to the discursive meanings attached to the fact that people describe their travels on the Way of St James and along the Hippie Trail as such.

In the next chapters, I will trace these discursive features in extracts from travel literature reporting about the Way of St James and the Hippie Trail. First, I shall briefly introduce the two routes and their history. I will also give an overview of the source material and my small sample thereof. Following that, I will present a few quotations from the sources that illustrate the discursive meanings of various types of pilgrimage mobility and their hierarchical ordering. Four tropes will be followed: (1) the idea of a temporary break with everyday routines, (2) the distinction of the authors and their co-travellers from other sorts of travellers such as 'mere tourists', (3) the idea that being on the move is more important than arriving at the destination, and (4) the irrelevance of the journey home.

Routes travelled and reported about

The Way of St James

The Way of St James, or Route to Santiago, has been taking pilgrims to the alleged tomb of Apostle James in the western Spanish town of Santiago (i.e. St James) de Compostela since about the 10th century CE. Major routes connected Central Europe with Santiago early on; reports and notices about pilgrims from the German-speaking world date back as early as 930 [Herbers (1991) 2011]. During the Middle Ages, the pilgrimage to Santiago (as well as to Rome and Jerusalem) flowered. The pilgrims' motivations ranged from piety, through the fulfilment of vows, to penalty for both religious and secular offenses. Though reporting on the travels in a published form was rare and restricted to the upper classes, returning home from pilgrimage may have probably increased one's social status by means of achievement and opportunities to tell tales. Early written and published reports from the German-speaking countries include those of Sebastian Ilsung (travelled in 1446), Leo von Rožmittal (1466), Hermann Küning von Vach (ca. 1490) and Arnold von Harff (1496–1498). With the Reformation and ensuing religious and territorial wars throughout Europe, pilgrim numbers decreased considerably. While the Reformation brought a harsh criticism of ritualism and outward display of religiosity, including pilgrimage, wars blocked the routes and to the dangers of travelling added that of being forcefully drafted into any military force met along the way. Pilgrimage to Santiago was revived again in the mid-19th century amidst the Catholic revival of this time. From the late 1930s on, St James became the patron saint of Spain, and Santiago became the country's national pilgrimage centre. It reached a new pan-European status in the 1980s with two visits by Pope John Paul II in 1982 and 1989. Meanwhile in 1987, the European Commission announced the network of Ways of St James to be the first European Cultural Route. In 1993 the architectural ensemble of Santiago and the Camino Francés were declared UNESCO World Heritage sites. These events helped the Route to Santiago gain new popularity all over Europe and worldwide.

The major route starts in the French town of St Jean Pied de Port in the Pyrenees and then passes through northern Spain to Santiago de Compostela. Four major feeder routes from France merge into the Camino Francés (French Way) at St Jean and Roncesvalles in Spain. These, in turn, are fed by a dense network of St James routes that spreads all over Europe. Most of the pilgrims from the reports start their route in St Jean, though some set off from one of the classic departure points in France (Paris, Vézelay, Le Puy and Arles) and some even from home, taking three months or more.

Pilgrims mostly travel on foot. Only a few make the route by bicycle, fewer even with other means of travel (such as horses, donkeys or footboard). However, the tourist industry, including most major travel agencies, has developed a wide variety of all-inclusive package tours on foot, by coach, by car, and even using air travel when only the last 100 kilometres will be covered in order to receive the Compostela, an official certificate documenting that one has rightfully made a pilgrimage.

In the Middle Ages and the early modern period, travel reports often served mainly as inspiration, information and a guide book for later pilgrims. Only very few passages of the texts contain accounts of personal adventures and less even report anything about religious experiences. Today, the scene has changed considerably, as there are libraries full of specialised travel guides on the Way of St James and its various branches. Travel accounts cover such material less and are more concerned with personal stories. Though they still contain passages that resemble guide book recommendations or warnings, pilgrim's reports today focus more on the individual experience of the pilgrimage, reflections on oneself, one's pains and tortures of the walk, sights visited and people met. In addition to books, websites, blogs and social media provide more space for images that at times even supersede verbal reporting.

Out of the vast literature, books by professional travel journalists or writers (e.g. Freund 1999; Moore 2006) are exceptional as they usually do not refer extensively to a spiritual, individualist search for meaning. Moore even uses this trope when reflecting on the connection between him and his donkey Shinto, and the transformations that he and the relationship go through on the journey. Catholic religiosity or alternative spiritualities do not play a role in such accounts. Rather, one could uphold the thesis that some travel writers regard the Route to Santiago as a topic that promises some readership and commercial success, even without spiritual content.

Rudolf Gruber's 1976 book is an early account on the Way before the great infrastructural developments. He writes of villages without a *refugio* (38), 'lonesome' roads and a ubiquitous respect of pilgrims. The Austrian pilgrim who is honouring a vow made to Slovak partisans in World War II stirs attention among the local populations wherever he comes, even in religious institutions: all the nuns of a convent 'want to see the pilgrim of St. James coming from Austria' (41). His pilgrim's book is filled with personal notes and benedictions instead of simple stamps that today's pilgrims collect in their book at each and every station of their journey as proof that they have made the journey to receive the Compostela. Gruber is even the subject of a long newspaper report upon arrival in Santiago (82). He concludes his account with a sort of prophecy: 'Maybe the "camino antiguo de Santiago" will become a modern "European hiking and pilgrimage trail" in the decades to come' (87). He was right in this, but this development led to immense changes in the attitudes of pilgrims and of the locals towards them. They came along with the infrastructural development and the commercialisation, or what Stausberg (2011, 64–68) calls the 'touristification of pilgrimage'. Recent reports refer to these processes in different ways. Oftentimes, pilgrims are grateful for the variety of opportunities of accommodation. But they also complain about the alleged lack of spiritual sincerity brought about by commercialisation both in the local attitude towards pilgrims and of pilgrims towards their own enterprise.

Three books have been especially influential for the modern history of the Route to Santiago: Paulo Coelho's *The Pilgrimage* (1995), Shirley MacLaine's *The Camino* (2001) and, in the German-speaking world, Hape Kerkeling's *Ich bin dann mal weg* (2006). The latter may have significantly contributed to a rising popularity of the Camino to German pilgrims. The years immediately following the book's publication saw a significant rise in the numbers of registered German pilgrims, doubling from roughly 8,000 to nearly 16,000 between 2006 and 2008. Since then, the number has remained stable around 13,000–14,000 per year. This has led some observers to speak of a 'Kerkeling Effect', though others doubt this and trace the growing numbers back to a generally increasing interest in the route.

From the mid-1990s on, more and more books reporting on the Camino were published. Many of them made reference to one, or all, of the three 'big books'. The most common feature across the board is the attempt to underscore the individuality of the pilgrimage experience. Most obviously, this happens through highlighting individual characteristics of the travelling person, such as being a 'career woman' (Dankbar 2009), having a certain disease to additionally cope with along the way, such as diabetes (Suckow 2011) or Parkinson's (Brass 2011). Others highlight special 'equipment' like travelling in special shoes (jakobsweginchucks.wordpress.com), by kickboard (bikehard.wordpress.com) or with a donkey (Moore 2006). Even more obvious, many reports bear the title or subtitle 'My Camino' (Bischoff 2008). The German 'Mein Jakobsweg' gives a list of some 20,000 hits on a basic search engine; the English 'My Camino' results in some 70,000. It is also noteworthy that many pilgrims take their reports as relevant to themselves and other pilgrims insomuch as they publish them as *books on demand* even if institutional publishers have declined taking them into their programmes. In most cases, individuality is also produced through reference to the respective author's motivation and personal background, recounted in both biographical sketches and personal reflection interlaced with the reports. In order to present some general features of the literature in the next chapter, I have chosen a few titles from the list of some 3,000 German language books and around 10,000 blogs about the Camino.

The Hippie Trail

Inspired by a century-long history of the reception of Indian religious ideas in America and by the poets of the beat generation (Prothero 1991; Sterritt 2013), a huge number of American and European youths started travelling the world as Hippies in the 1960s and 1970s. India had been seen as the motherland of spirituality since the late 18th century in Europe and was presented as such by Indian gurus visiting Europe and America since the late 19th century. For young people in search of a different lifestyle and religious purpose of life, India seemed to be a land of dreams. Already in 1967, Stuart Hall remarked that 'the identification with "East" as opposed to "West" [as] often taken literally: the numbers of Hippies – American, British, Swedish and German – who pass between India and Nepal . . . has [sic] been calculated in recent years as nearing the 10,000 mark' (Hall [1967] 2007, 151). One of the most important routes led them from Europe overland via Greece to Turkey, touching Istanbul and Lake Van, farther on into Iran and through Afghanistan (where many remained in Kabul and became heavily addicted to various kinds of hallucinogenics), then on to Pakistan and India. Paths split there. Depending on their respective religious or other interests, travellers moved on to Goa, Nepal or Thailand, or they went to holy places of India such as Benares, Tiruvannamalai, Vrindavan or Rishikesh. A significant number of people from Australia also took the reverse route from South East Asia overland to Europe (see Wheeler 1970). Remarkably few of them developed a similar spiritual interest as Europeans and Americans whose destination was Hindu or Buddhist South and South East Asia.

The Hippie Trail was open through the 1960s into the early 1970s. After that time, regional conflicts shut some countries for shorter or longer periods of time, and travelling became harder. After the Iranian revolution in 1979–1980, the overland route was no longer passable for travellers. Only in the early 2000s did the route open for a brief period of time, when some started off again, including a few travel journalists such as Rory Maclean (2006), who comes up with some interesting theses on the influence that the Hippies had on the countries they visited.

During the first years, the journey was purely individual, and its success depended notably upon how one fared with the locals. Among the travellers, loose associations formed for a short time and chunks of the route only to dissolve again. Travelers and seekers met inadvertently as 'like-minded people from similar social networks' (Urry 2002, 260). As the travellers were often on individual quests, these associations mostly served pragmatic purposes such as safety, finding accommodation or moneymaking, and they tended to dissolve quickly. However, travel along the route changed remarkably as soon as the numbers of travellers increased. From the late 1960s onwards, travelling overland to Asia became more and more of a business of its own, which also changed the face of the journey considerably. Locals discovered that the travellers brought at least some money, and they started businesses for the growing groups of Westerners. Some travellers started their own businesses after their return, buying cars or minibuses and offering regularly scheduled overland services (like Magic Bus, Hughes Overlanders or Sundowners), mostly from some European spot to Kathmandu and back. The best known business offspring from the Hippie Trail is probably Lonely Planet. Its first guide book was Tony Wheeler's *Across Asia on the Cheap*, published in 1970. Thenceforth the company developed rapidly.

Travel along the Hippie Trail mostly consisted in hitching and riding local buses and trains, the cheaper the better. When, in the seventies, some parts of the route were closed, distances were bridged by flying over the crisis areas. People slept in cheap hotels and sometimes in private accommodations. Amongst travellers, recommendations of where to sleep, eat, shop, meet other travellers or get drugs were passed on by word of mouth. Indeed, the backpackers 'may fruitfully be viewed as constituting an ad hoc community of storytellers. The unique structural features of the backpacking trip result in a social context which is highly conducive to narrative identity work' (Noy 2003, 81). This also crystallises in the ex post narrations of the reports that the travellers have started to publish since the late 1980s. Among them are a variety of texts. Their style and intention varies considerably, ranging from a slightly revised edition of the old travel diary nourished by some additional tourist information (Worrall 1988), through a report on the adventures and hardships of individual travel (Brady 2013), to a distinctly theological treatise that places the journey in the framework of a clear-cut spiritual path (Swami 2013).

Hierarchising mobilities

Chosen liminality

In their groundbreaking anthropological work on Christian pilgrimage traditions, Victor and Edith Turner (1978) argued that pilgrimage is performed in a state of liminality. Pilgrims leave their everyday lives behind, including friends, relatives, work and the respective social and economic status. 'Taking a break', 'escaping the daily routines', 'taking time for oneself' or 'preparing a decision' are common phrases in which the authors describe both the apartness of their situation and the ideas behind the choice for the pilgrimage. In accordance with such perception, they reflect about purposes, expectations and personal intentions in connection with the moment of departure and the preparation in some detail. Thus, they let their readers take part in the process of separation that leads into the liminality pilgrimage.

Most often, people hear about the Camino from friends or by reading accounts of it. They mostly link the ultimate decision to embark upon the pilgrimage with such a first acquaintance (e.g. Dankbar 2009, 18; Kunigo 2014, 11). However, there is always an account of some aim and/or a trigger event. For Dankbar (2009), dissatisfaction with her career and love life spawned the need for a prolonged time-out. Being a declared atheist, Kunigo (2014, 10) wants to prove 'not only, how much stresses and strains he can inflict' on himself, 'but also, how little luxury' he needs 'in order to be in harmony' with himself and the world around him.

Travelers on the Hippie Trail also report on the motives that led them on the way. For many, word of mouth about adventurous travels, free love and cheap drugs were the main attractions for going on the journey, with Jack Kerouac's *Dharma Bums* and *On the Road* being constant references. Others report they were looking for deep religious or spiritual experiences that they did not expect to find at home. Thus, Radhanatha Swami (2013) followed a long felt calling in search for God. Brady (2013), on the other hand, first rambles around Central and South America before returning home and leaving again with some vague idea of getting to India one day. Still, he describes his experiments with all kinds of hallucinogenic substances and with meditation practices in terms of a spiritual search he hopes will be finally solved when he reaches India. Worall (1988) reports that he wanted to see and learn more of the planet he was living on, taking 'more time than is allowed by convention'. While Radhanath Swami and Ananda Brady travelled on their own or with small, spontaneous groups, Worrall reports on an organised tour on a Hughes Overland minibus. For all of them, taking leave from family and friends is also a general topic that illustrates their preoccupation with entering a state of being different from the quotidian circumstances back home. Nearly all the reports contain scenes of farewell and reflection about the family. Brady (2013) spends a few pages on his seemingly difficult relationship with his father (176–179), which he obviously was able to positively restructure during his travels and in his account. For him, the radical break that somehow again reconciles him with his family in a loose way happens before he sets out on his travels to North Africa and Asia, when his father tells him, 'Of course you're welcome to come back any time to visit, but not to live. Burn your bridges . . .' (179). Radhanath Swami recounts the reluctance of his parents to let him go and their worries about his safety (Swami 2013, 29–30). Worrall just mentions the reactions of incomprehension to his 'unconventional' decision and a somehow uncomfortable farewell scene with his parents. However, even for him, the breakaway from routines has a taste of definiteness: 'Think of bursting out of the mould and dropping it, discarding it without looking back' (Worall 1988, 598).

Leaving generally means a break from one's daily routines, an alienation from family and friends. This is a generally reflected topic in the reports on the Camino as well. Reactions by friends and family to the decision to walk the Camino are narrated, with the scenes of farewell described. The longer the journey lasts, the more distance travellers construct between themselves and the home they have left behind, not only in geographic terms but virtually as well. 'Everything now seems so far away' is a common formulation found regularly in the reports.

Real pilgrims, other pilgrims and all the rest

In his book on religion and tourism, Michael Stausberg (2011) has argued that pilgrimage centres have grown into important tourism centres with the rise of modern tourism. The traditional places, architectural marvels, or pilgrim rites make pilgrimage sites attractive to tourists. Indeed, 'pilgrimage technically is a branch of the tourism sector' (57). This, however, means that different categories of travellers are present at pilgrimage sites, and they will be distinguished by the industries and pilgrimage officials. More importantly, for our purposes, pilgrims often make clear hierarchical differentiations between themselves and the 'tourists' and even between themselves as being 'real pilgrims' and other, 'false pilgrims' who are not doing the right thing.

Kunigo (2014, 212) accounts that on the last 100 kilometres of the route, they were 'permanently surrounded by Sarria-pilgrims', meaning those who do only these last 100 kilometres from Sarria to Santiago on foot in order to fulfil the necessary minimum for receiving the Compostela. They are looked at with measurable disdain by those who do the complete Camino Francés or come from even farther away. Sarria-pilgrims, Kunigo writes, can be recognised not only by their equipment but also by their walk: 'People who have only a hundred kilometres before them, walk completely differently than those who undertake five or ten times as much' (ibid.). Two of the Sarria-pilgrims 'make a beautifully absurd impression' but 'at least they just walk and don't perform some unworthy crap' (ibid.). Indeed, these pilgrims are more like 'tourists' (213). Worse still are 'taxi-pilgrims' whom he deems 'ridiculous': 'Having yourself driven from hostel to hostel in order to collect stamps for a certificate is nearly unsurpassably nonsensical' (ibid.).

In his popular *Ich bin dann mal weg* (2006), German comedian Hape Kerkeling defines the real pilgrims as those who are willing to question their identity and to be open towards the experiences to come. Who does not do that, he states, can just as well stay at home. Other pilgrims wonder about how the Camino is used as a sort of marriage market among pilgrims, how some people spend lots of time on their smartphones twittering and messaging to the world, or how they seek as much luxury as possible instead of sticking to the rule of simplicity during a 'real pilgrimage'. All reports feature a number of criteria by which the author claims to distinguish himself as a real or good pilgrim compared to 'false' pilgrims. Following Hervieu-Léger (2004), this can be interpreted as enhancing the process of validation of the individual experiences. The pilgrims read other pilgrims' books, blogs and tweets, and they comment on them, thereby creating a virtual community in which they mutually validate their experiences and set standards of 'real pilgrimage'. This also includes openly and harshly criticising those who seem not to stick to those standards.

Among the Hippie Trail reports, Worrall (1988) is most clearly preoccupied with his status 'under way', being a traveller in comparison with tourists. The first instance occurs when their van is overtaken by two minibuses in Yugoslavia, and they are told that these were only doing European trips: 'Huh. Mere tourists' (Worall 1988, 596). In writing this, Worrall creates a critical distance between himself as author and the traveller he was back then. According to Worrall, one major difference constructed by the travel group was that tourists informed themselves about the places they visited, just to find only what they expected, while the travellers didn't know a thing and went for the 'real experience'. In his report, however, Worrall gives his readers a good deal of tourist information about the places with an interesting narrative strategy: he lets one of his co-travellers read the information to everyone. Any such occurrence, however, ends with a lapidary, 'We did not know all that.'

For Radhanath Swami (2013), the distinction works along a different line of argument. He defines his journey to India as a god-guided spiritual route along which he slowly learns to follow certain rules of a spiritual life, such as refraining from sexuality, not using drugs, living as a vegetarian or meditating as often as possible. Anytime a new behavioural change occurs, there is a new distinction from other travellers who block their own spiritual paths by not giving up these habits.

Both in India and in Santiago, at the end of the respective journeys, the distinction between different kinds of travellers once again becomes virulent. Pilgrims often report on the overcrowded daily Pilgrims' Mass in Santiago. Being happy to arrive in front of the cathedral after an arduous walk of 1,000 kilometres or more, they most commonly are disappointed by the Mass, the preachers and the bureaucratic procedure of obtaining the official pilgrim's certificate. Pilgrims and tourists are distinguished in terms of mobility and immobility. While the tourists just look and travel onward, they 'block the way' and hinder 'real spiritual activities'. Pilgrims, on the other hand, are described as being on the move in both geographical and virtual space. Their journey is about changing one's physical location in order to also transform one's location in social and spiritual spaces.

Travelling matters more than arriving

Disappointment at what happens after arriving at one's destination is a common theme. Brady (2013) reaches India after some years of travelling, but he does not find the spiritual awakening he had hoped for all that time. Only when travelling to India again 30 years later does he find a guru whom he trusts and from whom he receives formal initiation as a spiritual student. Radhanath Swami (2013) is shocked to see accomplished yogis in India show off with their abilities, and only his own guru, Srila Prabhupada from the International Society for Krishna Consciousness, is able to convince him of his sincerity. Pilgrims to Santiago often find the place crowded, the Mass seems disgustingly dull to them, the tourists and would-be pilgrims are in the way. Reflecting on their feelings upon arrival, many of the travellers come to the conclusion that now they know what it means to say that the way is the destination. (German: *Der Weg ist das Ziel.*) This common saying runs like a thread through all texts on the Camino and the Hippie Trail. Indeed, physical pains, challenges and all kinds of discomforts along the way are constantly reinterpreted as a variation of that theme. Without these hardships, the way could not be the destination. Whenever blisters occur, the path becomes unbearably steep, the weather too hot or too wet, it is time for reflection about the reasons for 'doing this to oneself' (Bischoff 2008, 54). Spiritual insights and realisations about oneself occur regularly in conjunction with reported hardships of travel. The same holds true for the Hippie Trail books as well. Radhanath Swami (2013) makes his decisions to abide to certain principles of a pure life in times of trouble. Ananda Brady (2013) is always reminded of his spiritual quest and his plan to go to India when things go wrong in a place that he had liked for a while.

All personal change, in the end, is interpreted by the authors as a result of being underway, of moving, not of arriving at a predetermined destination. This trope holds true as well for the internal, personal and spiritual changes brought about during the journey. In the end, the travellers realise that life is about constant change instead of reaching a stable state of the self. The process of personal development is more relevant.

Travelling home is short

In Ian Reader's attempt to explain the recent popularity of pilgrimage in 2007, he accounted for technical development in transportation as one of the major reasons. In fact, he said, '[C]ontinual improvements in mass transport systems have made pilgrimage sites increasingly accessible' (Reader 2007, 216). However, reading pilgrims' and travellers' reports, we may have to formulate this more precisely. It seems that with mass transportation, pilgrimage sites have become more accessible for tourists, cultural travellers and other people. For pilgrims who seek what they call an original adventure, or experience, it seems more relevant that the sites have become more 'leaveable'. After a long journey on foot, by bike, or by hitchhiking, it is easy to return home in a fast and comfortable way.

Looking at the sources, it is clear that travelling back is quantitatively irrelevant. As the journey itself matters most, the time after the arrival is marginalised. This is true even for the medieval and early modern reports when the home journey lasted as long as the pilgrimage itself but merely figured in the reports in passing. In present-day reports, the home journey is most often relegated to single sentences and brief interpretations: 'Three hours on the plane geographically reverse two months of walking. What strange worlds we live in' (Freund 1999, 129). In Pia Brodmann's report, there is not even an attempt to revise the diary style when mentioning the return journey: 'Return journey by bus. Yearningly, I look out of the window. A bit of the pilgrimage route is visible' (Brodmann 2002, 246). In the Hippie Trail reports, the return journey is never even mentioned. The authors merely report very briefly about being back home without mentioning how they got there. Only Brady (2013, 566) mentions a farewell scene at an airport, which suggests that he flew back to the United States and thus returned to a more normal life after nearly a decade on the road.

Conclusions

Reports on the Camino and the Hippie Trail do share a lot of characteristics with other travel writings. There is a much wider boom of reporting about 'decelerated mobility': pilgrimage, hitch-hiking, long-haul hiking trails, adventure holidays and individual tourism are constantly being distinguished hierarchically from mass transportation, mass tourism and everyday commutation between home and work. Thus, it comes as no surprise to find at least one of the Hippie Trail reports (Worrall 1988) to be not that much different from other kinds of travel literature. Many of the blogs and books about the Camino are also structurally indistinguishable from other travel books. This fact can indeed be interpreted as evidence for the growing 'touristification of pilgrimage' (Stausberg 2011) and of so-called individualised travel. The sheer mass of reports about the Camino de Santiago in comparison with other travels, however, also points to the fact that pilgrimages, the individual search for meaning and writing about both have become deeply interwoven. The internal journey described in the accounts can be afforded only through travelling in person. According to the ideology of mobility underlying the reports, pilgrimage is necessarily a form of 'corporeal travel' (Urry 2002, 256). The spiritual and other transforming experiences can be brought about only through co-presence with other pilgrims ('face-to-face') on the way to a specific place ('face-the-place'). Not only do pilgrimage sites 'need to be seen "for oneself", to be experienced directly' (Urry 2002, 261), but there is a shift from place to route. The journey itself has to be made 'for oneself'; the route and its hardships have to be experienced directly. In addition to facilitating co-presence (Urry 2002, 262), pilgrimage also necessitates forms of involvement and commitment to be displayed in certain behaviours. These are constantly being surveyed, described and criticised by all the co-present pilgrims. 'Co-presence affords opportunities to display such attentiveness and hence commitment, and simultaneously to detect where there is little commitment in others' (Urry 2002, 259).

The reports, then, indicate how the search for religious, or spiritual, identity during the journey is framed in terms of mobility. While travelling, pilgrims are consciously mobile in contrast to the non-conscious forms of everyday mobility. To create such consciousness, it is necessary to escape the daily routines, to 'drop out', as the Hippies would have it (Hall [1967] 2007, 148), and to express the continual process of moving and transforming. While the mobility of pilgrimage and individual travel bears a strong dynamic, everyday mobility always remains the same. The latter should be left behind for an experience of real, decelerated mobility. As Frello (2008, 34) has clearly put it: '[h]ierarchical distinctions between movements are not only encountered when travellers of various kinds attempt to distinguish themselves in relation to mass tourism or even avoid the "tourist" label altogether, as when organisers as well as participants in heritage tours prefer to interpret their travel in terms of a "pilgrimage"'. These hierarchical distinctions of mobilities occur regularly and in various forms throughout the reports. Pilgrimage and other forms of 'slow travel' are thereby marked in a double way, as Howard (2012, 12) has argued: 'On the one hand, a pilgrimage or other slow journey may signify a very personal endeavour aimed at introspection and self-transformation, while on the other, may be seen as a meta-critique and indirect subversion of the existing social order'. Pilgrims implicitly in their journey and explicitly in their accounts criticise the everyday commutations and oscillations as stressful and meaningless mobility that lacks awareness. They contrast such 'hypermobility' not with sedentarism or other forms of determined non-mobility but with a different, older and more conscious form of mobility that focuses on deceleration and growing awareness.

Sources

Bischoff, Barbara. 2008. *Mein Jakobsweg: Verlangen nach lichterem Sein*. Norderstedt: Books on Demand.

Brady, Ananda G. 2013. *Odyssey: Ten Years on the Hippie Trail: My Decade of Overland Travels in the 70s*. Chula Vista, CA: Aventine Press.

Brass, Karl-Heinz. 2011. *Jeder Schritt zählt . . ..: 1006 km Jakobsweg trotz Parkinson*. Pfungstadt: Klarigo.

Brodmann, Pia. 2002. *Zu Fuss nach Santiago de Compostela: Erlebnisse – Begegnungen – Gedanken – Erkenntnisse: 9. Juni bis 15. August 2001*. Ufhusen: Warmisbach.

Coelho, Paulo. 1995. *The Pilgrimage: A Contemporary Quest for Ancient Wisdom*, translated by Alan Clarke. San Francisco: HarperOne.

Dankbar, Sabine. 2009. *Karriere oder Jakobsweg? Wegezeit – Wendezeit: Mein Weg nach Santiago de Compostela*. Dülmen: Laumann.

Freund, René. 1999. *Bis ans Ende der Welt: Zu Fuß auf dem Jakobsweg*. Vienna: Picus.

Gruber, Rudolf. 1976. *Tagebuch eines Pilgers nach Santiago de Compostela: Herausgegeben im "anno sancto Compostelano" 1976*. Linz: Wimmer.

Kerkeling, Hape. 2006. *Ich bin dann mal weg: Meine Reise auf dem Jakobsweg*. Münster: Piper.

Kunigo, Maori. 2014. *Vom Schisser zum Glückspilz in 26 Etappen: Noch ein Reisebericht vom Jakobsweg*. Norderstedt: Books on Demand.

Maclaine, Shirley. 2001. *Der Jakobsweg: Eine spirituelle Reise*. Münster: Goldmann. [Original: *The Camino*]

Maclean, Rory. 2006. *Magic Bus: On the Hippie Trail from Istanbul to India*. London: Penguin.

Moore, Tim. 2006. *Travels with My Donkey: One Man and His Ass on a Pilgrimage to Santiago*. New York: St. Martin's Griffin.

Suckow, Beate. 2011. *Wohin die Sehnsucht mich trägt: Als Diabetikerin allein auf dem Jakobsweg*. Leipzig: St. Benno.

Swami, Radhanath. 2013. *The Journey Home*. San Rafael, CA: Mandala.

Wheeler, Tony. 1970. *Across Asia on the Cheap*. Oakland, CA: Lonely Planet ebook (2010).

Worrall, John. 1988. *Travelling for Beginners – To Kathmandu in '72*. Amazon Digital Services.

References

Coleman, Simon. 2008. Do you believe in pilgrimage? Communitas, contestation and beyond. *Anthropological Theory* 2(3): 355–368.

Frello, Birgitta. 2008. Towards a discursive analytics of movement: On the making and unmaking of movement as an object of knowledge. *Mobilities* 3(1): 25–50.

Gebhardt, Winfried. 2013. Die Selbstermächtigung des religiösen Subjekts und die Entkonturierung der religiösen Landschaft. In *Religionshybride: Religion in posttraditionalen Kontexten*, edited by Peter A. Berger, Klaus Hock and Thomas Klie, 89–105. Wiesbaden: Springer VS.

Hall, Stuart. (1967) 2007. *The Hippies: An American 'Moment'.* CCCS Selected Working Papers 2: 146–167.

Herbers, Klaus. (1991) 2011. Der erste mitteleuropäische Jakobspilger zu Beginn des 10: Jahrhunderts und die Beziehungen der asturischen Monarchie zu Süddeutschland. In *Pilger, Päpste, Heilige: Ausgewählte Aufsätze zur europäischen Geschichte des Mittelalters,* edited by Klaus Herbers, 341–349. Tübingen: Narr.

Hervieu-Léger, Daniele. 2004. *Pilger und Konvertiten: Religion in Bewegung.* Würzburg: Ergon. [Original title: *Le Pèlerin et le converti: La religion en mouvement.* 1999. Paris: Flammarion.]

Howard, Christopher. 2012. Speeding Up and Slowing Down: Pilgrimage and Slow Travel through Time. In *Slow Tourism: Experiences and Mobilities,* edited by Simone Fullagar, Kevin Markwell and Erica Wilson, 11–24. Bristol: Channel View.

Noy, Chaim. 2003. This trip really changed me: Backpackers' narratives of self-change. *Annals of Tourism Research* 31(1): 78–102.

Prothero, Stephen. 1991. On the holy road: The Beat Movement as spiritual protest. *The Harvard Theological Review* 84(2): 205–222.

Puschmann, Norbert. 2012. Pilgern als Metapher moderner Religiosität. In *Pilgern gestern und heute: Soziologische Beiträge zur religiösen Praxis auf dem Jakobweg,* edited by Patrick Heiser and Christian Kurrat, 45–73. Münster: Lit.

Reader, Ian. 2007. Pilgrimage growth in the modern world: Meanings and implications. *Religion* 37: 210–229.

Schützeichel, Rainer. 2012. Über das Pilgern: Soziologische Analyse einer Handlungskonfiguration. In *Pilgern gestern und heute: Soziologische Beiträge zur religiösen Praxis auf dem Jakobweg,* edited by Patrick Heiser and Christian Kurrat, 19–43. Münster: Lit.

Stausberg, Michael. 2011. *Religion and Tourism: Crossroads, Destinations and Encounters.* London: Routledge.

Sterritt, David. 2013. *The Beats: A Very Short Introduction.* Oxford: Oxford University Press.

Turner, Victor, and Edith Turner. 1978. *Image and Pilgrimage in Christian Culture: Anthropological Perspectives.* New York: Columbia University Press.

Urry, John. 2002. Mobility and proximity. *Sociology* 36(2): 255–274.

3 Instrumentalising the 'mobility argument'

Discursive patterns in the Romanian media

Camelia Beciu and Mirela Lazar

Introduction

The intra-European Union migration from the Eastern European countries that recently joined the EU bears analytical relevance to the logics underlying the instrumentalisation of migration and mobility in the public spheres of both the sending and the receiving countries. Thus, in the home countries such as Romania, the migration issue has been strategically used in the political and media spheres as a resource for legitimisation and identity construction, triggering diverse forms of interpellation and public discourses on the state of the nation. The media have played a structuring role in this process, fostering over time certain dynamics in the way the migration issue is posed.

In this chapter we investigate an aspect generally overlooked in current research: the framing of transnational mobility in media discourse in connection to migration as a public issue. One assumption of this chapter is that labour migration in the EU cannot be dissociated from the analysis of the public spheres in the sending countries. More specifically, it cannot be dissociated from the media's role in defining mobility and immobility and in legitimising the subjects' positions in relation to transnational ties – various scales of belonging and actions at a distance (Frello 2008). Starting from the idea that public spheres are formed through competing discourses and that the media in the main give visibility to these discourses, this research answers a key question: how do the Romanian media use transnational mobility as a discursive resource to problematise migration? What representations of mobility do the media construct, and how are they used to redefine migration as a matter of public interest?

We distinguish first between migration 'considered a complex (and turbulent) process' (Easthope 2009, 62), produced under particular economic and social circumstances and specifically appropriated by individuals within this process, and mobility understood as 'an integral aspect of social life' (61) and of identity construction. The ontology of mobility is materialised into socio-spatial trajectories, lifestyles and practices of 'multiple mobilities' (Sheller and Urry 2006, 212).

Second, migration and mobility have to be considered according to various discursive conditions, one of them being the public negotiation of meanings and representations. To a certain extent, the arenas of public visibility and various social imaginaries shape the attitude that social actors have towards mobility. Public discourses instrumentally construct 'regimes of mobility' (Glick Schiller and Salazar 2013, 183). In other words, they legitimise meanings and forms of mobility and introduce specific distinctions and interrelationships between mobility and temporal, spatial and social scales. Thus, representations of mobility are built through institutional policies and regulations, imaginaries and discursive practices. As a result, it becomes relevant how public discourses (media, politicians, NGOs, etc.) incorporate migration and the various experiences taking shape in this specific field of unequal relationalities, and how, under certain circumstances, they give meaning to fixity (place) in relation to movement and to the 'other' or to 'in-betweenness' (Easthope 2009, 68).

In the first part of the chapter, we discuss the analytical relationship between transnationalism, migration and mobility in the context of Romanian labour migration in the EU. After presenting the methodological design of the research, we analyse a collection of articles from serious Romanian press between 2011 and 2014 to highlight patterns of meaning and visibility of mobility in this particular context.

Transnationalism, migration and mobility: contexts of research

Analyses of mobility in the context of migration are often linked with the transnational paradigm (Bailey et al. 2007; Bauböck and Faist 2010; Mügge 2012; Vertovec 2009). In this light, according to Faist (2010, 16), three conceptual approaches can be considered in defining transnationalism: descriptive-analytical (focusing on questions such as mobility and networks), transnational phenomena (substantiated by 'socially constituted formations') and sociocultural conditions (transnational practices). In his view, cross-border mobility and interactions within networks have structuring effects on the agency of groups and communities 'within global structures' (Faist 2010, 33). For authors like Boccagni (2012) and Georgiou (2006), this paradigm serves to analyse the configuration of 'fluid' identity spaces through interactions and social experiences at a distance, characterised by simultaneity and therefore by a proximity–distance dialectic.

We shall further discuss some implications of the use of this paradigm. To start with, one of the problems raised by the transnational paradigm is the need to avoid a catch-all use of the concept that would indiscriminately subsume actions at a distance and conflate migration, diasporic practices and mobility (Bauböck 2010; Boccagni 2012; Georgiou 2006). To Boccagni (2010), transnationalism should be understood as 'a potential attribute of social relationships, rather than a substantive entity' (119). Seen as such, transnationalism more widely reflects 'combinations of ties and their substance positions' (Faist 2010, 13), which are structured beyond the sovereign states' boundaries through various types of 'actions at a distance'. In this respect, we argue that mobility as a site of policies, practices and discourses highlights some of the processes that structure the transnational character of the social agents' actions, both grassroots and institutional. This research perspective could avoid an approach that takes transnationalism for granted. Thus, mobility is appropriated by social actors in practices of movement and non-movement under specific circumstances, migration being one of them. Such practices reveal strategies of the representation and negotiation of collective identities in connection to 'here' and 'there' – within the frame of relationality between hegemonic discourses and individual agency.

Furthermore, researchers also highlight the contradictions between (1) images acknowledged in both academic and public discourses on transnationalism, mobility and globalisation (the celebration of the mobility society and of fluid trajectories) and (2) the various constraints that actually define the practices of migration and mobility. In this regard, O'Reilly (2007, 277) points out the 'series of contradictions indicative of the tension inherent in a mobility–enclosure dialectic'. Therefore processes that emphasise mobility (globalisation, new technologies, etc.) must be linked to others that restrict mobility (unequal access to employment, etc.), establishing symbolic boundaries (intra-EU migration is the example we will consider).

Not least, the paradigm of transnationalism is often discussed in terms of its explanatory potential, particularly with regard to understanding ties and actions at a distance as emergent, distinct realities, not as mere extensions of national frameworks or 'container-societies' (Beck 2000). From this point of view, transnationalism is often opposed to 'methodological nationalism' (Beck 2000). Some scholars argue that the transnational approach 'de-naturalises' aspects predefined mostly from a national angle, building the framework for the definition of migrants and other non-state actors 'as crucial agents' (Faist 2010, 14).

With this in mind, it should be clarified how the perspective of the sending country could be analytically constructed (including the practices of non-movement) so as to be relevant for the analysis of migration and transnational interactions. An operational concept in this regard could be 'regimes of mobility' (Glick Schiller and Salazar 2013). It introduces a type of analysis that (1) 'addresses the range of actors within specific situations, including, but not exclusively, state actors' (196) who participate in the legitimisation of meanings and forms of mobility and that (2) takes into consideration 'movement and settlement in constant and reconstituting interrelationships' (193) and 'in relationship to forces that structure political economy' (192).

We analyse here the ways in which public discourses in the countries of origin build meanings for mobility and practices for visibility of the migrants, acting among spaces and belongings: 'Rather than being evaluated as either good or bad, migration can be discussed as part of broader transnational processes within which nation-states are enmeshed and to which they contribute' (Glick Schiller 2010, 110). In the analysis of media representation of mobility, we do not introduce a predefined national angle but stress the dynamics of the national angle in the media public sphere and in connection with certain forms of simultaneity of the debates held in both the origin and destination countries. In other words, we consider the findings in the context of a public sphere that has evolved in terms of practices of debate and framing of intra-EU migration. In this sense we focus on a highly debated topic in the European countries: the lifting of labour market restrictions in the EU for Romanians and Bulgarians on 1 January 2014.

Methodology and corpus

The methodological framework draws on elements of critical discourse analysis (Chouliaraki 2006; Fairclough 2003; Van Leeuwen 2008) in order to emphasise discursive choices in the media construction of mobility in relation to intra-EU migration. We refer mainly to two conditions for these discourses, representation and evaluation. They are both organised by particular discourse strategies used to construct public issues.

The representation of the world (actors, events, relations, etc.) is a key dimension of discourse in terms of including/excluding actors, actions, practices and values (Wodak 2010). In discourse studies, representation, as a practice of mediated visibility, conditions the production of 'power discourses' and ideologies: 'Representation has to do with knowledge but thereby also with "control over things"' (Fairclough 2003, 28). 'Moreover, if ideologies are primarily representations, they can nevertheless also be "enacted" in ways of acting socially, and "inculcated" in the identities of social agents' (9). The ideological work of discourses, as argued by Fairclough, consists in 'seeking to universalize particular meanings in the service of achieving and maintaining dominance'. (56) This hegemonic process of building meaning, within representational strategies as signifying practices, attempts 'to secure discursive or ideological "closure"' (Hall 1997, 245). But meanings 'can never be finally fixed' (270), and there is always a discursive work to 're-appropriate' them (reversing interventions, counter-strategies) in order to construct new ones. Thus, what takes precedence in this study is the analysis of the discursive strategies that the media adopt to legitimise meanings and hierarchical forms of mobility and immobility in terms of subjects' positions and membership categories.

Evaluative statements (value judgements, commonsensical frames) express various ways in which individuals define social action under specific circumstances, placing it in a perspective of both generality and engagement, that is in a public interest area. Thus, evaluations can establish ideological patterns of meaning. 'Ideological' points to those patterns of meaning 'involved in (an) aspect(s) of social "reality" (in particular, in the realm of social relations in the public sphere), felt to be commonsensical, and often functioning in a normative way' (Verschueren 2012, 10). Ideological meanings may have structuring effects on social life when 'beliefs and concerns which are associated with the interests of particular social groups come to be general beliefs and concerns' (Fairclough and Fairclough 2012, 100).

By using critical discourse analysis, we are able to underline the reproduction of meanings and contexts of mobility in relation to strategies employed to establish normative patterns: the naturalisation of certain aspects; the definition of hierarchies and distinctions or similarities; the legitimation of membership categories and the strategic use of an identity repertoire. In particular, we analyse how the media produce ideological meanings of mobility, as actors playing at the crossroads of two fields of power: 'the media logic' as the 'production of issues according to criteria of competitiveness' (Landerer 2013, 243) and the mobility-related field of struggle between various actors: international institutions, media in the origin and destination countries, political-national discourse, European positioning, etc.

Based on these premises, the research investigates how mobility is built as an argument in redefining the public issue of migration, considering:

- The representation of migrants from the perspective of the social worlds in which they are involved (ways of being and acting) and of their mobility-immobility practices (personal and collective identities in connection with movement, place, proximity and distance);
- The referential strategies used: the modes of assignment and categorisation of the social actors of migration through the use of certain pronouns, metaphors, nominal phrases, adjectival phrases;
- The evaluations of mobility in the context of migration (the construction of the journalists' perspective).

The corpus consists of four Romanian quality newspapers (*Evenimentul Zilei, Cotidianul, Adevarul, Jurnalul National*) and covers the period 2011, 2013–2014. It is worth noting that the Romanian media overall, including quality newspapers, can be placed within a paradigm of commercial logic and political polarisation. We selected articles focusing explicitly on the theme of labour migration, according to two criteria: articles on macro events that dominated the media agenda in 2013 (full access to the EU labour market for Romanians starting with 1 January 2014) and articles focusing on various aspects of migration as part of the daily editorial policy on labour migration coverage. Throughout 2013, the media in Romania referred extensively to the implications of ending restrictions on the free movement of workers from Romania and Bulgaria. They adopted a particular angle of framing: the reactions of the press, politicians and the public opinion in the European countries that were to open their labour market, of which the UK was the most publicised. The coverage of this event intensified by January 2014, when each of the previous four newspapers published an average of three articles per day, and this number occasionally reached five or six articles in the same edition of one newspaper. The corpus on the opening of the UK labour market comprised 119 articles in 2013 and 75 in January 2014. The corpus on various aspects of labour migration in the EU includes 60 articles in 2011 and 51 in 2013.

Discursive patterns of transnational mobility: building a politics of visibility

Essentialising the geography of mobility

In the Romanian media discourse, mobility is constructed along certain regularities (thematic, contextual and evaluative) that generate patterns of visibility in terms of places (cities, countries), routes (images of circular mobility), social imaginaries (ways in which individuals and groups build their mobility) and processes (mobility as a mechanism for identity construction or as a means to institutionalise norms and practices).

As a trend, newspaper articles emphasise the 'mobility-settlement' dialectic (the reference to the city/country as a strategy to legitimise the migrant's status) and 'mobility as a process' (various aspects in connection to economic mobility and its negotiation in the public sphere). The print media also build mobility meanings through implicit images, which are discourse effects resulting from the general framing of migration.

After 2007, migrants and the various issues associated with this phenomenon acquired visibility in contexts assumed to have implications for the so-called image of the country. Trajectories and situations experienced by migrants are described and evaluated through their impact on the symbolic capital of the nation (Beciu 2012). A series of categories are thus legitimised, such as the migrants who have stood out in the destination countries through positive behaviour and actions ('the heroes'), recognised by the local communities. This category is counterposed on the one hand to the migrants (1) who, in a way or another, have fallen victim to untoward events or (2) who were involved in crime and on the other hand, (3) to 'us', the Romanians who have remained in place. Thus, the media define a symbolic hierarchy of those acting in (non-) migration contexts. An overlap between different forms of migration and mobility also results, and they generally encompass the symbolic capital of the nation. The discourse of self-perceived identity therefore structures the representation and problematisation of migration, and the media also use discursive patterns of mobility to construct it, as we will show.

The press provides visibility to migration mainly through day-to-day news reporting and feature articles that give a particular thematic focus. The news stories approach the migration topic as an outcome of a disruptive event involving Romanian protagonists in the destination country (Italy, Spain, Great Britain, Germany, etc.). The repertoire of these events is limited: offences, accidents, violence, negative stories in the host countries' media, statements made by politicians in those countries, TV shows giving a negative image of the Romanians through stereotyping. The articles take the form of reports that present only the chronology of the incidents, with the significance reduced to formulae of the type: 'two Romanians in Zaragoza', 'Romanians in Sicily', 'a group of Romanians from London'. The place emphasised in the headline and the story (cities and regions in the main destination countries) is not linked to further information about the migrants' engagement with these particular areas.

Within the 'mobility-settlement' nexus, the media construct global representations of the social actors through their association with the city or the region in the country of destination where they have settled, naturalising 'routes of the Romanians' in European countries in the – implied – context of labour migration. Through this representation, emphasis is placed on 'the Romanians' and less on the social actors of migration. By making 'routes', 'regions' and 'cities' visible, this discursive mobility geography creates 'groups' and categories of 'Romanians'. Mobility becomes significant in terms of the Romanians' presence in various European areas. Thus, the press establishes a politics of visibility within a social field of mobility-settlement, with individuals and groups being represented as national actors. This homogeneous social space, consisting of typical characters and actions, generates a 'phatic morality . . . created by long-term, habitual, ambient forms of mediated connectivity' (Frosh 2011, 383).

The feature articles value mobility as an identity path of anonymous individuals, a path with obstacles, risks and trauma ending in a miraculous/spectacular success of these people turned into heroes or in an even greater accumulation of difficulties: 'A young Romanian of Roma origin, Anina Ciuciu, who arrived illegally in France with her parents, is currently studying law at the Sorbonne and she dreams of becoming a magistrate.' (*Cotidianul*, 3 May 2013). Feature articles usually favour two images of the migrant: the hero of positive actions, outstanding in terms of drama and final outcome; the victim of seemingly preordained, inescapable situations. A series of expressions serve as evaluations of the individuals' path ('A Journey through Hell', *Evenimentul Zilei*, 5 January 2014) including the personal success or drama embedded in a trajectory of movement-settlement. This trajectory is invested with a symbolic dimension, authenticating the individual's success or failure in the context of migration, and legitimising her categorisation status.

Both day-to-day news reporting and feature articles introduce an essentialisation of mobility, reduced to abstract places and distances. We encounter a repertory of spatial trajectories that legitimises groups and categories of migrants as national actors. It is, however, a repertory that circumvents the ways in which these actors foster meaningful relationships and roles in practices developed in relation to others and to different forms of ' "locality" in the country of immigration and/ or in the sending country' (Dahinden 2010, 51). On the other hand, this representation mode highlights the sensational/dramatic side of migration (categories of winners, victims and culprits, and dichotomies such as the migrant hero versus the migrant victim). Instead, the migrants' lifestyles and their emergent practices do not enter in. The two types of articles are embedded in an editorial strategy to produce discourse about migration, namely the serialisation and the narrativization of events which become relevant to a permanent media agenda. This strategy, which became significant in 2013, is still shaping the media discourse.

Mobility through patterns of competitiveness

In 2013, the press in Romania began intense writing on an event with structural consequences for intra-EU labour migration, namely the lifting of work restrictions on 1 January 2014. Journalists initiated a discourse of anticipation throughout the year 2013, creating around this event a number of micro events that were periodically resumed.

The impact of the economic recession on migration-related policies in some European countries (Spain and the UK, in the first place) was constantly debated in correlation with the reconfiguration of the labour market, including the target occupations of Eastern and Central European migrants before the beginning of the crisis. The media reported the implications of these processes for the Romanian migrants, such as job loss and difficulty of finding employment in the destination countries or upon return to their countries of origin. At the same time, the press quantified the political and media reactions in the countries of destination, as well as the reactions of European officials, dwelling on the viewpoints expressed by British journalists and the British political class against a possible influx of Romanian migrants after 1 January 2014. The serialisation of each of these events is likely to develop, among other things, representations of mobility used in defining public issues.

We identify a pattern of meaning according to which mobility is associated to economically measurable trajectories – capital flows related to flows of the workforce within the EU. Mobility, in this case, is an abstract reality defined through social actors-entities (social groups, ethnic groups) whose path is measured in terms of effects on the economies-entities. Mobility and its impact on the economies of the home and destination countries, in the context of the crisis, are described in the form of seemingly invisible forces acting under objective mechanisms and in specific contexts. The metaphor of the 'flow' – the only element of concreteness to represent this kind of mobility – defines the magnitude of the phenomenon of migration, its inevitability and its implications for the source and host states. Through the use of this metaphor, abstract representations of migrants (as statistical categories) become legitimised, along with a specific interpretation of the economic recession's impact on migration: the crisis is associated with the undesirable consequences of a drop in migration and with Romania's changing position in the hierarchy of the countries that generate labour migration.

'If you look at the movement of workers from one country to another, the number of those who came from Romania and Bulgaria has decreased considerably in recent years', the EC spokesman said today.

(*Adevarul*, 25 July 2011)

In just two years of crisis, the flow of Romanians who left for other countries halved from 453,000 to only 255,000.

(*Adevarul*, 13 July 2011)

The continuous rise of Romanian residents in Spain and their high level of unemployment have had an impact on the ability of Spain to absorb new influxes of workers.

(*Evenimentul Zilei*, 11 November 2011)

Changes in the labour market, in the context of the economic recession, gave way to a new media discursive practice, that is the representation of mobility as a *competitive structure* of opportunities within an emerging 'parallel immobility regime' (Turner 2007, 289). A series of articles portrayed mobility in terms of more or less strategic choices the migrants make as to the place and the country of destination. Such framing of mobility also introduces competitive relations between the countries of destination, between the countries of origin and of destination and among the countries of origin, as well as a presumed hierarchy of the destination countries.

> Spain, the main destination for Romanian migration.
>
> > (*Adevarul*, 17 July 2011)

> Romanians renounce Spain for the Nordic countries, where they earn 1,200 Euros per month.
>
> > (*Evenimentul Zilei*, 28 July 2011)

> The Bulgarians and the Chinese might steal our jobs in Spain.
>
> > (*Evenimentul Zilei*, 9 August 2011)

> Britain preferred by young Romanians looking for work.
>
> > (*Adevarul*, 10 June 2013)

> The country for which tens of thousands of Romanians leave annually to make a good living could soon become a state unfriendly to Romanians, like Spain. The economic problems of Italy make those who leave for work turn to other destinations.
>
> > (*Evenimentul Zilei*, 22 September 2011)

> The profile of the Romanian worker that the British look for. Stories of young people "begging" for a day's work.
>
> > (*Jurnalul National*, 12 March 2013)

In the context of migration controls, the media employ a gains-and-losses frame to construct this competitive field of economic mobility. What is relevant in this regard is that the impact of the crisis on labour market access is transferred to the country of origin, to 'us' Romanians who actually lose jobs in the destination countries, which ensues in the *naturalisation of migration*. As such, the crisis and the undesirable consequences of decreasing migration become the theme that requires debate and both political and collective responsibility. Journalists focus more on Romania's status as a sending country in relation to the destination countries than on the social actors' perspective.

Migrant mobility and symbolic boundaries of identity

As Hall (1997) argues, in representing 'difference', both its positive and negative meanings are necessary to construct identities, but, 'at the same time, it is threatening, a site of danger, of negative feelings' (238). Based on this approach, we investigate the ways in which Romanian newspapers' representations of intra-EU mobility/migration invest the production of 'difference' with a negative connotation, establishing a 'site of danger' as a symbolic marker of identity boundaries. The newspapers reproduce the foreign media's categorisations of Romanian labour migrants and of their mobility patterns. The ideological underpinnings of these discursive categorisation strategies, with their focus on negativity, challenge the question of the nation's representation. Otherness and negativity as symbolic boundaries for Romania's image abroad are turned into a newsworthy theme for political and public debates in the national arena. The media discourse on the mobility of the migratory flows (as a 'produced movement' according to Cresswell 2001, 20 in Frello 2008, 30) establishes and instrumentalises hierarchies of (political, legal) status: powerful countries, having a voice, versus weak, voiceless countries; citizens having full rights versus second-class/vulnerable citizens.

The Romanian newspapers delineate labour mobility, as part of the constructed identity of the migrants' community, according to two axes: the supranational axis (the European Union) and the local axis (the destination countries). On the EU axis, the collective identity (of the migrant group extended to the nation) is related to EU citizenship (the latter being defined in terms of rights within the competitive field of mobility). The newspapers bring to the fore a derogatory European identity reserved for the imagined community of the people who leave for work abroad and also for their co-nationals (the inclusive 'we Romanians'). This construction is given legitimacy (Van Leeuwen 2008) by reference to the self- and external perception–labelling discourses that use authority arguments as well as experience-based testimony.

'We believe that a wave of criticism, since the beginning of the year, is aimed at labelling these citizens as second-class Europeans who present a risk just because they exercise their basic right to freely move and work', wrote European Parliament [Romanian] members.

(*Adevarul*, 3 February 2013)

'The EU benefits are not for Romanians', she [a Romanian migrant] says with frustration. 'You're part of a community, but you cannot work as other Europeans. We are always labelled as being Bulgarians or Romanians.'

(*Cotidianul*, 8 May 2013)

The YouGov poll for Sky News . . . found that around two thirds (64%) of British adults thought Romanians and Bulgarians should not be allowed the same working rights in Britain as those from other EU countries.

(*Jurnalul National*, 4 March 2013)

This categorisation pattern for the Romanian migrants' status, ranked as inferior European citizens (being identified as an obstacle to their intra-EU mobility), ideologically reconstitutes the relations of inequality and the Romania's political voice's loss of authority within the European Union.

'When it comes to decisions, especially in the last three years of the economic recession, Sofia and Bucharest have hardly been seen. . . . When it comes to important decisions, aggressiveness in entering the inner circle that makes these decisions is a game for tough people', said another European diplomat quoted by Reuters.

(*Cotidianul*, 8 May 2013)

On the axis of the destination countries, mobility is represented in the social interaction (relationships and practices) of Romanian migrants with the host societies, as a means of distinguishing between 'us' and 'them'.

The press relates mobility, its limitation and the uncertainties of Romanian migrants' settlement (social and territorial exclusion/eviction, expulsion) to the precariousness of their legal and socio-economic status, delineated mainly through the categorisation scheme 'poor, low-skilled, uneducated and uncivilised Romanians posing a threat to the host population'. This scheme is also legitimised through references to public and political discourses in the host countries. 'Poverty immigration' is a pattern of categorisation used by the Western media to cast Romanian migrants into 'otherness':

> Romanians and Bulgarians are the 'poverty immigrants' and they could be expelled from Germany. . . . They will be banned from travelling, according to realitatea.net.
>
> (*Evenimentul zilei*, 8 June 2013)

> 'Romanians and Bulgarians are warned to stay away from the British city of Brighton if they have no jobs or homes', theargus.co.uk writes.
>
> (*Jurnalul National*, 8 February 2013)

> The evacuation of Roma people that took place last Sunday was considered a great success.
>
> (*Adevarul*, 28 July 2013)

At the same time, discourses that shape identity on the basis of difference are ideologically recontextualised (the Romanian otherness) in order to strengthen the boundary markers of Romanian nationality (the inclusive 'us'):

> '. . . the Romanian "otherness" took shape in the imagination of the British public, and this great and educated nation was reduced to several inflammatory stereotypes. Even the word Romanian is too often uttered with a sneer', says Dunlop [a British historian, a writer and a TV producer].
>
> (*Evenimentul zilei*, 1 April 2013)

A 'rhetoric of inferiority' is premised by Romanian journalists on the stereotypes of collective perceptions and on attitudes of distrust and fears emerging towards the Romanians' mobility in host societies:

> . . . the hysteria caused by the British tabloids in which Romanians and Bulgarians are labelled as thieves, crooks and profiteers that will flood the UK by the thousands after labour market restrictions are lifted next year. . . .
>
> (*Cotidianul*, 3 February 2013)

The 'threat' of free movement by Romanian workers is legitimised through rational reasoning about pressures from migrants on the social security services and on jobs in the destination countries: According to Asscher [Dutch Minister of Social Affairs], there is "a big problem" with the free movement of workers [including Romanians] in Europe because it leads to "a downward spiral in the working conditions and lower minimum wages".

(*Evenimentul zilei*, 1 April 2013)

The newspapers instrumentalise a strategy of pole reversal in the binary opposition victim–perpetrator: from victims of inequalities and domination in the receiving countries, the Romanian migrants become 'invaders' who threaten the host population who in turn becomes a victim.

The press gives visibility to the ideologically based representations of the migrants' mobility in the host countries shared by some Romanians from previous immigration waves – old settlers – who also use a hyperbolic rhetoric of calamity (the 'invasion', the 'flooding' of the threatening Romanian immigrants) to justify restricting the access to Romanian newcomers:

'The invasion of those who will take advantage of the state aid system is imminent. I have warned the Romanian authorities to take the necessary measures to prevent the exodus of Roma', said Daniel Teau [president of the Federation of Romanian Associations in Europe].

(*Evenimentul zilei*, 1 January 2014)

The ethnic identity obstacles to exercising the right to free movement and work draw on stereotypes predicated on the logic of xenophobia and exclusion:

Politicians compete in making bellicose statements on the issue of nomads, while on the internet a 'game' has appeared called 'hurt the Gypsy'.

(*Adevarul*, 10 February 2011)

Without being a dominant construction in the Romanian newspapers, a discursive counter-strategy appears to redefine the mobility-settlement nexus in view of recovering the symbolic capital of national identity. Through positive metaphorical meanings, mobility is reinvested with value, reputation for competence and meritocracy assets:

Angela Gheorghiu, Nadia Comaneci, Alina Cojocaru, Norman Manea or Adrian Mutu, they, too, are Romanians, Mr. Boris!, Sir, Lord Mayor of London, have you forgotten?

(*Adevarul*, February 3, 2011)

Newspapers use the 'self-esteem–self-assessment/symbolic branding' counter-approach to communicate our revalorised national/collective identity to others:

Enescu and Eugène Ionesco, they are both great Romanians, Sir! Thousands of British honoured and heard these Romanians.

(*Adevarul*, 3 February 2011)

The Romanian newspapers recover speeches and views (usually coming from institutional authorities) that endeavour to neutralise or reverse the negative schema underlying the mobility-settlement interrelationship. As a trend, they exploit this counter-discourse in order to extend the interpretation of identity with a sense of collective contribution, beyond the individual experience of success:

> Constantly mentioned as a scarecrow for the British when it comes to opening the labour market from 1 January 2014, Romania is trying to counteract the media attacks.
>
> (*Jurnalul National*, 1 April 2013)

> Our ambassador in London writes articles in the British press to restore the Romanians' image.
>
> (*Jurnalul National*, 1st April 2013)

> [Romanian Minister of Foreign Affairs] Corlățean said that most Romanians already living and working in the UK 'are well-integrated into the British society'.
>
> (*Jurnalul National*, 4 March 2013)

> He [Romanian ambassador Jinga] states that over 4,000 doctors and nurses from Romania educated in our universities are now working in the National Health Service. . . . Tens of thousands of highly skilled Romanian construction workers found jobs in Great Britain.
>
> (*Jurnalul National*, 1 April 2013)

Mobility as a political metaphor: configuring national identity and country status

By repeatedly quoting British sources that express only one type of positioning, the newspapers in Romania legitimise the idea of a dominant discourse in the UK. One of the main ways to impose this discourse is to reproduce and isolate an image of mobility introduced by the British tabloids: mobility as an 'invasion' of the British territory (*Evenimentul zilei*, 1 January 2014) by the 'masses' of Romanian immigrants. Thus, a pattern of meaning is legitimised: mobility as a means of survival, the extreme solution for disadvantaged social groups; hence, the introduction of a categorisation such as the 'Romanians, the immigrants of poverty' (*Evenimentul zilei*, 8 June 2013) or 'poverty immigration' (*Adevarul*, 5 January 2014). This meaning of mobility is reproduced by giving prominence to a particular vocabulary: 'invasion', 'siege', 'exodus', 'hordes of Romanian immigrants' (*Jurnalul National*, 14 March 2013), 'influx of low-skilled workers from Romania and Bulgaria' and 'an army of out-of-work Romanians' are the kinds of terms consistently used by the Romanian journalists, most of them taken from the British press (e.g. *The Sun*, 3 February 2013); others are introduced by the journalists themselves in order to point out the intensity of negative opinions in the

UK (for example, the term hysteria used in reference to the attitude of the British newspapers):

> The scandal of the Romanian invasion.
>
> (*Jurnalul National*, 3 February 2013)

> *DAILY MAIL*: The population of two Romanian villages will move to the UK when restrictions are lifted on 1 January.
>
> (*Evenimentul Zilei*, 11 November 2013)

> Germany complains of the Romanians' assault.
>
> (*Evenimentul Zilei*, 5 February 2013)

> Ion Jinga, the Romanian Ambassador to London: 'Romanians do not want to "conquer" Britain'.
>
> (*Evenimentul Zilei*, 25 January 2013)

The Romanian newspapers also produce a metanarrative, pointing, especially through headlines, to each change of tone or reframing in the British press. For example, from the global image of danger ('The British people are terrified: "Romanian Gypsies will invade Britain"', *Evenimentul Zilei*, 1 January 2014), the newspapers switch to a narrower angle, that is the Romanians facing a nightmare journey to Britain ('Romanians' bus trip from Hell to Britain: Between "customs bribery" and "the predatory Hungarian customs officers"', *Evenimentul Zilei*, 5 January 2014). Ultimately, the newspapers introduce the outcome, namely 'the invasion did not occur' (this time quoting Britain's non-tabloid press):

> At home with Victor Spirescu, the only Romanian who invaded Britain: I just came to work, not to steal.
>
> (*Adevarul*, 2 January 2014)

> The *Independent* reacts to the hysteria in Britain: 'Your guide to immigration rhetoric'.
>
> (*Adevarul*, 4 January 2014)

> Top Gear star mocks Romanian INVASION of Britain.
>
> (*Evenimentul Zilei*, 4 January 2014)

> Romanian Invasion of Britain completely deflated.
>
> (*Adevarul*, 2 January 2014)

> [*The Guardian*] Ion Jinga, the Romanian ambassador in London, mocks MPs and media waiting for immigrants: 'Waiting for Godot'.
>
> (*Adevarul*, 3 January 2014)

By strategically using polyphony (the press, the public opinion and the political class in Britain), the Romanian newspapers develop an identity discourse on the theme of access to the labour market. It legitimises not only a relationship of symbolic inequality between the countries involved in this economic process but also collective attitudes in these countries, expressed in the stereotyped perception of the migrants' home country.

The subject of economic mobility is approached as an extension of the imagined community – the 'us'. The events and situations faced by migrants are reframed in terms of national and collective identity in relation to the nation's image abroad. We note a specific pattern to designate the migrants ('our Romanians', 'our workplaces') that reflects an essentialist inclusion strategy in a collective 'we'. On the other hand, this inclusion strategy establishes power relations between 'us' and 'them' – a kind of symbolic 'ownership' over the actors of migration and their belonging to a collective identity – and between 'we' and 'the host countries'. It is important to note that the Romanian journalists comment on the evaluations in the British press through identity utterances such as, 'We are under attack again in the British press' (*Evenimentul Zilei*, 10 March 2013) or, 'Why the British do not give a damn about us' (*Cotidianul*, 13 February 2013).

Through this type of utterances, the newspapers also evaluate the impact of possible restrictions that some countries have adopted regarding the European labour market access:

> Could we still go to work in the Iberian Peninsula?
>
> (*Evenimentul Zilei*, 22 July 2011)

> Spanish employers still want our workforce in agriculture and construction, despite the announcement that we will be received only with work permits.
>
> (*Evenimentul Zilei*, 10 August 2011)

> If Italy is in trouble, will our immigrants return?
>
> (*Evenimentul Zilei*, 22 September 2011)

In constructing migration as an identity issue, the Romanian newspapers use a particular representation of mobility endorsed by the media in Britain: the 'assault'. The media discourse thus emphasises the argument of 'the other' in order to warn, in a sensational and schematic way, about the difficulties posed to those planning to find a job in the new labour market. Simultaneously, this discourse legitimises categories: migrants as vulnerable social actors; migrants as resource for the destination countries ['the Romanian migrants useful to Europe for holding jobs rejected by the population in the rich countries' (*Evenimentul Zilei*, 11 November 2011)] and as a symbolic resource for the home country (the heroes of 'success stories'); 'us' versus 'them', as collective attitudes and identities.

Within some debates initiated by newspapers (between journalists and politicians – for example *Adevarul* in 2014) in order to redefine the 'invasion of migrants' as a meta-public issue, the journalists argue that these rhetorical and ideological stances have overemphasised the issue in the Romanian press:

> Alex is right when he says that the bubble has been more inflated here, in Romania, than abroad. Because in Romania, why not admit it, we are still obsessed with having a good image worldwide, wondering whether the Romanians living abroad represent us or not. Other countries do not do it; they are not interested, for instance, in watching the image of the Germans, of the Italians, of the Swedes in the press in Slovakia.
>
> (Deputy chief editor of the *Dilema veche* weekly,
> *Adevarul* Live, 2 January 2014)

It can be argued that, through the instrumentalisation of mobility from the perspective of identity and country status issues, the media staged a broader debate on the political-institutional systems of the country, on the one hand, and the reconfiguration of social ties and collective solidarity, on the other. Within this debate, through a populist discourse, journalists assume an interpellation role in relation to the political field, while questioning the 'we' identity.

Conclusions

An important question that this research attempts to clarify, as a contribution to the study of mobility, refers to building a relationship between migration and mobility (as a practice of migration) within the dynamics of the public spheres in the countries of origin and destination. We tackle this question through an analytical discussion on the role that the sending countries (as actors) play in the processes of mediating transnational ties and interactions.

We bring out the transnational dimension by examining how public actors (namely media) position themselves towards migrants' circular mobility in the EU and how public discourse in this respect is constructed in the country of origin. Avoiding an opposition between transnationalism and the methodological nationalism approaches, we analyse the (re)construction of the national angle. We do this by looking at the dynamics of the visibility and reification practices in the country of origin ('here') regarding various types of migrant actions at a distance. The media place migrants in regimes of mobility, building 'reference points' of transnationalism (Boccagni 2012, 118) that they relate to: what awaits them in the destination countries and what implications their actions 'there' might have on the country's image and on Romanians' status in general. They position migrants within a field of power and ascribe them a moral responsibility for the country of origin.

We have considered a meaningful context for labour migration dynamics: the full opening of the European labour market for Romania and Bulgaria, starting 1 January 2014, reframed by the media in the context of the economic recession. The European debate on the subject shows some forms of simultaneity, involving the European institutions, the media and the political classes in the countries of origin and destination, and highlights the symbolic negotiation of issues and meanings.

It should also be noted that this economic context introduces specific types of constraints on migration and mobility: objective constraints (the economic recession) and symbolic constraints (the free access to labour markets would generate various positions, some negative, in some destination countries, ensuing in a discursive construction of mobility as a 'site of danger' long before it materialises as a 'movement' starting 1 January 2014).

Considering this field of symbolic power, we analysed the media construction of images and meanings of mobility and the ways they were used to redefine migration as a public issue, that is an issue that had already been provided with some patterns of visibility and interpretation in the Romanian public sphere. More specifically, we were interested in highlighting how the media hegemonically legitimise meanings of mobility and subjects' positions in terms of movement/ non-movement and movement/settlement, under circumstances of constraint.

The main finding of this research shows that the media build a particular pattern of mobility: journalists interpret mobility in turbulent economic contexts as competitive relations between the sending and destination countries. The representations of the social actors of migration (under polarised identities, categories), as well as of their movement practices (abstract trajectories of movement/ settlement), and the journalists' engagement with the anti-immigration media campaigns in the countries of destination (the sending country seen as a victim of stereotype perceptions) follow a rule of specific discursive production that points to the sending country's position/status. In other words, 'the assessment of movement as movement' (Frello 2008, 27) is based on the discursive construction of the self-perceived national identity in relation to a series of actors, policies and actions at the European scale.

First, the disruptive effects of these contexts on the migrants' access to the European labour market are reframed from an identity perspective: 'us' (the citizens) and the state. The economic recession and restrictions on mobility affect Romania's position in terms of economic losses and gains within a hierarchy of the sending countries. Consequently, the movement practices are represented in an abstract and essentialist way (the presentation of places and distances indicating the 'flow of movement'). Individuals are subject to the same representation, discursively constituted as statistical categories or groups relevant for Romanians' mobility. Migrants acquire visibility in the frame of various incidents that occur in regions and cities emerging as spaces disconnected from the social worlds in which individuals and groups act. This modality of representing and interpreting mobility introduces, on the one hand, a relationship of symbolic 'ownership' by the national community over the migrants – a relation that incorporates 'them' (the migrants) into 'us' (as a collective identity, as a state ranked unfavourably in the European recession environment). On the other hand, an effect of naturalisation of migration appears. It should be noted, in this respect, that the press often reports the European officials' releases to call attention to the migrants' contribution to the economy of the destination countries. The media discuss less the labour migration causes and the social actors' experiences and focus more on the conditions of economic mobility as an individual and a collective resource, both being related to Romania's status in the context of European policies.

Second, the media strategically mobilise labelling, an anti-immigration rhetoric and especially a particular metaphor of mobility (the 'assault'), reproduced from the press in some destination countries, to legitimise identities: migrants as vulnerable social actors, or as an economic resource for the destination countries, and so on. In particular, mobility is represented as a 'site of danger' by reframing a metaphorical vocabulary used in the media of the destination countries; this is meant to contribute to the discursive production of this asymmetrical and competitive relation between 'us' (the state, the national community) and the 'other' (the destination countries, the media and public opinion in those countries), established by means of status and stereotypical images of collective identity. This approach to mobility cannot be separated, to some extent, from the increasing marketisation of the Romanian quality press, a trend that has occurred, among other mechanisms, through the hybridisation of genres and the framing of antagonistic positions.

Lastly, the fact that the media use the representations and meanings of economic mobility to legitimise competitive relations between the sending and destination countries is likely to be related to the development, over time, of certain patterns in the problematisation of migration in the media sphere in Romania. A dominant pattern associates the migrants' actions in the destination countries to Romania's international image. Labour migration is debated, among other aspects, in relation to the migrants' actions viewed as 'entrepreneurs' of the nation's symbolic capital. In the context of full labour market access, the issue of the nation's symbolic capital is preserved but is no longer predominantly related to the migrants' actions. A new angle is used to reframe the issue of migration through the construction of mobility as an argument, namely the statutory and identity repositioning of the country of origin.

Acknowledgement

This work was supported by a grant of the Romanian National Authority for Scientific Research, CNCS–UEFISCDI, project number PN-II-ID-PCE-2011–3–0968, Diaspora in the Romanian Media and Political Sphere from Event to the Social Construction of Public Issues.

References

Bailey, Olga G., Myria Georgiou and R. Harindranath. 2007. *Transnational Lives and the Media Re-Imagining Diaspora*. Farnham: Palgrave Macmillan.
Bauböck, Rainer. 2010. Cold Constellations and Hot Identities: Political Theory Questions about Transnationalism and Diaspora. In *Diaspora and Transnationalism: Concepts, Theories and Methods*, edited by Rainer Bauböck and Thomas Faist, 295–323. Amsterdam: Amsterdam University Press.

Beciu, Camelia. 2012. Qui fait la diaspora? Le problème de l'identité dans les recherches sur les diasporas. *Romanian Journal of Communication and Public Relations*, special issue, edited by Camelia Beciu, Malina Ciocea, and Alex I. Cârlan 14(4): 13−29.

Beck, Ulrich. 2000. The cosmopolitan perspective: Sociology of the second age of modernity. *British Journal of Sociology* 51(1): 79–105.

Boccagni, Paolo. 2010. Private, public or both? On the scope and impact of transnationalism in immigrants' everyday lives. In *Diaspora and Transnationalism: Concepts, Theories and Methods,* edited by Rainer Bauböck and Thomas Faist, 185–205. Amsterdam: Amsterdam University Press.

Boccagni, Paolo. 2012. Rethinking transnational studies: Transnational ties and the transnationalism of everyday life. *European Journal of Social Theory* 15(1): 117–132.

Chouliaraki, Lilie. 2006. Towards an analytics of mediation. *Critical Discourse Studies* 3(2): 153–178.

Cresswell, Tim. 2001. The production of mobilities. *New Formations* 43: 11–25.

Dahinden, Janine. 2010. The Dynamics of Migrants' Transnational Formations: Between Mobility and Locality. In *Diaspora and Transnationalism: Concepts, Theories and Methods*, edited by Rainer Bauböck and Thomas Faist, 51–71. Amsterdam: Amsterdam University Press.

Easthope, Hazel. 2009. Fixed identities in a mobile world? The relationship between mobility, place, and identity. *Global Studies in Culture and Power* 16(1): 61–82. doi:10.1080/1070289080260.5810.

Fairclough, Isabela, and Norman Fairclough. 2012. *Political Discourse Analysis: A Method for Advanced Students*. London: Routledge.

Fairclough, Norman. 2003. *Analysing Discourse: Textual Analysis for Social Research*. London: Routledge.

Faist, Thomas. 2010. Diaspora and Transnationalism: What Kind of Dance Partners? In *Diaspora and Transnationalism: Concepts, Theories and Methods*, edited by Rainer Bauböck and Thomas Faist, 9–34. Amsterdam: Amsterdam University Press.

Frello, Birgitta. 2008. Towards a discursive analytics of movement: On the making and unmaking of movement as an object of knowledge. *Mobilities* 3(1): 25–50. doi:10.1080/17450100701797299.

Frosh, Paul. 2011. Phatic morality: Television and proper distance. *International Journal of Cultural Studies* 14(4): 383–400.

Georgiou, Myria. 2006. *Diaspora, Identity and the Media: Diasporic Transnationalism and Mediated Spatialities*. Cresskill, NJ: Hampton Press.

Glick Schiller, Nina. 2010. A global perspective on transnational migration: Theorising migration without methodological nationalism. In *Diaspora and Transnationalism: Concepts, Theories and Methods*, edited by Rainer Bauböck and Thomas Faist, 109–129. Amsterdam: Amsterdam University Press.

Glick Schiller, Nina, and Noel B. Salazar. 2013. Regimes of mobility across the globe. *Journal of Ethnic and Migration Studies* 39(2): 183–200. doi:10.1080/1369183X.2013.723253.

Hall, Stuart. 1997. *Representation: Cultural Representations and Signifying Practices*. London: Sage.

Landerer, Nino. 2013. Rethinking the logics: A conceptual framework for the mediatization of politics. *Communication Theory* 23: 239–258.

Mügge, Liza. 2012. Ideologies of nationhood in sending-state transnationalism: Comparing Surinam and Turkey. *Ethnicities* 13(3): 338–358.

O'Reilly, Karen. 2007. Intra-European migration and the mobility-enclosure dialectic. *Sociology* 41(2): 277–293.

Sheller, Mimi, and John Urry. 2006. The new mobilities paradigm. *Environment and Planning A* 38(2): 207–226.

Turner, Bryan S. 2007. The enclave society: Towards a sociology of immobility. *European Journal of Social Theory* 10(2): 287–303. doi:10.1177/1368431007077807.

Van Leeuwen, Theo. 2008. *Discourse and Practice: New Tools for Critical Analysis*. New York: Oxford University Press.

Verschueren, Jef. 2012. *Ideology and Language Use: Pragmatic Guidelines for Empirical Research*. Cambridge: Cambridge University Press.

Vertovec, Steven. 2009. *Transnationalism*. London, New York: Routledge.

Wodak, Ruth. 2010. 'Us' and 'Them': Inclusion and Exclusion – Discrimination via Discourse. In *Identity, Belonging and Migration*, edited by Gerard Delanty, Ruth Wodak and Paul R. Jones, 54–77. Liverpool: Liverpool University Press.

4 The discursive accomplishment of rationalities in the automobility regime

Laura Bang Lindegaard

Introduction

Today, a century after the introduction of the Model T, automobility has proven to be a severe, if not unsurpassable problem for contemporary Western societies. The physical infrastructure in large cities is under constant pressure, and expansion of the existing capacity simply generates additional traffic and pushes the problem to a not so distant future. Ironically, then, the fascination with 'the flying car' in 20th-century science fiction is not simply an extrapolation of the automobile's technological development but also, and perhaps even foremost, the extrapolation of an inherent antagonism in automobility and a desire for a neat technological fix. Indeed, if automobility were in fact universalised, then the pursuit of individual mobility would probably end in infrastructural congestion and collective immobility. In addition to what are, after all, merely practical problems, automobility is intimately linked with contemporary society's dependency on fossil fuels and, by implication, the current climate crisis. According to Van der Hoeven et al. (2012), the transport sector accounted for 22 per cent of the world's energy-related CO_2 emissions in 2010, and road transportation accounted for almost three-quarters of the transport sector's overall emissions.

Considering the blatant fact that automobility accounts for such an extremely high amount of human-caused environmental pollution and CO_2 emissions, it may be no surprise that reducing energy use and mitigating climate change both feature prominently on the current academic transport research agenda. Recent studies within this domain emphasise the need to broaden the research perspective beyond narrower disciplinary boundaries. For example, both Schwanen et al. (2011) and Banister et al. (2012) speak from the point of view of transport studies, such as transport geography, but they both point out that transport research would benefit tremendously from insights, concepts and methods from other disciplines, especially the social sciences. Yet, considering such developments within transportation research, surprisingly there are still relatively few studies focusing on reducing energy use and climate change mitigation not only within the more designated field of mobilities research but also within the social sciences as such. However, some work has been done on sustainable mobility (Freudendal-Pedersen 2009; Geels et al. 2012) and on climate change and future fuel systems (Urry 2008, 2011). A few somewhat *critical* studies have also been made on automobility (Böhm et al. 2006; Conley and McLaren 2009; Cresswell 2010; Paterson 2007; Scott 2013; Sheller and Urry 2000; Urry 2004). Urry (2004), for instance, argues that Western societies are 'locked' in 'systems of automobility', that is 'self-organising, self-generating, non-linear world-wide systems of cars, car-drivers, roads, petroleum supplies, and many novel objects, technologies, and signs', (27). He suggests that change will come about only if a whole range of minor, unpredictable turning points happen at the same time, thereby causing a tipping point that will lead to new systems 'after the car'.

While I acknowledge the relevance of material configurations, I do not understand social change (or the lack thereof) as merely a consequence of the blind and unpredictable happenstance of complex systems. It is also the result of current forms of governing within the diagram of advanced liberalism (Rose 1999). Within this diagram of governance, governing is characterised by an understanding of the human actor as an entrepreneur of his or her own self and by an understanding of freedom as autonomy (Rose 1999, 142). That is, governing is understood as intertwined with a 'freedom as autonomy' discourse. Accordingly, this chapter proposes to conceptualise our current, car-dependent living as a regime of automobility (cf. Böhm et al. 2006, 6) embedded in advanced liberalism and bound up with the 'freedom as autonomy discourse'.[1] Furthermore, it proposes a methodological approach to the study of this regime. In particular, it suggests that by connecting studies of governmentality with ethnomethodological discourse analysis, one can study how the more overall, powerful discourse 'freedom as autonomy' is accomplished in everyday discursive interaction.[2] Empirically, the chapter reports on a qualitative study in a small Danish village engaged in a municipal sustainability project aimed at 'greening' its citizens' transportation practices. The analysis shows that while the municipality attempts to govern the citizens not by crushing their capacity to act but by using it to get the citizens to choose to act differently, the citizens skilfully exploit this way of governing to accomplish themselves and their transportation practices as already as sustainable and, by implication, as licit as possible. The analysis demonstrates how the villagers negotiate the municipality's advanced liberalism strategy in ways that merely sustain their car-dependent lives and the regime of automobility.

Conceptualising and approaching rationalities of the regimes of automobility

Studies of governmentality

Foucault's concept of governmentality sees the population as representing more than the power of a sovereign; it is seen not merely as the subject of needs but also as the object utilised to fulfil these needs (Foucault 2007, 100). The notion is often explained through the related notion of the 'conduct of conduct' and the insight that the exercise of power should be understood as 'a way of acting upon an acting subject or acting subjects by virtue of their acting or being capable of action' (Foucault 1983, 220).[3] Power is thus understood as exercised only in the presence of *freedom* (Foucault 1983, 221). Within current studies of governmentality, Rose (1999, 139f.) demonstrates that such an understanding of governing characterises the current, dominant diagram of governance. He calls this diagram 'advanced liberalism' (Rose 1999, 139) and relates it to a discourse of freedom as autonomy. That is, he observes that advanced liberalism is accomplished through the utilisation of autonomous individuals, thereby pointing towards that power as the *obligation* to be free, the obligation to make appropriate, responsible choices and the obligation to actualise oneself eternally. As Rose also puts it, freedom today is an 'imperative of self-realisation' (Rose 1999, 87). Furthermore, by implication, governing today means governing through informed and knowledgeable subjects and through an individually infused 'logic of (responsible) choice' (Rose 1999, 88).

Dean (2010) emphasises that this way of governing relies on the construction, maintenance and negotiation of different regimes of practices. In short, the Foucault-inspired notion of regimes of practices denotes the apparently coherent and necessary sets of ways of going about things that constitute any given society at a given time and place (Foucault 2000). Dean (2010, 31) mentions, among others, punishment, relieving poverty and maintaining mental health as regimes of practices in contemporary advanced liberal societies.[4] In this context, I would suggest that one may also speak of the commonsensical way we currently handle everyday mobilities as displaying a regime of automobility. Furthermore, Dean (2010, 33) points out that regimes of practices come into existence and survive insofar as they succeed in maintaining four interdependent dimensions: fields of visibilities; forms of knowledge, logics, moralities and rationalities; the mobilisation of technologies; and, lastly, the production of subjectivities.

Drawing inspiration from Rose and Dean, I propose that in order to attain a better understanding of the automobility regime, one must investigate its intertwined relationship with advanced liberalism, particularly with the discourse of 'freedom as autonomy'. However, in the aim to go beyond simply presupposing and reifying the significance of this powerful discourse, I pursue its possible accomplishment and contestation in actual everyday discursive interaction at the most molecular level of governing. Although scholars of governmentalities have indicated in various ways their wish to examine how regimes of practices are accomplished in discursive interaction at the molecular level (Dean 2010, 20f.; Miller and Rose 2008, 7; Rose 1999, 32), this ambition remains to be achieved due to a lack of appropriate methods. This is why I have found it fruitful to connect my governmentality perspective with ethnomethodology. Not only does ethnomethodology provide a thoroughly tested springboard to analyse discursive interaction at the molecular level, it also implies certain theoretical assumptions that render it useful for enquiries, particularly into one of the dimensions of regimes of practices, namely the production of rationalities.[5]

Ethnomethodology

Ethnomethodology has grown from the work of Garfinkel (1967). It is founded on the assumption that social order is continuously accomplished in interaction, and

Garfinkel's main ambition was to describe the 'ethno methods' through which this is done. Consequently, ethnomethodology represents a rather different approach from social order, which implies that certain terms are used with a quite specific meaning; for instance, accountability and reflexivity. While accountability in ordinary speech is often associated only with liability, here it also denotes intelligibility or explainability, in the sense that actors are supposed to design their actions in such a way that their sense is explicable on demand (Garfinkel 1967, 50). Thus, the understandability and expressability of an activity as a sensible action are, at the same time, an essential part of that action. Garfinkel uses the term reflexivity to focus on this aspect of social actions. He observes that rationality should be understood as the phenomenon that is observable straightforward when people demonstrate the reasonableness of their achievements, for instance by making use of practices such as those he calls 'et cetera' or 'unless' (Garfinkel 1967, 3). In terms of this chapter, they may be practices such as justifying or exemplifying one's everyday transportation practices.

Coulter (1979, 1991) and Jayyusi (1984, 1991), respectively, respecify the classic problems of logic and morality in order to elaborate this ethnomethodological agenda. Not only do they expound that the categories (or, in more Foucauldian wording, subjectivities) of rationality and morality are closely related phenomena accomplished in interaction, they also indicate how this accomplishment can be made available for enquiry. Particularly, drawing both on Garfinkel's seminal work and on Sacks' (1992) work on the two ethnomethodological research strands, membership categorisation analysis and conversation analysis, Coulter and Jayyusi provide arguments for endogenous approaches to logic and morality. In turn, drawing on their research, this chapter discusses a case of sequentially displayed category work that establishes licit membership categories and predicates for everyday transportation practices. As such, it enquires into the way rationalities are accomplished in the currently hegemonic regime of automobility.

Considering commensurability

Studies of governmentality and ethnomethodology are often seen as incompatible since the former is understood as a historical and more macro-oriented approach whereas the latter is seen as a situational and micro-oriented approach. However, as I have argued elsewhere (Lindegaard 2012), a merger of the two positions can be sustained theoretically.[6] Therefore, I draw on ethnomethodology to pursue the local accomplishment of the more global phenomenon of freedom as autonomy.

A car-dependent site

This chapter reports on a recent ethnographic study in a small village in Denmark (Lindegaard 2012) in order to demonstrate the proposed approach to regimes of automobility. Horslunde is a village with 750 inhabitants in which most everyday needs can be fulfilled; for instance, it has a supermarket, a local shop and a bakery, two schools (one private, one public), a kindergarten and a nursing home for elderly people. Furthermore, it has craft shops, an art society, leisure and sports associations as well as a church. However, there are very few jobs in the village, and most adults commute to work elsewhere, as do teenagers attending upper secondary school. The infrastructure in the village's area is inherently automobility generated and automobility generating. From a Danish perspective, the village must be characterised as rural and in a highly decentralised municipality. Although it is set only 10 kilometres from Nakskov, the closest larger town, Nakskov is pointedly a *town*, not a city: there are almost no educational opportunities beyond upper secondary school level, and even though people can begin public transit trips from Nakskov to other parts of the country, they cannot commute directly to any larger city. Furthermore, buses between Nakskov and Horslunde are rare, do not run after 9 p.m. on weekdays and run only a couple times over the weekend. Accordingly, life in Horslunde revolves around car dependency.

Horslunde is indeed a good site for a study of advanced liberalism. The village is designated a 'demonstration project' in the Land of Opportunity project (2009), a six-year partnership project among the strategic, philanthropic foundation Realdania and three Danish municipalities, one of which is Lolland in which Horslunde is located. The partnership project is inspired by the OECD construction of The New Rural Paradigm (Crosta et al. 2006), which arose from the observation that a traditional focus on financial redistribution and agriculture-based policies is 'not able to harness the potential' of a new globalisation-generated 'range of economic engines for growth' (Crosta et al. 2006, 3). Following this observation, the OECD recommends a new approach to rural policy, requiring 'a less "defensive" approach to rural policy and stronger co-ordination across sectors, across levels of government, and between public and private actors' (Crosta et al. 2006, 3). Significantly, the new paradigm focuses on government as a dispersed process at all levels and on making use of the *freedom* of the governed in generating economic growth.

Focusing on Horslunde, the project concerned how the village could be transformed into an *energy village*. The realisation phase was initiated in early 2010, and October 2010 featured the first of five so-called theme months focusing on different opportunities for energy savings in everyday life in Horslunde. November 2010 focused on transportation practices whereby the municipality attempted to inform citizens about different 'greener' and more energy-efficient forms of daily mobility. In other words, it attempted to conduct the transportation conduct of the citizens in this car-dependent village. The campaign consisted of a flyer informing local residents about different aspects of greener driving and a transportation theme day where the townspeople had the possibility to talk to a green driving expert and to participate in a contest with the opportunity of winning a green driving course. The flyer was displayed and made available at different spots in the village, like the bakery, and the theme day took place on a Saturday in the parking lot in front of the supermarket.

Considering that Energy Village Horslunde represented an obvious case to study how the regime of automobility is intertwined with advanced liberalism and the discourse of 'freedom as autonomy', I conducted a focus group study in the village. This decision was partly a consequence of Rose's observation that focus groups can themselves be seen as a tool of governmentality. Rose (1999, 189) observes that focus groups can be seen as one of a whole array of little devices and techniques that have been invented to make current communities real, and he points out that in focus groups citizens are called upon and comply as they map out new spaces of culture, clarify current values and virtues and insert them into the deliberations of authorities. Hence, focus groups can be understood as an accounting-oriented device that magnifies the accomplishment and negotiation of rationalities; that is, as a vehicle that emphasises the call to point out and account for positions. Accordingly, focus groups appeared to be an obvious choice for a study of the contested accomplishment of rationalities that co-constitute the regime of automobility.

Considering the study's construction and my ethnomethodological starting point, it made little sense to speculate about conventional sampling procedures. From an ethnomethodological perspective, in principle it is not possible to have an idea about whether one group or another will provide this or that kind of insight *prior* to the actual investigation (Benson and Hughes 1991; Sacks 1984). In other words, ethnomethodology eschews traditional, sociological concerns with the *demographic* subject and is instead concerned with the accomplishment of *social* actors (Rawls 2005, 165). Bearing this caveat in mind, here are a few details regarding the construction and design of my study.

I spent June and July 2010 getting acquainted with life in Horslunde through several forms of observation in the village and conversations with citizens. I simply walked around the small village, knocking on doors and asking people if they had a couple of minutes to tell me about themselves and their lives in Horslunde. Hence, in the first few weeks I was invited into quite a few homes and gardens for a cold drink and a story about life in Horslunde today as well as several decades ago. Moreover, I also conducted a few unstructured interviews in which I more specifically asked people what they knew and thought of the energy village project, and, similarly, I organised a single unstructured focus group session on the same topic. Whereas I 'sampled' people for individual interviews by knocking on doors, I contacted the citizens for the groups through random door knocking and telephone calls, and although most of the calls were indeed random, a few came from references by citizens who had already expressed their interest (yet, in standard qualitative research terms, these citizens were still random in that they were not selected as a result of any sampling principle – other than simply being citizens of Horslunde). Whenever I asked people if they would like to participate, I told them that my research interest in the village was related to the energy village project, thereby providing them with a reasonable idea about the nature of the group interviews I was asking them to participate in.

Although I worked with two groups of citizens, this chapter draws on data from just one group, so I shall only mention its composition. The group included three women and three men, all retired. Although this composition is fairly representative of the citizens in the village (one reason for the area's vulnerable demography is a remarkably elderly population), it should again be underlined that the 'sampling' was not the result of any a priori idea of the importance of certain imposed categories. I had several sessions with this group, but here I draw on data from a single session carried out after the municipal transportation theme month. In this session, I asked broadly about the citizens' reactions to the municipal transportation theme month, focusing on how they related the strategy to their own practices. Hence, at the most general level I asked about their overall experience of the transportation theme month, about their experience of the transportation theme day and about their views on green driving as suggested by the municipal flyer. The aim here was to make the accomplishment of automobility rationalities available for enquiry when citizens were faced with the complex call to account for their own and others' everyday transportation practices.[7]

It is important to note that the study did not concern all aspects of the citizens' practices generated by and generating automobility but only the discursive aspect of these practices. Yet this is no banal or insignificant facet of these practices. I again emphasise that practices should be understood as co-constituted by various aspects, including the discursive interaction in which rationalities are negotiated. Not only is this insight, as already pointed out, shared by studies of governmentality, it is also commonly accounted for within other disciplines, such as discourse studies (e.g. Berger and Luckmann 1966; Fairclough 1992) and practice theory (e.g. Reckwitz 2002). Furthermore, this focus on the discursive co-constitution of the rationalities of everyday transportation practices can be understood in terms of Kaufmann's (2002) notion of motility (see also Kaufmann and Montulet 2008; Kesselring 2006; Sheller 2011; Urry 2007). Kaufmann (2002, 38) suggests that motility can be defined as the potential side of mobility, comprising three interdependent aspects: access, skills and appropriation. In this context, the third aspect, appropriation, is of particular relevance since it has to do with how people interpret access and skills, and how they legitimise or deem appropriate potential means of access. In fact, since this chapter demonstrates how appropriation can be approached and studied in practice, I would suggest that it can be seen as a contribution to research into potential mobility.

Method

As anticipated, I draw on the ethnomethodological methods of conversation analysis (CA) and membership categorisation analysis (MCA) throughout the analysis of the focus group data in order to study the accomplishment of rationalities in the automobility regime. CA is concerned with the sequential organisation of interaction in everyday and institutional settings, while MCA is concerned with the social organisation of knowledge in categories. Following Watson (1997), I understand these two methods as complementary perspectives. For clarity, however, I will introduce a few concepts from each of the two separately.

The basic element in the MCA apparatus is what Sacks (1992) calls membership categorisation devices. According to Sacks, a membership categorisation device is a collection, on the one hand, of categories for referring to persons and, on the other, of rules of application (Sacks 1992, 246). Collections are not just any set of categories but of categories that are considered routinely and commonsensically to go together. Accordingly, 'mother' and 'baby' are examples of categories, and 'family' is an example of a membership categorisation device. Moreover, Sacks describes two rules of application with regard to membership categorisation devices. The first, the economy rule (Sacks 1992, 244), holds that while I am often, in one sense, ascribable to more than one category – for instance, 'woman', 'left winger', 'Dane' and 'assistant professor' – I am not always performing these categories in equally relevant ways. What comes off as relevant in a given situation depends on the situation that is constituted. In particular, one category will provide a sufficient description of me in any actual situation; which one is a matter of a certain kind of consistency. The second, the consistency rule (Sacks 1992, 244), points out that if somebody else has been ascribed to the category 'Swede' from the device nationalities, I should be categorised with one from the same device, most likely the category 'Dane'. Sacks adds one more feature to the apparatus, namely category boundedness and category-bound activities.[8] Category-bound activities are activities that are expectedly carried out by the member of a given category. 'Speaking Danish', for instance, is expected from members of the category 'Dane' in the membership categorisation device 'nationalities'. It is important to note that category-bound activities and categories are co-selected. The activity provides for the category, and the category provides for the activity. Hence, the membership categorisation analysis system does not constitute an ordered approach; that is, it does not and cannot provide the analyst with a guide as to where to begin his or her analysis. The relevant membership categorisation device is accomplished in situ as a complex assemblage of co-constituting categories and category-bound features; none can be said to be of a priori higher relevance than others.

As mentioned, MCA is inevitably intertwined with the insight that such interaction is displayed sequentially. Whenever one or the other category is invoked, its accomplishment is always a matter of how it is taken up and carried on. Whether or not a certain category is accomplished depends on how respondents relate to the projection of the category (and, in principle, this is continually open for negotiation). On the other hand, whereas respondents can do all sorts of things in response to a certain projection, whatever they do will be understood as exactly that: a response to the projection. Hence, seeing category analysis as co-constituted by sequential analysis, the following paragraphs discuss two aspects of particular relevance to sequential analysis.

Firstly, introducing the notion of sequence organisation, conversational turns do not occur in isolation but are organised retrospectively and prospectively in sequences of turns. According to Schegloff (2007, 13f.), the basic unit of sequence organisation is the adjacency pair, which is organised into a first pair part and a second pair part. Examples of first pair parts can be questions, requests, offers and so on (including, importantly, all sorts of less vernacular terms for actions), while examples of second pair parts can be answers, acceptances, refusals and the like. This leads to pair types such as question-answer, request-accept/refusal, offer-accept/refusal, and so on. One adjacency pair sequence structure of particular relevance for this chapter is the *topic-proffering sequence*. It comprises a first pair part, a topic proffer, and a second pair part, a response to this proffer. In any case, however, the basic idea is that the production of a given first pair part projects a context whereby the relevant next turn is the production of a second pair part of a type that corresponds with the type that was produced in the first turn.

Secondly, considering the notion of preference, this aspect concerns the insight that the production of one kind of response, or second pair part, is preferred, while the production of another is 'dispreferred' (Pomerantz 1984). Consequently, although a greeting does not always elicit a greeting, it does make a return greeting normatively relevant. Accordingly, if a greeting is not met with a greeting, it is noticeably absent and, by implication, accountable. Hence, this preference structure is an 'oriented-to phenomenon' made observably relevant by members in interaction. Again, considering in particular the topic-proffering sequences that feature prominently in my data, such sequences are characterised by contingencies that are different from those found in most other types of sequences. Whereas it is ordinarily the case that dispreferred seconds are expansion relevant (due to the fact that they are commonly mitigated and accounted for in different ways), in topic-proffering sequences the sequential environment tends to display a systematic reversal of this ordinary differential expansion relevance of preferred and dispreferred second pair parts (Schegloff 2007, 169). In other words, in topic-proffering sequences, mainly preferred seconds are expanded.

Analysing the discursive accomplishment of rationalities in the automobility regime

The analysis shows two different ways in which the citizens negotiate the municipal attempt to govern them through use of the 'freedom as autonomy' discourse. It shows how the citizens skilfully exploit this way of governing in their discursive accomplishment of a rationality in which they are *already* subjects who are as sustainably and licitly mobile as possible. The first part of the analysis shows how the citizens rationalise the municipal strategy as one that is not really aimed at them but at others, that is it shows how they *transfer* their rational accountability to someone else. The second part of the analysis demonstrates the accomplishment of a slightly different rationality in that it shows how the citizens *pre-empt* their rational accountability by accomplishing themselves as already licit, sustainable movers. The interaction represented in the excerpts is from the early phases of the same focus group session, and it displays the participants' first responses to the moderator's proffer of the first topic concerning their overall experience of the municipal transportation theme month.

While the following analysis concerns the detailed examination of only a few instances, in the case study from which these examples are drawn (Lindegaard 2012), both the transferring rationality and the pre-emption rationality appear quite often. Considering transference, we find, for example, an instance in which a participant transfers accountability, saying that she does not need information on green driving but that younger and older drivers might. Similarly, a couple of retired men make their age observably relevant in accounting their preference for having a car of their own, thereby indirectly transferring accountability for considering shared cars and public transportation to younger people. Thirdly, a participant quite simply transfers accountability for using the bus to those who depend on the bus, and, lastly, the case study points to an instance in which two women deliver similar accounts, transferring accountability to people who live in other, less dispersed areas. Considering the pre-emption rationality, the case study touches upon numerous other instances in which participants pre-empt the municipal strategy. I am not aware of any other instances in which this is done as in the following analysis, namely by direct reference to category membership. On the other hand, there seem to be quite a few instances in which participants pre-empt the strategy by referring to their own already existing 'dispositions', as such rendering the municipal strategy less relevant. For instance, the case study comprises three excerpts in which two different women invoke their own and other's personal feelings and mentalities as reasons why they and others drive as they do. It contains five excerpts in which three different participants each, though quite differently, show that they already hold the suggested knowledge about proper conduct of transportation conduct.

Transferring accountability

In the interaction represented in the three snippets of Excerpt 1, the participants ascribe to memberships that are *not* accountable for knowing about the transportation theme month and invoke certain other memberships that *are* accountable for knowing, namely those bound by predicates such as 'using public transportation' and 'going to work'. In this way, the municipal strategy is accomplished as aimed at conducting some *other* members' transportation conduct. As such, the analysis demonstrates how the participants make use of certain available categories and category-bound features in order to insulate themselves from being held accountable for awareness of the campaign. The analysis focuses on the response by one of the participants, Svend, to the moderator's proffer and, in particular, on the category work co-constituting his three, interrelated accounts for why his lack of knowledge of the theme month is appropriate.

Excerpt 1a; sve = Svend:[9]

29	sve	But it's not . . . Since I never
30		use public transportation I
31		didn't pay that much attention

When Svend initiates his first account, it has already been established, in the first few minutes of the focus group session, that none of the citizens have in fact noticed the municipal theme month (despite the fact that this group of citizens had an earlier session with the moderator in which the moderator reminded them of the upcoming theme month). Svend initiates his explanation of why he did not really observe the transportation theme month with the turn construction unit 'but it's not'. As the conjunction can be heard as marking a distance to the preceding interaction (through the disjunctive coordination conjunction 'but'), the unit can be heard as projecting a dispreferred action, and, as it is, the subsequent interaction does have a typical dispreference structure. Through the antecedent 'since I never use public transportation' and the consequent 'I didn't pay that much attention', lines 29–31 display an accounting mitigation of Svend's knowledge about the transportation theme month. In greater detail, in the antecedent of the conditional clause ('since I never use public transportation') the predicate 'using public transportation' is made observably relevant. Drawing on Sacks' consistency rule, it is reasonable to hear the predicate as bound to a membership category belonging to what is by then an already accomplished topical device, namely 'the transportation theme month'. This membership is invoked, as Svend *resists* its bound predicate and the membership as such. Secondly, in the consequent ('I didn't pay that much attention') some sort of category-bound right or obligation is invoked. This happens when Svend infers from his *non*-membership of categories bound by the predicate 'using public transportation' that he did not pay much attention. In an ordinary logical hearing, the antecedent is heard as justifying or grounding the consequent, and, by implication, Svend's non-membership is treated as justifying his lack of attention. Hence, Svend resists membership of a category bound by the predicate 'using public transportation' and by the obligation 'to pay attention to the theme month'. However, when he resists the categorisation, he also invokes it, thereby projecting a group of people who do use public transportation and who are *specifically* accountable for knowing about the transportation theme month. Further, since no one mentioned public transportation before Svend's category work, it comes off as a specifically *reached for* contribution to the ongoing accomplishment of the theme month: Svend specifically reaches for an understanding or notion of the month that mitigates his obligation to know about it, reflect on it and, eventually, *act* on it.

Excerpt 1b; mod = moderator; sve = Svend:

41	sve	because,
42		as you know, I'm not going to work or
43		anything
44	mod	no
45	sve	at all of course,
46		luckily

Svend's second account comes off as clearly elaborating the insulating category work accomplished in the first account. In lines 41–46 he says, 'because, as you know, I'm not going to work or anything at all of course, luckily', thereby resisting membership of a category bound by the activity 'going to work or anything'. Importantly, it is *not* collaborative to hear this as invoking just any unemployed category. Rather, resistance of the 'going to work' predicate comes off as negative, invoking Svend's membership in 'retired people'. In and through the 'shared knowledge' displaying adverb 'you know', Svend displays that everyone present already knows that he does not have to go to work, and thereby he makes it observably relevant for the people present to draw on their background knowledge, namely that Svend happens to be retired. Furthermore, the appraising adjective 'luckily' supports this hearing in that all other forms of unemployment but retirement are generally conceived of as very *un*lucky. Lastly, as Svend *negatively* categorises himself, he naturally invokes the complementary *positively* invoked category of people who are, on the other hand, bound by the predicate 'going to work' and who are, it must be assumed, accountable for knowing about the transportation theme month. Consequently, through this contrasting pair of categories, Svend further establishes that he himself cannot be held accountable for knowing about the transportation theme month, whereas some other people, namely those who go to work, can.

Excerpt 1c; mod = moderator; sve = Svend:

47	mod	you had-
48		you just had a feeling that it was
49		something about some public
50		transportation
51	sve	yes well I
52		thought it was a survey
53		for people that truly use the
54		public- that was how I interpreted it

In the proceeding interaction, Svend suggests that the theme month consisted of a survey aimed at people who *truly* rely on public transportation. He then delivers his third explanation for why he should not be seen as belonging to the people whom the municipality attempts to conduct through the transportation theme month. By saying, 'yes well I thought it was a survey for people that truly use the public' (lines 51–54), he invokes a membership of people bound by the predicate 'to truly use public [transportation]' (lines 53–54), once again using it to resist personal accountability. Furthermore, the stressed and accentuating premodifier 'truly' comes off as reached for as it strengthens the bond between category and predicate and displays that the predicate is no mere random predicate but rather an obligating, category-bound activity. Hence, the stress limits the scope of accountability to members obliged to use public transportation as a *category*-bound activity, thereby insulating Svend from accountability, even if he *happens* to use public transportation once in a while.

In summary, the analysis has demonstrated how the participants, notably Svend, use the interactional opportunity to transfer their rational accountability in order to isolate and spare themselves from being held accountable for knowing about the municipal theme month. As part and parcel of this task, certain membership incumbents were invoked for the practical purpose of transferring accountability: the non-accountable and the accountable. Due to the individual features of these memberships, the transportation theme month has thus been accomplished in a specific way, namely as a theme month on public transportation and commuting to work and school, not as something of any relevance for the citizens who participated in the focus group.

Pre-empting accountability

As mentioned, this second part of the analysis demonstrates accomplishment of a slightly different rationality, namely a pre-emption rationality. This occurs as the citizens seem to infer that the municipal attempt to conduct their transportation conduct is not really necessary, since they already comply with the suggested conduct, due to their specific memberships. The data displayed in the two snippets from Excerpt 2 represent the interaction that takes place only three minutes after the exchange in Excerpt 1. Consequently, the parties involved are still in the business of accomplishing a round prompted by the moderator's proffer of the first topic [except that, between these two excerpts, the second question on possible experiences of the transportation theme day has been made briefly relevant as part of the general topic talk on (not) observing the strategy].

In the interaction represented in the two snippets from Excerpt 2, *green driving* is accomplished as advisable, and the point of the analysis is to demonstrate how this is done in a remarkable way. The analysis points out how the participants ascribe to a 'retired' category, thereby accomplishing their own driving as *already* as green as possible. This happens as Svend and Carin skilfully negotiate what could otherwise have challenged their insulation from the municipality's conduct of their conduct. This part of the analysis demonstrates, first, how Hans problematises the earlier transference of accountability as he orients to the green driving course previously mentioned by the moderator as a potential and relevant path for learning to drive differently and, secondly, how the other participants negotiate this challenge of the otherwise established collective isolation by drawing on a 'retired category'.

Excerpt 2a; han = Hans; mod = moderator:

13	han	the green driving course . . . that um did
14		I also take special notice of because I'd
15		um- I'd like to
16		learn that
17		((short pause))
18	mod	yes
19	han	because I have ever never been a . . . um-
20		a hundred per cent good driver

In line 13, Hans self-selects and delivers the turn construction unit 'the green driving course'. By treating the reference 'the' as anaphoric rather than deictic (there is nothing in his non-verbal interaction to suggest that the reference should be to a physical manifestation of, or an index to, such a course), Hans treats the 'green driving' course as something that has already been mentioned. Consequently, the reference ties back to something that was previously made relevant in the session, presumably to a point not long before, when the moderator mentioned that the theme month included the opportunity of winning a 'green driving' course. From the middle of line 14 to line 16, Hans substantiates and accounts for his response as he classifies himself as someone who would like to learn green driving. Literally, he merely says, 'because I'd like to learn that', but since he uses the utterance to qualify his reopening of this subtopic, his wish to learn comes off as related to the topic concerned, namely the 'green driving' course. Further, in lines 19–20, Hans further substantiates his answer saying, 'because I have ever never been a . . . um- a hundred per cent good driver'. The premise marker 'because' (line 19) presents what follows as an explanation for his wish. The explanation, then, is Hans's reference to the fact that he has never been a very good driver. The reference to a long time span invokes Hans' membership of a category that is somehow similar to the category already negatively invoked, namely the 'retired' category bound by the activity '*not* going to work or anything'. Secondly, by resisting the assessment 'a good driver', Hans invokes the predicate 'driver' as bound to this category. Particularly, since the appraising adjective 'good' comes off as inextricably bound to the predicate 'driver', Hans's work presupposes that the predicate 'driver' does already apply to him (and to other memberships within the device). Through this category work, Hans suggests that with regard to his incumbency, the category is characterised by the predicate 'to wish to learn to drive greener'. Thereby rendering the theme month relevant, Hans challenges the otherwise accomplished isolation. However, it should be noted that he ascribes the new predicate only to himself. Consequently, 'green driving' is displayed as a voluntary aspect of driving; you can consider learning it if you feel like it, but the phenomenon is not in any way treated as something car drivers need or ought to consider. Hence, Hans's categorisation work does not specifically entail a *moral* evaluation of categories characterised by the driver predicate.

Excerpt 2b; sve = Svend:

39   sve   at your age, Blom, you are a green
40   driver

Nevertheless, the other participants do treat Hans's interest in the green driving course as problematic, and they do so in a remarkable way, as they co-construct a more specified version of the 'retired' category, namely a version that is already bound by a 'green driving' predicate, which renders it irrelevant for members of the category to even consider considering a 'green driving' course. In lines 39–40, Svend says, 'at your age, Blom, you are a green driver', and by referring to Hans's[10] age, Svend invokes the 'retired' category (once again according to Sacks' economy rule). However, whereas Hans invoked the 'retired' category in relation to the predicate 'driver', Svend invokes it in relation to the more specific predicate 'green driver'. Consequently, being or not being a green driver is presented as a question of age, not as a question of green driving courses. This evidently challenges Hans's self-ascription to a membership of drivers who want to *learn*, since it pre-empts any such wish: you cannot learn to do something you already know how to do. Since the 'retired' category is accomplished as a collectivity category, Svend's work not only ascribes something to Hans; rather, when it is ascribed to Hans, it is simultaneously ascribed to the entire collectivity. Hence, if Svend succeeds in rejecting Hans's claimed topic-embracing resources (his wish to learn), his work will automatically insulate him and the other participants from this possibly threatening topic extension. The entire 'retired' collectivity, it must be assumed, is already characterised by a 'green driving' predicate that pre-empts any reasons for considering a green driving course.

In the end, then, the citizens approach the municipal strategy as governmental, as a strategy aimed at governing through the conduct of conduct, and they fulfil this strategy in and through their pre-emption of it. The 'retired' category not only pre-empts the municipal strategy aimed at green driving; naturally, it also accomplishes it. Further, the analysis demonstrates how the citizens 'take advantage' of the governmental utilisation of their freedom by subtly negotiating the rationality of the governmental strategy. Through the use of the 'retired' category as a pre-emption resource, green driving is accomplished as nothing beyond how members of this membership category already drive. This governmental strategy is accomplished when the other citizens treat Hans as a kind of *deviant* case when he displays interest in the green driving course and refers to green driving as something he would like to learn. In other words, the very pre-emption of the municipal strategy is accomplished in the interactional negotiations of and resistance to Hans's orientation to the strategy as aiming at something that is *not* already fulfilled. This only supports the hypothesis that it is of primary importance to the citizens to pre-empt any rational accountability invoked by the municipal strategy or, more specifically, that it is of primary importance to the citizens to negotiate the municipal strategy in a way that gives them the opportunity to align with it but without exploiting their autonomous freedom. In this way, the analysis shows how the regime of automobility is maintained rather than challenged.

Discussion

The analysis has demonstrated how citizens of Horslunde accomplish certain rationalities that in effect transfer and pre-empt the municipal attempt to conduct the conduct of the citizens. Accordingly, the analysis has demonstrated how two varieties of the 'freedom as autonomy' discourse are readily accomplished and used to forestall any change of the citizens' everyday transportation practices. Without presupposing and reifying the significance of the 'freedom as autonomy' discourse, the analysis has demonstrated the intertwined relationship of the automobility regime and this powerful discourse as it is accomplished and contested in actual, everyday discursive interaction at the most molecular level of governing.

Of course, in these pages only a few examples are analysed to underpin these claims. Furthermore, even though both the transferring rationality and the pre-emption rationality appear quite often in the case study from which these examples are drawn (Lindegaard 2012), in this chapter I am concerned with a question slightly different from the ordinary question of generalisability. Considering the ordinary question of generalisability, the concern is whether a particular practice is more or less likely to be generalisable to other settings.[11] Conversely, the most prominent concern of this chapter is rather the theoretically based outline of an approach to study how a presumably significant discourse is made relevant and maintained in the local discursive accomplishment of rationalities in the automobility regime.[12]

Conclusion

This chapter has suggested that in order to properly understand the currently dominant regime of automobility, it is necessary to investigate how it is intertwined with advanced liberalism and the discourse of 'freedom as autonomy'. The chapter has also suggested that in order not to hypostasise the significance of this discourse, its accomplishment should also be studied in actual, empirical interaction at the mundane, molecular level where people discursively rationalise their own and others' everyday transportation practices.

Based in this theoretical and methodological proposal, the chapter has shown how residents in a small, Danish village negotiate a municipal strategy aimed at conducting their transportation conduct. Concluding, I would suggest that the findings of this analysis have generated a critical question of importance beyond the local focus group setting in a Danish municipality: seeing as the discourse of 'freedom as autonomy' is readily accomplished and utilised to forestall any change of one's transportation practices, what should we do to ever end the regime of automobility?[13,14] Whereas current car-dependent living is, of course, inevitably intertwined with phenomena such as infrastructure, technology and economy, it is, apparently, simultaneously intertwined with the continuous maintenance and negotiation of advanced liberalism and the 'freedom as autonomy' discourse. Accordingly, I would like to suggest that we must also acknowledge the more ephemeral and illusive, everyday discursive accomplishment of rationalities in the automobility regime in order to ever end the regime.

Notes

1 Others also point out that car-dependent living is somehow intertwined with the notion of autonomy. See, for instance, Böhm et al. (2006); Conley and Tigar McLaren (2009); Merriman (2006); Paterson (2007); Urry (2004).

2 See, for instance, Alvesson and Kärreman (2000) for a discussion of the theoretical and methodological challenges of 'climbing the ladder of discourse' (1139), that is, of connecting a study of the everyday accomplishment of local discourses with broader interpretations in terms of more muscular and grandiose Discourses (Alvesson and Kärreman 2000, 1147). See McHoul (1986) for a discussion of the distinction between discourse and Discourse in relation to Foucault's work.

3 Playing on the double meaning in the French verb *conduire*, Foucault suggests that the equivocal nature of the term conduct in itself expresses the 'doubled' understanding of exercise of power, as a matter of actions upon actions.

4 Dean (2010, 10) adapts the term advanced liberalism from Rose (1999).

5 Note, again, that Dean considers *practices* to be the more overall type of regime or assemblage, whereas rationality is only one of the co-constituting dimensions of this assemblage. Accordingly, Dean (2010, 32) observes that while practices exist in the milieu of thought, they have a material and institutional locale as well. Correspondingly, my point is not that rationalities and practices are coinciding phenomena but rather that Dean's use of Foucault's notion of regimes of practices demonstrates that rationality is *one* important and inevitable dimension of regimes of practices.

6 For other studies connecting Foucauldian studies and ethnomethodology, see, in particular, Laurier and Philo (2004), McHoul (1986, 1996) and Summerville and Adkins (2007).

7 Ethnomethodologists are often sceptical of the use of interview data such as focus groups. This chapter, however, relies on my argument laid out elsewhere (Lindegaard 2014) that it is in fact possible to do thoroughly ethnomethodological studies of focus group data that demonstrate how members in a focus group setting accomplish certain rational orders and, significantly, how they do so by using certain *available* resources.

8 The notion of category boundedness was later expanded by, among others, Jayyusi (1984), Sharrock (1974) and Watson (1978). Watson (1978) was among the first to point out that Sacks' notion of CBAs should be understood as just one type of category-bound predicate. Hence, additional predicates that can be expected to be ascribed to the members of a given category are rights, entitlements, obligations, knowledge, attributes and competencies (Hester and Eglin 1997, 5).

9 See Lindegaard (2012) for a complete conversation analytical transcription of all the original Danish data.

10 Since Hans' surname is 'Blom', Svend is without doubt referring to Hans. Of course, all names, including this surname, are anonymised.

11 As pointed out by Peräkylä (2004) and Sacks (1984, 22; 1992, 485), the strict, ethnomethodological answer to this question would be that if a given practice occurs, then it is an undeniable part of culture and implies, as such, the potential for happening again. See also Rawls (2005, 165, 187f.) for a discussion of the notion of generalisability from an ethnomethodological perspective.

12 See Silverman (2013, 146) for a discussion of theoretical generalisations.

13 I am here taking inspiration from Foucault's (1995) phrase "if this were really the case, what would you do?" to express the belief that even the most 'indifferent' description has a normative potential in that it demonstrates the obvious possibility for something to happen. Whereas this is not always acknowledged in Foucauldian studies, it is almost never so in ethnomethodological studies. However, as discussed elsewhere (Lindegaard 2012), a few scholars within ethnomethodological research do contemplate the idea of politicising ethnomethodology. See in particular Freund and Abrams (1976), Jayyusi (1991) and McHoul (1986, 1990, 1994, 1996).

14 Rapley (2001, 318) discusses the critical potential of pointing out the *availability* of certain resources – such as, I would suggest, the readily available resources to maintain the 'freedom as autonomy' discourse.

References

Alvesson, Mats, and Dan Kärreman. 2000. Varieties of discourse: On the study of organizations through discourse analysis. *Human Relations* 53: 1125–1149.

Banister, David, Tim Schwanen and Jillian Anable. 2012. Introduction to the special section on theoretical perspectives on climate change mitigation in transport. *Journal of Transport Geography* 24: 467–470.

Benson, Douglas, and John Hughes. 1991. Method: Evidence and Inference – Evidence and Inference for Ethnomethodology. In *Ethnomethodology and the Human Sciences*, edited by Graham Button, 109–136. Cambridge: Cambridge University Press.

Berger, Peter L., and Thomas Luckmann. 1966. *The Social Construction of Reality*. Harmondsworth: Penguin.

Böhm, Steffen, Campbell Jones, Chris Land and Mat Paterson. 2006. Introduction: Impossibilities of Automobility. In *Against Automobility*, edited by Steffen Böhm, Campbell Jones, Chris Land and Mat Paterson, 3–16. Malden, MA, Oxford, Victoria: Blackwell.

Conley, Jim, and Arlene Tigar McLaren. 2009. Introduction. In *Car Troubles*, edited by Jim Conley and Arlene Tigar McLaren, 1–17. Farnham, Burlington, VT: Ashgate.

Coulter, Jeff. 1979. *The Social Construction of Mind*. London, Basingstoke: Macmillan Press.

———. 1991. Logic: Ethnomethodology and the Logic of Language. In *Ethnomethodology and the Human Sciences*, edited by Graham Button, 20–50. Cambridge: Cambridge University Press.

Cresswell, Tim. 2010. Towards a politics of mobility. *Environment and Planning D: Society and Space* 28: 17–31.

Crosta, Nicola, Andrew Davies and Karen Maguire. 2006. *The New Rural Paradigm: Policies and Governance*. Paris: OECD.

Dean, Mitchell M. 2010. *Governmentality: Power and Rule in Modern Society*. London: Sage.

Fairclough, Norman. 1992. *Discourse and Social Change*. Cambridge: Polity.

Foucault, Michel. 1983. The Subject and Power. In *Michel Foucault: Beyond Structuralism and Hermeneutics*, edited by Hubert L. Dreyfus and Paul Rabinow, 208–226. Chicago: University of Chicago Press.

———. 1995. *Discipline & Punish: The Birth of the Prison* (Second Vintage Books Edition). New York and Toronto: Random House.

———. 2000. Questions of Method. In *Power*, edited by James D. Faubion, 223–238. London: Penguin.

———. 2007. *Security, Territory, Population: Lectures at the Collège de France 1977–78*. New York: Palgrave.

Freudendal-Pedersen, Malene. 2009. *Mobility in Daily Life: Between Freedom and Unfreedom*. Farnham, UK, Burlington, VT: Ashgate.

Freund, Peter, and Mona Abrams. 1976. Ethnomethodology and Marxism: Their use for critical theorizing. *Theory and Society* 3(3): 377–393.

Garfinkel, Harold. 1967. *Studies in Ethnomethodology*. Cambridge: Polity.

Geels, Frank W., René Kemp, Geoff Dudley and Glenn Lyons. 2012. *Automobility in Transition? A Socio-Technical Analysis of Sustainable Transport*. New York, London: Routledge.

Hester, Stephen, and Peter Eglin. 1997. Membership Categorization Analysis: An Introduction. In *Culture in Action: Studies in Membership Categorization Analysis*, edited by Stephen Hester and Peter Eglin, 1–23. London: International Institute for Ethnomethodology and Conversation Analysis and University Press of America.

Hoeven, Maria Van der (2012). *CO_2 Emissions from Fuel Combustion. Highlights*. Annual report from the International Energy Agency, IEA. Accessed 17 June 2014. www.iea.org/publications/freepublications/publication/CO2emissionfromfuelcombustionHIGHLIGHTSMarch2013.pdf.

Jayyusi, Lena. 1984. *Categorization and the Moral Order*. Boston, London, Melbourne, Henley: Routledge, Kegan Paul.

———. 1991. Values and Moral Judgement: Communicative Praxis. In *Ethnomethodology and the Human Sciences*, edited by Graham Button, 227–251. Cambridge: Cambridge University Press.

Kaufmann, Vincent. 2002. *Re-thinking Mobility.* Farnham, Burlington, VT: Ashgate.
Kaufmann, Vincent, and Bertrand Montulet. 2008. Between Social and Spatial Mobilities: The Issue of Social Fluidity. In *Tracing Mobilities: Towards a Cosmopolitan Perspective*, edited by Weert Canzler, Vincent Kaufmann and Sven Kesselring, 37–56. Farnham, Burlington, VT: Ashgate.
Kesselring, Sven. 2006. Pioneering mobilities: New patterns of movement and motility in a mobile world. *Environment and Planning A* 38(2): 269–279.
Land of Opportunity, Project Summary. (2009, 12). Accessed 7 March 2012. www.mulighe dernesland.dk/#/41956/.
Laurier, Eric, and Chris Philo. 2004. Ethnoarchaeology and undefined investigations. *Environment and Planning A* 36: 421–436.
Lindegaard, Laura B. 2012. *Automobility at the interface of discourse and governmentality: A study of the accomplishment of rationalities that co-constitute car-dependent mobility in the face of climate change.* PhD dissertation, Aalborg University.
———. 2014. Doing focus group research: Studying rational ordering in focus group interaction. *Discourse Studies*, doi:10.1177/1461445614538563.
McHoul, Alec. 1986. The getting of sexuality: Foucault, Garfinkel and the analysis of sexual discourse. *Theory Culture Society* 3: 65–79.
———. 1990. Critique and description: An analysis of Bogen and Lynch. *Journal of Pragmatics* 14: 523–532.
———. 1994. Towards a critical ethnomethodology. *Theory, Culture & Society* 11: 105–126.
———. 1996. *Semiotic Investigations. Towards an Effective Semiotics.* Lincoln, London: University of Nebraska Press.
Merriman, Peter. 2006. 'Mirror, Signal, Manoeuvre': Assembling and Governing the Motorway Driver in Late 1950s Britain. In *Against Automobility*, edited by Steffen Böhm, Campbell Jones, Chris Land and Mat Paterson, 75–92. Malden, MA, Oxford, Victoria: Blackwell.
Miller, Peter, and Nikolas Rose. 2008. *Governing the Present.* Cambridge, Malden, MA: Polity.
Paterson, Mat. 2007. *Automobile Politics: Ecology and Cultural Political Economy.* Cambridge: Cambridge University Press.
Peräkylä, Anssi. 2004. Reliability and Validity in Research Based on Naturally Occurring Social Interaction. In *Qualitative Research: Theory, Method and Practice*, edited by David Silverman, 283–304. London: Sage.
Pomerantz, Anita.1984. Agreeing and Disagreeing with Assessments: Some Features of Preferred/Dispreferred Turn Shapes. In *Structures of Social Action: Studies in Conversation Analysis*, edited by J. Maxwell Atkinson and John Heritage, 57–101. Cambridge: Cambridge University Press.
Rapley, T. J. 2001. The art(fulness) of open-ended interviewing: Some considerations on analysing interviews. *Qualitative Research*, 1(3): 303–323.
Rawls, Anne W. 2005. Garfinkel's conception of time. *Time & Society* 14(2/3): 163–190.
Reckwitz, Andreas. 2002. Toward a theory of social practices: A development in culturalist theorizing. *European Journal of Social Theory* 5: 243–263.
Rose, Nikolas. 1999. *Powers of Freedom. Reframing Political Thought.* Cambridge: Cambridge University Press.
Sacks, Harvey. 1984. Notes on Methodology. In *Structures of Social Action. Studies in Conversation Analysis*, edited by J. Maxwell Atkinson and John Heritage, 21–27. Cambridge: Cambridge University Press.

———. 1992. *Lectures on Conversation* (Vol. 1). Malden, MA: Blackwell.

Schegloff, Emanuel A. 2007. *Sequence Organization in Interaction.* Cambridge: Cambridge University Press.

Schwanen, Tim, David Banister and Jillian Anable. 2011. Scientific research about climate change mitigation in transport: A critical review. *Transportation Research Part A* 45: 993–1006.

Scott, Nick A. 2013. Like a fish needs a bicycle: Henri Lefebvre and the liberation of transportation. *Space and Culture* 16: 397–410.

Sharrock, Wes. 1974. On Owning Knowledge. In *Ethnomethodology*, edited by Roy Turner, 45–53. Harmondsworth: Penguin.

Sheller, Mimi. 2011. Mobility. *Sociopedia.isa* doi:10.1177/205684601163.

Sheller, Mimi, and John Urry. 2000. The city and the car. *International Journal of Urban and Regional Research* 24(4): 737–757.

Silverman, David. 2013. *Doing Qualitative Research.* London: Sage.

Summerville, Jennifer, and Barbara Adkins. 2007. Enrolling the citizen in sustainability: Membership categorization, morality and civic participation. *Hum Stud* 30: 429–446.

Urry, John. 2004. The 'system' of automobility. *Theory Culture Society* 21: 25–39.

———. 2007. *Mobilities.* Cambridge: Polity.

———. 2008. Climate change, travel and complex futures. *British Journal of Sociology* 59: 261–279.

———. 2011. *Climate Change and Society.* London: Polity.

Hoeven, Maria Van der. 2012. *CO_2 Emissions from Fuel Combustion. Highlights.* Annual report from the International Energy Agency, IEA. Accessed 17 June 2014. www.iea.org/publications/freepublications/publication/CO2emissionfromfuelcombustionHIGHLIGHTSMarch2013.pdf.

Watson, Rod. 1978. Categorization, authorization and blame-negotiation in conversation. *Sociology* 12(1): 105–113.

———. 1997. Some General Reflections on 'Categorization' and 'Sequence' in the Analysis of Conversation. In *Culture in Action: Studies in Membership Categorization Analysis*, edited by Stephen Hester and Peter Eglin, 76. London: International Institute for Ethnomethodology and Conversation Analysis and University Press of America.

Part II
Mobile subjects

5 Who does the move?

Affirmation or deconstruction of the solitary mobile subject

Katharina Manderscheid

Introduction

Within the discussion of Michel Foucault's oeuvre, the term governmentality has gained much attention in general social science debates (amongst others, Dean 1999; Lemke 2002; Rose 1999) and in mobilities research in particular (Bæren-holdt 2013; Böhm et al. 2006b; Bonham 2006; Dodge and Kitchin 2006; Packer 2003, 2008a; Paterson and Stripple 2010). With this term, developed in his lectures at the Collège de France between 1977 and 1979 (Foucault 2007, 2008), Foucault linked his two interests, the genealogy of the state and the genealogy of the subject (cf. Foucault 1983, 1992). The most commonly used definition of governmentality characterises it as the conduct of conduct and thus as a term that ranges from governing the self to governing others. All in all, in his history of governmentality, Foucault shows how the modern sovereign state and the autonomous individual co-determine each other's emergence (Lemke 2002, 50f.). The subjectification or the active constitution of the subject, then, means that:

> the subject constitutes himself in an active fashion, by the practices of the self, [but] these practices are nevertheless not something that the individual invents himself. They are patterns that he finds in his culture and which are proposed, suggested and imposed on him by his culture, his society and his social group.
>
> (Foucault 1987, 122)

The figure of the subject is a radically social as well as modern one in the sense that s/he discursively emerged together with the specific modern sociopolitical context. The modern subject is further specified as the author of agency, which is framed within the terminology of causality and rationality (Otto 2014, 17f.). Yet the modern subject is continuing to develop and, as governmentality studies have elaborated for the era of so-called neoliberalism, the last decades have witnessed an even more acute ascription of responsibilities to the subject, along with a resulting moral necessity for self-management, thereby eclipsing social structuring and embeddings (Bröckling et al. 2000; cf. Dean 1999; Miller and Rose 2009).

This idea of a co-evolution and mutual determination of sociopolitical and spatial formations on the one hand and specific subjects on the other has been applied (with and without reference to Foucault) to the field of mobilities studies, especially to the object of *automobility*, highlighting its centrality within modern Western states and subject formations of the 20th century. Automobility, as Sheller and Urry (2000, 738f.) defined it, consists of six aspects: (1) the *car industry* from which key concepts such as Fordism have emerged and that produces (2) the manufactured *object of the car* as the major item of individual consumption after housing; (3) a *powerful machinic complex* constituted through the car's technical and social interlinkages with other industries and services, ranging from car parts to tourism, leisure activities and suburban home building; (4) a *predominant global form of mobility*; (5) a *dominant culture* that sustains major discourses of what constitutes the good life and that provides powerful literary and artistic images and symbols; and finally (6), automobility constitutes the main *cause of environmental resource use*. Thus, from a mobilities studies' point of view, automobility is fundamentally interwoven with the modern state formation, the economy, material landscapes, culture and knowledge and social practices. Moreover, in the light of governmentality studies, the automobile subject (in a literal and metaphorical meaning) as the solitary author of decisions and moves, detached and detaching him/herself from social, material and historical contexts, constitutes an effect of automobility in this broad sense. Concepts of planning, policy making and transportation research, in particular, are part of the production of the very subject they presuppose:[1] These disciplines and institutions tend to model personal mobility – be it residential migration, commuting patterns, transportation mode choice, leisure or tourist travel[2] – as derived from set demands. The origin of transportation and residential choices is seen in conscious rational decisions of autonomous subjects, taking costs and available options into consideration against the background of their individual demands and preferences (e.g. Bamberg 1996; for an overview, Schwanen and Lucas 2011). This conceptualisation corresponds to the modern understanding of the subject as one that chooses rationally and is equipped with autonomous agency (cf. Reckwitz 2006). The demands, options and activities, however, that make travel necessary – social contacts, work, school, shopping – are treated as givens, external to the analysis of transport behaviour (Van Acker et al. 2010, 230).

In the following, I will focus on the subject conceptualisations within mobilities research. In order to strengthen the argument of the co-constitution of social formations and mobile subjectivities, I will highlight the role of automobility in constituting prototypically modern subjectivity. In opposition to the 'rational subject' appellation, the works subsumed under the mobilities paradigm outline a theorem of mobility as a relational practice that will be sketched in the second part. This central concept entails a fundamental critique of the autonomous mobile subject and thus the modern rational subject in general. However, there seems to be a cleavage between the theoretical assumptions and the research practice of mobilities scholars, as will be highlighted in the third section. By privileging certain methods and perspectives on what is social, segments of mobilities research implicitly affirm the solitary mobile subject by ignoring conditioning contexts and dependencies. In the conclusion, I will then suggest developing further some methods and methodologies that account for a more relational subjectivity and agency.

The automobile subject as paradigmatic for the modern subject

The co-constitution and co-emergence of socio-spatial order and subjectification have been elaborated by numerous mobilities scholars in relation to automobility. On this token, the motorised car cannot be reduced to a mere technological add-on of Western modernity but must be understood as part and parcel of this specific social formation with its specific spatialities – the internally integrated bound nation state – and with its specific regime of accumulation – the capitalist Fordist national economy (Böhm et al. 2006a; Paterson 2007; cf. Urry 2004). As Rajan (2006, 113f.) elaborated, the car as a principal technology of liberal democratic societies, with its promise of freedom (of choice) and individuality, reinforces the modern teleology by establishing characteristically that which is modern and, by definition, permanently desirable. Thus, automobility constitutes a crucial element of the governance and production of the very subjectivities, desires and lifestyles within which its legitimisation is grounded. This complex automobile-social formation came about during the 20th century in the Western world and is continuously changing and adapting its organisation.[3]

Looking back, it often seems that the motor car was simply the most suitable technology to organise the movement of people from home to work within national territories and therefore became the dominant mode of mass transportation. Automobile passenger travel has gained the aura of 'naturalness', and '[m]any people maintain that cars are the evolutionary epitome of transportation, the ultimate technological extension of free human movement' (Goodwin 2010, 66; Manderscheid 2014a, 7; cf. Henderson 2009). However, as research into the history of automobility has shown, many elements used to explain the success of individual motorised transport, at a closer look, turn out to be an effect of the latter.

At the time of their first appearance in Western cities, automobiles were not seen as the means of future mass transportation but rather the opposite, as something for the affluent bourgeoisie, 'the motor car provided fantasies of status, freedom and escape from the constraints of a highly disciplined urban, industrial order' (McShane 1994, 148; quoted in Paterson 2007, 132). Cars were too expensive (and not reliable enough) to be a means of commuting or of far travel for the working class. It was not until the reorganisation of the labour process as part of a new accumulation regime that cars became affordable for the masses, making them 'the commodity form as such in the 20th century' (cf. Paterson 2007, 107; Ross 1995, 19). The Fordist era of capitalist growth has been described as one characterised by the state's distinctive role in securing full employment in a relatively closed national economy mainly through demand-side management.

Social policy with the aim of reproducing labour power had a distinctive welfare orientation, promoting mass consumption, family wages and thereby the integration of the working class into capitalist society (Aglietta 1979, 152; Jessop 1999; Paterson 2007, 111f.). In this context, the car and suburban housing constituted central elements of consumption norms, as Michel Aglietta highlights:

> The structure of the consumption norm thus coincides with its conditioning by capitalist relations of production. It is governed by two commodities: the standardized housing that is the privileged site of individual consumption; and the automobile as the means of transportation compatible with the separation of home and workplace.
>
> (Aglietta 1979, 159)

What is more, this economic regime and its spatial organisation are inseparably interwoven with the nuclear family and its asymmetric gender relations, which constitute both the precondition for the reproduction of the labour force and the individualising counterweight to Taylorist discipline and heteronomy (Aglietta 1979, 159f.; Kohlmorgen 2004, 120; cf. Meißner 2011). In this context, the private car, made affordable to most social strata through mass production, can be described as an 'equaliser', providing not just the elite with generous amounts of personal space while expanding opportunities (Rajan 2006, 114):

> At least on the face of it, automobility appears to have the built-in mechanisms to fulfil contemporary liberal society's promise of delivering both freedom and equality in several of those places that have embraced capitalist theory and practice.
>
> (Rajan 2006, 118)

Yet this freedom took the form of individualisation as the disembedding of the individual from social collectives such as class, neighbourhood, religious communities and extended families (Beck 1992). During the 20th century and supported by a range of social, cultural, economic and political means, automobility became deeply ingrained in many social practices, lifestyles and living arrangements (Henderson 2009; cf. Seiler 2008). The inclusion of broad social strata into the qualified labour force with rising wages and the expansion of social welfare during the second half of the 20th century meant also an adoption of formerly socially exclusive consumption and lifestyles by the majority of the population. Thus, within the self-description of Fordist societies, the middle classes with their individualist aspirations, values of self-fulfilment and lifestyles – including a suburban home and a car – played an important part, whereas the cleavage between the working class and the bourgeois capitalist class lost its identificatory and descriptive power for the life realities of the masses. Correspondingly, the promotion of home ownership as well as the provision of infrastructures for private car traffic became central elements within post-war Western public policies, constituting a central part of Fordist regulation (Gegner 2007; Kuhm 1997;

Seiler 2008). In this view, the Fordist class compromise and the degree of territorial social cohesion to a large part are rooted in individual mobilisation and motorisation of the masses. This constitutes both the precondition and the effect of the individual integration into the system of productive employment (cf. Miller and Rose 2009). Yet this 'elevator effect' (Beck 1992) in Western societies came at the price of increasing individual responsibilities and risks, thus forcing people to become solitary authors of their movements, professional careers, life projects and social inclusion. In this context, automobility constitutes a central element within a broader technology of spatial mobilisation and social individualisation. The topographical separation of working and dwelling that makes car driving and thus car owning necessary for large parts of the workforce in Western societies did not just 'naturally' happen but is itself at the same time the cause and effect of the modern spreading of car mobility. As John Urry phrased it:

> [a]utomobility divides workplaces from homes, producing lengthy commutes into and across the city. It splits homes and business districts, undermining local retail outlets to which one might have walked or cycled, eroding town-centres, non-car pathways and public spaces. . . . Automobility is thus a system that coerces people into an intense flexibility. It forces people to juggle fragments of time so as to deal with the temporal and spatial constraints that it itself generates.
>
> (Urry 2004, 28)

This schema suggests that the late modern addressing and performative interpellation of the individual by a regime of automobility is part and parcel of the constitution and embodiment of the modern subject. The governmental formation and privileging of the automobile subject in current Western social formations creates both a social normality and its flip side, several deviant and problematic subjectivities: whereas up until the late 1960s and early 1970, only a minority of households owned a private car (for Germany, cf. Kuhm 1997, 185), by now, within the old EU states, on average fewer than two people share a passenger car, that is more than 500 cars per 1,000 inhabitants (Wikipedia 2014; Worldbank 2014). Car owning and driving thus constitute almost an unquestioned matter of course that is deeply ingrained in the fabric and organisation of the social realm. Paradigmatically, passing the driving test and receiving a driver's license (rather than the right to vote) marks the entry into adulthood as a full member of modern societies (Packer 2008b; cf. Rajan 2006; Seiler 2008). Thus, against the background of Foucault's understanding of governmentality and subjectification, the argument may be summarised as constituting the modern subject as an automobile subject, which is aided by the car's supporting institutions – the highway and gasoline delivery infrastructure, traffic rules, parking structures, licensing procedures and highway patrol officers. Jointly, they serve as 'training wheels' to prepare the individual to become a mature citizen in a material and spatial society (Rajan 2006, 122). Yet it is not the automobile subject per se but the *economically productive automobile subject* – driving for work or consumption – that deserves full social admission (cf. Manderscheid and Richardson 2011). Looking at work-fare policies, the argument works as well the other way round: being a productive thus employable person involves accepting to commute – by car.

Furthermore, the formation of the automobile subject entails constituting a hierarchy of mobile subject positions, differentiating between good and normal movements and moorings, symbolising socially accepted life organisations on the one side and subordinated, deviant or simply unproductive forms on the other – in other words, uncontrolled leisure traffic in relation to economically relevant com-mutes of the labour force, private car traffic and subsidised public transport (cf. D. Miller 2001; Seiler 2008). Other mobile subjects – pedestrians, public traffic users, cyclists, passengers – although co-products and derivatives of automobility, are of lower degree of generalisation and recognition. For example, among other state policies, urban and spatial planning assume and plan for automobile subjects and treat 'the others' as a category of problematic deviants, whose needs can be met only as far as public budget restrictions allow (cf. Manderscheid and Richard-son 2011). In a way, by taking individual automobility as a normal characteristic of modern subjects, the responsibility for being slow or immobile is assigned individually to the non-automobile subjects.[4] The moral prompt to be automobile is paradigmatically expressed in a quote attributed to Margaret Thatcher: 'a man who, beyond the age of 26, finds himself on a bus can count himself a failure' (HM Government 2003).

The specific modern and automobile subject is continuously affirmed by aggre-gated social practices and knowledge, as well as by policy and scientific dis-courses. As argued in the introduction, the rational autonomously mobile subject pervades transportation and planning. Yet as a discordant discourse, the theoretical foundations of the mobility paradigm[5] challenge this figure by stressing the rela-tional and embedded character of mobility practices and mobile actors, together with the relational character of the social in general. However, as I will show in more detail in the remainder of the chapter, there seems to be a gap between these epistemological claims and research practices within mobilities studies, which run the risk of reproducing or affirming the solitary mobile subject through their research designs and methodologies.

In order to elaborate this hypothesis further, I will now turn to the relational understanding of mobility that is a central epistemic axiom of mobilities research.

Mobilities as a relational practice: mobile subjects as embedded agents

One of the fundamental breaks of the mobilities paradigm from 'traditional' social theory consists in the focus on movement and fluidity rather than on territorially fixed social units (Hannam et al. 2006; Sheller and Urry 2006), which:

> challenges the ways in which much social science research has been "a-mobile". Even while it has increasingly introduced spatial analysis the social sciences have still failed to examine how the spatialities of social life

presuppose (and frequently involve conflict over) both the actual and the imagined movement of people from place to place, person to person, event to event.

(Sheller and Urry 2006, 208)

In this view, people, objects and symbols are understood as travelling virtually, physically and imaginatively in multiple ways. *Mobility*[6] encompasses a wide range of movements that can be seen as a continuum, ranging from the daily routine movements around the home at one end of the spectrum to long-distance migration and virtual mobility at the other end (Pooley et al. 2005, 5). Persons thus move physically on a frequent and regular basis in their everyday life and maybe once or twice a year for holidays; they relocate permanently or temporally to new dwellings, and they move virtually by communicating and connecting through the Internet, mobile phones and the like. These different forms of movement require a broad range of technical artefacts and infrastructures, norms and regulations. Correspondingly, movement or mobility can be understood only in relation to its material foundation. Thus, movement as a practice has to be *contextualised within specific material, geographical and broader spatial environments*. As Urry states:

> [t]he human and the material intersect in various combinations and networks, which in turn vary greatly in their degree of stabilisation over time and across space. . . . In such an account the human is highly decentred and is not to be seen as separate from the non-human.

(Urry 2000, 78)

Maybe these statements on the hybrid character of mobile agents are where the difference and opposition to the modern conceptualisation of an autonomous rational subject become most visible. By this token, Büscher and Urry (2009, 100) consider the analysis of mobilities as 'an example of *post-human* analysis' (emphasis K.M.). More specifically, they presume 'that the powers of "humans" are co-constituted by various material agencies, of clothing, tools, objects, paths, buildings, machines, paper, and so on' (Büscher and Urry 2009, 100).

In addition, the common disregard of *location-specific spatial*, especially *infrastructural inequalities*, on different scales assumes and thus corroborates the ideologically infused ideal of equal chances and restraints to being mobile across territorial and social spaces like national societies, thereby affirming equally motile subjects. However, this assumption no longer (if ever) holds true for most Western countries in which, starting at different levels of spatial homogeneity and integration, processes of spatial and infrastructural differentiation and splintering are taking place (Graham and Marvin 2001). Spatial differentiation can be observed at the global, national, regional and urban scales, which means that, depending on the analytical interest, movement has to be contextualised within the matching scale(s). Yet the infrastructure equipment of places should not be seen as meaningful or 'equalising' per se, even though its effect on people's lives depends on their life-geographies and the spatial extent of personal networks

(Cass et al. 2005; Frei et al. 2009; Larsen and Jacobsen 2009; cf. Urry 2003): Not everyone needs to move physically in order to be socially integrated, and not everyone's social ties are long distance. What is more, the degree to which people can compensate for a lack of publicly provided access to services and infrastructures depends on their economic, cultural or social capital (Bourdieu 1986) or their network capital (Urry 2007, 194ff.). Thus, together with the material context, the *individual's networks* and *socio-spatial positionality* should also be taken into consideration.

Furthermore, movements take place within a *spatially and historically defined sociocultural context*. Mobility, infrastructures and spaces are being constructed and made meaningful through a range of symbols, representations and discourses. The collective meaning of mobility – as well as the knowledge and representation of possible destinations and, more broadly speaking, of mobility practices – varies multidimensionally with one's position in time, space and society. Yet in the course of historical sedimentation and collective habitualisation, the social origin of the extensions and limitations of the realm of movement practices tend to become invisible, gradually being considered as a natural matter of course both by the actors within these contexts and by scientific analysis. Yet against this background, individual and collective mobility choices, such as modes of transportation, destinations, speed and their absence cannot be attributed sufficiently to conscious and informed individual decisions. Rather, mobilities are pervaded by preconscious and incorporated cultural discourses and knowledge (e.g. Freudendal-Pedersen 2007), infused with supra-subjective meanings and hierarchies. The moves and fixes that are thinkable, choose-able and 'do-able' by individuals, groups and larger social formations are thus prescribed by discursive formations at a given space and time (cf. Foucault 2002).

Moreover, movements also take place in specific *social contexts* within which these practices as broader mobility strategies involve further *rectified or alternative, dependent and relational forms of movement, mooring and stillness* (e.g. Hannam et al. 2006; Schneider et al. 2002). Thus, moves are rarely decisions taken in complete social isolation but should be conceptualised as negotiated more or less directly within personal networks of relations. For example, residential mobility affects and matters within personal relationships, families and other social networks (e.g. Larsen et al. 2006, 74f.; Schneider et al. 2002). Thus, the latter have an impact, one way or another, on residential choices. Other forms of travel also go hand in hand with dependent social immobilities: at starting, resting and end points of travel are places with people attached to them – families, lovers, work colleagues and partners, services, maintenance – which form the immobile social prerequisite for travel. The relation between moving and immobile people and bodies is intrinsically linked with power relations of class, ethnicity and gender (e.g. Malkki 1992; Weiss 2005; Wolff 1993).

Against this background, mobility practices emerge in specific social, cultural, material and geographic situations within collectively and personally shaped spatial relations. Elsewhere (Manderscheid 2012, 2014b), I suggest referring to this trans-individual background of practices as the 'mobility *dispositif*', and other authors refer to it as 'larger material and symbolic regimes' (D'Andrea et al. 2011, 158) or 'socio-technical systems' (Urry 2004). Yet what is of interest here are the methodological consequences of these outlined axioms of mobilities research, especially the conceptualisation and methodical operationalisation of mobile agency.

Having outlined the relevant ontological foundation of the mobilities paradigm, I will now turn to the practice of mobilities research. As an empirical base, I analysed the articles that appeared in *Mobilities* in 2013 as a sample of present contributions to mobilities studies. The analysis focused on the scale of the research object, the methods used and, if applicable, the conceptualisation of agency. The sample can be seen as representing state-of-the-art mobilities research, published in its central journal. The aim of this study was to underpin and illustrate rather general observations empirically.

Performing mobilities: missing links between theory and methods

Methods and methodologies, drawing on antipositivist, performative and holistic understandings of science, extend theoretical axioms into the empirical world (Diaz-Bone 2010; cf. Kuhn 1962). In this view, methods and scientific techniques are not understood as neutral instruments to be used and applied in order to analyse pre-existing social entities but rather as carriers of theoretical assumptions and trimmed models of the empirical world. Thus, rather than merely illuminating a world that exists independently, methods (co-)constitute their object of research. This performative view on methods and research plays a prominent role in French epistemology, which is rooted in the works of Gaston Bachelard (2002) and can be found in the works of, among others, Roland Barthes, Georges Canguilhem and Michel Foucault. The latter states this holistic and performative role of knowledge and discourses in general, which he sees not 'as groups of signs . . . signifying elements referring to concepts or representation . . . but as practices that systematically form the objects of which they speak' (Foucault 1972, 49). Or, as John Law and John Urry phrased it outside the French discussion, social research practices are performative, 'they enact realities and they can help to bring into being what they also discover' (Law and Urry 2004, 393).

From the very beginning, mobilities studies contained a strand on methods – referred to as *mobile methods* and *methods for mobilities research* (e.g. Ahas 2011; Büscher and Urry 2009; Büscher et al. 2011a; Fincham et al. 2010; Merriman 2013). In a Kuhnian view (Kuhn 1962), the development of new theoretical approaches, terminologies and methods marks the emergence of a new scientific paradigm, an idea that has been actively employed by mobility scholars in speaking of a 'mobilities paradigm' (e.g. Urry 2007, 39). By this token, Urry argues that 'research methods also need to be "on the move", in effect to simulate in various ways the many and interdependent forms of intermittent movement of people, images, information and objects' (ibid.). His emphasis on the ability of methods to follow people, images, information and objects constitutes an opposition to the assumption of fixity and sedentarism of 'traditional' social science research methods, which typically locate people through their residential address and more or less explicitly assume spatially fixed lives, social integration based on geographic proximity and spatial co-presence. These sedentary assumptions are reflected in many ways in social science data and in the classifications used, such as, amongst others, the discussion of analytical consequences of territorialising concepts of identity (e.g. Malkki 1992) or research on multilocal forms of dwelling (e.g. Hilti 2009) has brought to the fore. Traditionally, the social facet is conceptualised as contained within territorial units – the neighbourhood, the city, the region, the nation state – which then figure as sampling units for social science data collections. Mobile methods, on the other hand, aim at tracking the multiple movements of people, information and objects (Büscher and Urry 2009, 103ff.), thereby turning the very spatialities of the social into an object of empirical research. The suggested methods encompass a range of qualitative, partly technologically supported means of collecting data on moving systems (cf. Büscher et al. 2011a, 2011b, 7ff.; Fincham et al. 2010), aiming at overcoming the sedentary bias.

Yet constructing principally mobile rather than sedentary research units through social science methods is only one of the methodological issues raised by mobilities theoretical concepts. As outlined in the previous section, further elements comprise the *hybrid character of moving entities* – consisting of human-technical networks – and their *embedding* into *geographic* and *infrastructure contexts* and into *networks of social ties and obligations*, as well as their *position within a historically and culturally specific field of knowledge*. Although these issues form a prominent part of mobilities thinking, until now they hardly seem to be addressed by the suggested mobile methods. What is more, the performed ontologies of mobility research applying the idea of 'following the thing' (e.g. Adey 2010, 53) take the mobile thing's existence – be it a mobile human or an object – as a fact a priori that is defined by its movement: '[s]ubjectivities are mobilised prior to empirical investigation through this act of paradigmatic naming' (Bissell 2010, 55). Thus, what is other than mobile is regarded 'immobile' or 'moored'. The other exists only in relation to the moving things (ibid.), while the nature of its existence is always already predefined. This a priori existing mobile thing, followed by mobilities scholars, most often tends to be either an object of the material world or a human being. Thus, the theorem of hybrid sociotechnical formations gets lost in large parts of the discussion and application of these mobile methods. What is still less developed are methods 'to examine the many ways in which objects and people are assembled and reassembled through time-space' (Urry 2007, 50).

The analysis of all papers published in *Mobilities* in 2013 reveals that only 5 of 33 papers focused (more or less systematically) on the interaction between people and material objects, yet none questioned the ontology of its research object. This contributes to the observation that research designs and methods used in mobilities studies do not reflect systematically the idea of sociotechnical hybrids constituting and constituted through movement. Rather, as Savage and colleagues (2010, 6) observe, mobilities research practice shows an elective affinity with theoretically humanist methods like face-to-face conversations, moving with the research subject, ethnographic methods and participation in virtual interactions. These methods, stemming from qualitative understanding and phenomenological sociological traditions, tend to overemphasise the agency of humans, while the material and technological foundation of the various forms of mobility, their productivity and performativity, as well as their interaction with and embodiment by mobile humans, is not reflected within these methods and most research designs; thus, they remain largely unobserved (Schad and Duchêne-Lacroix 2013, 364).

In addition, there is the issue of contextualising the mobile things. As elaborated elsewhere (cf. D'Andrea et al. 2011; Manderscheid 2014b), the empirical focus of most mobilities research tends to be either the micro level of experiences, practices and motives or the macro level of flows and movements, their technological and material preconditions, past developments, political economies and potential futures, as well as links to specific constitutions of discourses and knowledge. Both methodological approaches undoubtedly have been of high value for the development of mobilities studies. However, whereas macro approaches run the risk of reading 'social life off external social forms – flows, circuits, circulations of people, capital and culture – without any model of subjective mediation' (Povinelli and Chauncey 1999, 7), micro sociological approaches try to excavate these subjective elements especially without systematic consideration of their positionality in space, time and the social realm. The analysis of the sample of *Mobilities* papers shows that less than a third of the papers apply a dual focus of practices and experiences at the micro level and of social and spatial structures of movement at the macro level. Amongst these papers, only one analysis explicitly highlighted the need to correct subjective statements by structural context information. Thus, it appears that to a large extent, mobility research analyses these two sides separately – either the experience and mobility practices or their discursive, spatial or structural foundation.

Furthermore, especially by applying narrative methods, a significant part of mobilities research implicitly reconstructs and affirms the actor of movement as a conscious, active and to some degree autonomous subject. Amongst the 33 *Mobilities* papers, 10 used interview material and five worked with ethnographic methods of participating observation that included communication with the researched subject. As Bissell (2010, 57) elaborated, the use of narration 'tends to privilege the active dimension of corporeal experience: I *walked*, I *ran*, I *watched*, I *talked*, I *remembered*'. These 'performative renderings of mobile subjects . . ., might have the effect of generating an *overanimated* mobile subject. This potential for movement and connection . . . privileges the body-in-action, as active and agentive.' What slips from this empirical focus are other, less conscious, less active and less reportable bodily experiences. Together with the point made before, especially the decontextualised focus on the micro level of subjective representations of movements, using solely interview-generated textual material runs the risk of overstating the role of conscious reasoning by individuals while at the same time eclipsing pre- and unconscious habitual and structurally shaped factors (cf. Bourdieu 2000).

Overall, the papers analysed display a peculiar tendency to abstract from social and spatial contexts in which mobility decisions and practices take place and to privilege the subjective view onto the social world. Very often without further consideration, within empirical mobilities research, the individual person is represented as the sole author of mobility practices. What is more, concepts and classifications used in mobilities (as well as other sociological) research carry highly normative assumptions on '*the good mobile subject*'. Beyond the analysed sample, this also becomes evident with research on children's mobility practices and usage of urban spaces, which tends to treat as a problem the decrease of public spaces in towns and cities where children can play as well as the increase of children transported by car to places of leisure and activities spread all over the town or the city. This line of argument can be traced back through the history of urban studies and is found in the writings of Mumford and Jacobs, as well as in the psychological writings of Piaget, Fromm and others. The more or less explicit ideal of a child's socialisation is seen in '*independent mobility*' (Katz 1994; O'Brian et al. 2000; Shaw et al. 2013; cf. Zeiher 1990), which is commonly defined as the 'freedom [of children] to travel around their own neighbourhood or city without adult supervision' (Shaw et al. 2013, 35). The purpose of these travels may be leisure, school or play. Researchers of children's mobilities, as well as children's health and development policies, agree on the mental and physical benefits of their independent mobility, which, on the other side, is limited by traffic landscape designs as well as by parental judgements, restrictions and 'licenses'. Yet, as Mikkelsen and colleagues (2009, 41) state in their critical review of the concept:

> the idea of children's independent mobility reflects a cultural and adult-centred focus on individual agency seeing independent mobility as a natural step in children. . . . In this understanding, childhood emerges as a phase in life in which children progressively grow up, and literally move out of the dependence of adults into independence. The cultural ideal is that children should be brought up to become an individual actor as opposed to a collective one.

Independence in this context is strongly biased to the absence of adults during journeys and outdoor movements. Other types of dependence affecting children's mobilities that arise from economic, political, material, cultural or other social relationships remain underexposed. Thus, the enmeshment of children's mobility practices with peer activities and their norms and rules (e.g. Goodman et al. 2013; Mikkelsen and Christensen 2009) is hidden behind this focus on accompanying adults. Furthermore, one may question whether it makes sense to talk about dependence or independence as a fixed status or if these concepts should be seen as part of social relations that are constituted through reciprocal actions (Mikkelsen and Christensen 2009, 41). Finally, independent mobility is often equalised to walking and cycling as forms of self-driven movement (Goodman et al. 2013, 276), whereas procedures of being moved – by public transportation as well as car-passengering – are framed as inferior and less autonomous. Taken together, the concept of independent children's mobility and its common application in

urban studies and social science research reflects the modern ideal of autonomous, independent mobility that finds its mature adult form in the solitary car
driver. The process of learning 'truly self-determined mobility', then, is seen as
initially requiring 'the company of peers' (Goodman et al. 2013, 288) as a necessary but immature stage within the process of becoming truly independently
mobile.

The concept of children's independent mobility is currently undergoing some
critique (e.g. Goodman et al. 2013; Mikkelsen and Chistensen 2009) that highlights the importance of mutual dependence on and relations with other travelling peers, as well as the cultural bias within the concept. Yet the connected
idealisation of adult independent mobility – especially by car – remains largely
untouched. However, as I highlighted in the previous sections, the automobile
subject should be understood as a powerful construction and abstraction, which
emphasises the autonomous and rational characteristics by eclipsing dependence
on infrastructure-material, spatial and social contexts, the preconscious and historically embodied desires, values and preferences and thus the socio-discursive
nature of the mobility order.

This cuspidal outline of methodological and conceptual issues within mobilities research practice relegates it to a gap between theoretical foundations and
their performative extension into the empirical. By drawing mainly on qualitative methods centred on humans, this research practice implicitly affirms the
autonomous mobile subject that emerged together with Western modernity and
whose embedding in, dependence on and interaction with social, spatial, material, cultural and historical contexts tend to be obscured. Therefore, in a way,
although mobilities research theoretically intends to criticise and deconstruct a
broader governmental invocation and formation of a figure, it is nevertheless an
essential part of it. As Foucault pointed out prominently throughout his oeuvre,
the production of knowledge is inseparably infused and interwoven with power
relations. Thus, neither theory nor methods can be regarded as neutral tools
applied to the search for the truth. Rather, they are part and parcel of social power
relations, shaped by and themselves shaping social realities. The emergence of
a concept such as the modern subject as an autonomous and rationally thinking
independent mind does not simply constitute a description of modern humans
in contrast to the collectively embedded premodern person but also expresses
a gendered and desocialised pre-scription of modern subjectivities as cultural
forms, suggestions, expectations, normalities and constraints on which empirical
individuals have to act.

Politics of methods: searching for alternatives

The claim of forming a new paradigm entails the development of appropriate theories, terminologies and methods. Furthermore, the key texts of mobilities research
contain a more or less explicit critical stance on the social world by, to mention
only a few critical topic examples, directing the focus on the sociocultural embedding and governing of movement practices and the rise in motorised mobilities,

thus criticising the one-dimensional approaches of transport studies and traffic policies that focus simply on individual behaviour modelled as rational choices. Against this background, the critique of concepts, terminologies and methods – such as the implicit affirmation of the 'rational autonomous mobile subject' manifest as the automobile subject (together with individualising governance in regard to social as well as environmental issues (cf. Paterson and Stripple 2010) and the search for technological quick fixes for ecological and transportation problems) – becomes a political strategy within the contestation of hegemonic views of the world and within the critique of the present mobility order. In this light, it seems crucial to develop and discover new methods and methodologies that are not only co-mobile with their object of research but that frame and perform the empirical object differently and in accordance with the outlined claims of its relational and hybrid character. Mobilities research would thereby constitute and signify a new reality of empirical objects in a more coherent manner.

Turning the outlined points of critique into points of departure for this search, I see some – although not yet fleshed out – sources of inspiration. Firstly, the *decentring of the subject in relation to its material environment* should be taken seriously, by working with post-human methods. Points of contact are the so called material turn (e.g. Bennett and Joyce 2013; Kazig and Weichhart 2009) and, of course, Actor-Network Theory (ANT) (Latour 2005; cf. Law 2002). In particular, ANT focuses explicitly on the processual interaction between human and non-human actants. Thus, ANT represents a non-humanist perspective, decentring the human subject. As an ecological theory, ANT rejects the sociological approach that sees the non-human world either as the material condition of our existence or as no more than a set of symbols forming the basis for human activities (Murdoch 2001, 116f.). The approach is based on an understanding of practices as effecting change rather than as an intentional action of a human subject. Within a temporally stabilised network, human feelings, ideas and intentions, as well as non-human entities like artefacts, machines, plants, animals and the like, are thus thought to have their own agency or practice potential. For example, transportation infrastructures, settlement structures, information and communication technology devices, as well as legal documents (passports, driving licence, rail card), contain formative potential as a pre-scription, which can take the form of permissions and grants (cf. Akrich and Latour 1992). The extent of these actor-networks and thereby the research object cannot be defined ex ante but constitutes one result of the empirical analysis. Furthermore, the empirical contributions of the actors involved in a specific mobile practice also constitute objects of a 'de-scription'.

However, even ANT-research practice also draws mainly on qualitative-ethnographic methods, thus privileging actors capable of speaking (humans) compared to unanimated objects and thereby only insufficiently capturing the stated symmetry between human and material actors (Murdoch 2001; Schad and Duchêne-Lacroix 2013, 269). Recently, the methodological approach of 'technography' (Jansen and Vellema 2011; cf. Kien 2008; Rammert and Schubert 2006) has gained some attention within the STS- and ANT-related discussion on how to integrate technological and social aspects more symmetrically. In this context, technology is understood as the use of skills, tools, knowledge and techniques to accomplish certain ends (Jansen and Vellema 2011, 169).[7] Rather than describing the elements of a network or array, the specific focus of technography is placed on the relationships themselves (Kien 2008). Or, as Vannini and Vannini (2008, 1299) phrased it, '[T]echnography is the study and the writing of technical structures of communication processes, both in their material and symbolic substance, and their potential for shaping social outcomes'. The approach has been described as consisting of three steps. First, the study of 'performance', which consists of a description of the material and social circumstances of technological practices and their interrelationships and thus of the processual technology in use (Jansen and Vellema 2011, 170f.). The second step analyses the task-related knowledge transmitted in a network and thus how the knowledge and skills of the different actors are mobilised and coordinated and how bearers of skills and knowledge are included or excluded from the performance or practice (Jansen and Vellema 2011, 171f.). Finally, the third step tries to excavate the rules, protocols, routines and rituals shaping the specific practices, their organisation and the inclusion of actors (Jansen and Vellema 2011, 172f.). Ideally, the descriptions are empirically grounded mainly in observations rather than in interviews with human actors, thus placing emphasis on the organisation of the networks and practices rather than their human rationalisation (Jansen and Vellema 2011, 174). Although up until now, only few technographic studies existed in relation to mobilities research (Schad and Duchêne-Lacroix 2013; Vannini and Vannini 2008), this approach seems to hold some potential for the performance of the post-human claim of mobilities research through empirical studies. For example, in relation to car mobility, it suggests an empirical take on the mobile body as an assemblage of social practices, embodied dispositions and skills as well as technological potential and affordances that are commonly taken for granted and treated as unremarkable (Dant 2004, 74; Jensen et al. 2014, 3).[8] This would substantiate an alternative view on automobility and agency regarding transportation and foster a more political understanding of technology and infrastructure policies.

The second shortcoming of mobilities research practice was seen in a lack of contextualisation of the mobile subjects and the lack of studies linking the micro level of experiences and rationalities with the macro level of discourses, infrastructures and social order. As D'Andrea and colleagues (2011, 155f.) stated, a 'significant challenge for mobilities studies is the systematic unbundling and formalisation of research protocols, methods and analyses that can integrate macro and micro components, rather than allowing these to continue developing separately'. As one strategy, the qualitative data collected on the micro level may be contrasted with information on the contextual structures. Elsewhere (Manderscheid 2014b; similarly Taipale 2014), I suggested using the statistical technique of multiple correspondence analysis to search for structuring dimensions underlying patterns of practices. Similarly, as one case within the sample of papers, Huete et al. (2013) argue that the subjective assessments of individuals may be skewed and are not sufficient as the sole analytical framework. Analysing the research differentiation between lifestyle and labour migration, the authors excavate an underlying ethnic-national elitism in the self-classifications of migrants from the UK and Northern countries to Spain who are claiming primarily non-economic factors as motivations for their residential mobility. However, a quantitative comparison of their residential mobility patterns over time brings the dependence on economic factors to the fore, rendering their mobility patterns strikingly similar to those of the so called labour migrants. Thus, using multilevel data can help correct for blind spots, preconscious knowledge, biased accounts or assumptions of one-dimensional effects on one level.

On this token, another interesting analysis technique could be social network analysis extended by a spatial dimension, applied to micro data as well as survey data. Larsen and colleagues (Larsen et al. 2006), for example, outline a form of qualitative spatial network analysis for individual cases, whereas the works of Axhausen and fellows (Axhausen 2007; Frei et al. 2009) are pioneering in the field of visualisation and analysis of social network geographies based on standardised survey data. They suggest some analytical techniques in order to compare network geographies between different social groups that form the backdrop for their differing mobility practices. These methods of spatial network analysis appear as promising tools to account more systematically for the socio-spatial embedding of mobile actors and the network effects of mobile practices.

These few suggestions may suffice to show, that, besides the development of further qualitative methods for mobilities research, it may also be worthwhile to rediscover standardised techniques that are suitable to contextualise mobility practices and thus re-embed the solitary mobile subjects into spatial and social structures in a nondeterministic way.[9] Taken together, the suggested advancements within this discussion of mobile methods and methods for mobilities research may contribute to the discursive deconstruction of the modern automobile subject.

Conclusion

Drawing on the Foucauldian understanding of governmentality and subjectification, automobility may be understood as a principal 'technology of contemporary liberalism' (Rajan 2006, 114), producing the very subjects it requires. The modern subject is characterised as an autonomously deciding rational actor, detached and detaching itself from social and spatial ties. Yet realities do not exist independently of their representation, and this representation of the social world is highly contested and continuously changing. Taking mobilities studies as a standpoint within the contestation of the mobile social order, my contribution has focused particularly on the construction and critique of this solitary mobile subject. From its very beginnings, the mobilities paradigm questioned and challenged this conception, which also pervades social sciences in general as well as transportation studies and policy making in particular. Taking the order of knowledge – to which scientific discourses continuously contribute – as a cultural space of definitions and productions of specific subjectivities (Reckwitz 2008, 26ff.), research practices should be understood not only as descriptors of empirical realities but also as techniques to effect and co-produce these very realities.

Against this background, I have analysed the methodological performance of mobilities studies, which show some incoherence in regard to some of the founding theoretical claims of the mobilities paradigm: by drawing mainly on narrative qualitative methods and by focusing mainly on the micro level of practices and experiences, segments of mobilities research risk implicitly affirming the mobile rational subject as a disembedded solitary figure by abstracting from his/her dependence on material, infrastructure, social, cultural and historic conditions. As sources for further development of methods for mobilities research I suggest to look more closely at the toolboxes of ANT and STS research, especially technography, as well as selected multilevel statistics that allow individual practices to be contextualised within broader structural backgrounds.

However, I am not claiming that mobilities research can change mobility realities simply by broadening their methodologies and analytical techniques. Sociocultural discourses and fields of knowledge suggest and impose specific patterns and subjectivities, even though they do not determine the empirical individual, who is always faced with multiple and contradicting expectations, forces and patterns. Yet, as part of the social struggle for the 'true' view on the social, mobilities studies contribute to the way we conceive mobility and thus may contribute to changing mobility itself.

Notes

1 In a more differentiated account, Doughty and Murray (2014) distinguish analytically between a technocratic and a right-to-mobilities strand, as well as strands of mobile riskiness, of speedy connectivity and of sustainable mobility pervading more or less powerful institutional mobility discourses.
2 I will focus on physical movement in geographic space. However, the argument could also be applied to virtual mobilities.
3 Within the context under discussion, however, what is of interest is not the historical evidence for this claim, which has been elaborated more systematically elsewhere (e.g. Packer 2008a; Paterson 2007; Rajan 2006; Seiler 2008), but an understanding of automobility as a technology, as a mode of subjectification.
4 This hypothesis runs parallel to the diagnosis of governmentality studies that observe a process of de-socialisation and conceptualisation of the individual as an active and responsible subject. As Nikolas Rose has argued in regard to unemployment, 'each individual is solicited as an ally of economy success through ensuring that they invest in the management, presentation, promotion and enhancement of their own economic capital as a capacity of their selves and as a lifelong project' (Rose 1996, 339).
5 Of course, the theoretical foundations of mobilities research are broad and rooted in heterogeneous strands of social theory. However, the claim of constituting a 'new paradigm' (Sheller and Urry 2006) comes with the assumption of some degree of common theoretical claims, especially some fundamental breaks with 'traditional' social theory.
6 Of course, considering the question of what constitutes movement and what is labelled immobility, the object, mobility, is itself the effect of social constructions and contestations (cf. Mincke, this volume; Frello 2008). Yet I am abstracting from this here, since my interest is to contrast the (implicit) ontologies of the mobilities paradigm with traditional social theory and transportation research.
7 The ends to be accomplished are themselves discursively produced and should not be seen as natural givens. Furthermore, it appears necessary to differentiate between seemingly obvious intentions, strategies and unintended effects of technologies.

8 Another interesting approach on the material side of the mobile social world consists in the concept of interactive metal fatigue (Pel 2014).
9 As the ongoing debate in human geography has shown, criticisms of quantitative methods very often conflate these unwarrantedly with positivist methodologies and epistemologies (Barnes 2004; Ellis 2009; Schwanen and Kwan 2009; cf. Sheppard 2001).

References

Adey, Peter. 2010. *Mobility*. London, New York: Routledge.

Aglietta, Michel. 1979. *A Theory of Capitalist Regulation. The US Experience*. London: Verso Classics.

Ahas, R. 2011. Mobile Positioning. In *Mobile Methods*, edited by M. Büscher, J. Urry and K. Witchger, 183–199. London: Routledge.

Akrich, Madeleine, and Bruno Latour. 1992. A Summary of a Convenient Vocabulary for the Semiotics of Human and Nonhuman Assemblies. In *Shaping Technology/Building Society Studies in Sociotechnical Change*, edited by Wiebe E. Bijker and John Law, 259–264. Cambridge, MA: MIT Press.

Axhausen, Kay W. 2007. Activity spaces, biographies, social networks and their welfare gains and externalities: Some hypotheses and empirical results. *Mobilities* 2(1): 15–36.

Bachelard, Gaston. 2002. *The Formation of the Scientific Mind*. Bolton: Clinamen.

Bærenholdt, Jørgen Ole. 2013. Governmobility: The powers of mobility. *Mobilities* 8(1): 20–34.

Bamberg, Sebastian. 1996. Zeit und Geld: Empirische Verhaltenserklärung mittels Restriktionen am Beispiel der Verkehrsmittelwahl. *ZUMA-Nachrichten* 38: 7–32.

Barnes, Trevor J. 2004. Placing ideas: Genius loci, heterotopia and geography's quantitative revolution. *Progress in Human Geography* 28(5): 565–595.

Beck, Ulrich. 1992. Risk Society: Towards a New Modernity. In *Nation. Vol. 2. Theory, Culture & Society Series*, edited by Mark Ritter. London: Sage.

Bennett, Tony, and Patrick Joyce. Eds. 2013. *Material Powers: Cultural Studies, History and the Material Turn*. London, New York: Routledge.

Bissell, David. 2010. Narrating Mobile Methodologies: Active and Passive Empiricisms. In *Mobile Methodologies*, edited by Ben Fincham, Mark McGuinness and Lesley Murray, 53–68. New York: Palgrave Macmillan.

Böhm, Steffen, Campbell Jones, Chris Land and Mat Paterson. 2006a. Introduction: Impossibilities of automobility. In *Against Automobility*. Special Issue: Sociological Review Monograph Series, edited by Steffen Böhm, Campbell Jones, Chris Land and Matthew Paterson, 3–16. Malden: Blackwell.

———. Eds. 2006b. *Against Automobility*. Malden, MA, Oxford, Victoria: Blackwell.

Bonham, Jennifer. 2006. Transport: Disciplining the Body That Travels. In *Against Automobility*, edited by Steffen Böhm, Campbell Jones, Chris Land and Matthew Paterson, 57–74. Malden, MA, Oxford, Victoria: Blackwell.

Bourdieu, Pierre. 1986. The (Three) Forms of Capital. In *Handbook of Theory and Research in the Sociology of Education*, edited by John G Richardson, 241–258. New York, London: Greenwood Press.

———. 2000. *Distinction. A Social Critique of the Judgment of Taste*. Cambridge, MA: Harvard University Press.

Bröckling, Ulrich, Susanne Krasmann and Thomas Lemke. Eds. 2000. *Gouvernementalität der Gegenwart: Studien zur Ökonomisierung des Sozialen*. Frankfurt am Main: Suhrkamp.

Büscher, Monika, and John Urry. 2009. Mobile methods and the empirical. *European Journal of Social Theory* 12(1): 99–116.

Büscher, Monika, John Urry and Katian Witchger. 2011a. *Mobile Methods*. London, New York: Routledge.

———. 2011b. Introduction: Mobile Methods. In *Mobile Methods*, edited by Monika Büscher, John Urry and Katian Witchger, 1–19. London, New York: Routledge.

Cass, Noel, Elizabeth Shove, and John Urry. 2005. Social exclusion, mobility and access. *Sociological Review* 53: 539–555.

D'Andrea, Anthony, Luigina Ciolfi and Breda Gray. 2011. Methodological challenges and innovations in mobilities research. *Mobilities* 6(2): 149–160.

Dant, Tim. 2004. The driver-car. *Theory, Culture & Society* 21(4/5): 61–79.

Dean, Mitchell M. 1999. *Governmentality: Power and Rule in Modern Society*. London: Sage.

Diaz-Bone, Rainer. 2010. *Die Performativität der Sozialforschung – Sozialforschung als Sozio-Epistemologie. 4*. Working Paper, Soziologisches Seminar, Kultur- und Sozialwissenschaftliche Fakultät, Universität Luzern. Luzern.

Dodge, Martin, and Rob Kitchin. 2006. *Code, vehicles and governmentality: The automatic production of driving spaces*. Maynooth, Ireland: NIRSA Working Papers Series 29.

Doughty, Karaolina, and Lesley Murray. 2014. Discourses of mobility: Institutions, everyday lives and embodiment. *Mobilities* (Online First).

Ellis, Mark. 2009. Vital statistics. *The Professional Geographer* 61(3): 301–309.

Fincham, Ben, Mark McGuinness and Lesley Murray. 2010. *Mobile Methodologies*. London: Palgrave Macmillan.

Foucault, Michel. 1972. *Archeology of Knowledge and the Discourse on Language*. New York: Pantheon.

———. 1983. *Der Wille zum Wissen: Sexualität und Wahrheit 1*. Frankfurt am Main: Suhrkamp.

———. 1987. The ethic of care for the self as a practice of freedom: An interview with Michel Foucault. *Philosophy & Social Criticism* 12 (2–3): 112–131. doi:10.1177/019 145378701200202.

———. 1992. *Überwachen und Strafen: Die Geburt des Gefängnisses*. Frankfurt am Main.: Suhrkamp.

———. 2002. *The Archaeology of Knowledge*. London, New York: Routledge.

———. 2007. *Security, Territory, Population: Lectures at the Collège de France, 1977–78*. London: Palgrave Macmillan.

———. 2008. *The Birth of Biopolitics: Lectures at the Collège de France, 1978–79*, edited by Michel Senellart. Houndsmills, Basingstoke, New York: Palgrave Macmillan.

Frei, Andreas, Kay W. Axhausen and Timo Ohnmacht. 2009. Mobilities and Social Network Geography: Size and Spatial Dispersion – The Zurich Case Study. In *Mobilities and Inequality*, edited by Timo Ohnmacht, Hanja Maksim and Manfred Max Bergman, 99–120. Aldershot: Ashgate.

Freudendal-Pedersen, Malene. 2007. Mobility, motility and freedom: The structural story as an analytical tool for understanding the interconnection. *Schweizerische Zeitschrift für Soziologie* 33(1): 27–43.

Gegner, Martin. 2007. Verkehr und Daseinsvorsorge. In *Handbuch Verkehrspolitik*, edited by Oliver Schöller, Weert Canzler and Andreas Knie, 455–470. Wiesbaden: VS Verlag für Sozialwissenschaften.

Goodman, Anna, Alasdair Jones, Helen Roberts, Rebecca Steinbach and Judith Green. 2013. 'We can all just get on a bus and go': Rethinking independent mobility in the context of the universal provision of free bus travel to young Londoners. *Mobilities* 9(2): 275–293.

Goodwin, K. J. 2010. Reconstructing automobility: The making and breaking of modern transportation. *Global Environmental Politics* 10(4): 60–78.

Graham, Stephen, and Simon Marvin. 2001. *Splintering Urbanism: Networked Infrastructures, Technological Mobilities and the Urban Condition.* London, New York: Routledge.

Hannam, Kevin, Mimi Sheller and John Urry. 2006. Editorial: Mobilities, immobilities and moorings. *Mobilities* 1(1): 1–22.

Henderson, Jason. 2009. The Politics of Mobility: De-Essentializing Automobility and Contesting Urban Space. In *Car Troubles. Critical Studies of Automobility and Auto-Mobility*, edited by Jim Conley and Arlene Tigar McLaren, 147–164. Farnham, Burlington: Ashgate.

Hilti, Nicola. 2009. Here, There, and In-Between: On the Interplay of Multilocal Living, Space, and Inequality. In *Mobilities and Inequality*, edited by Timo Ohnmacht, Hanja Maksim and Manfred Max Bergman, 145–164. Aldershot: Ashgate.

HM Government. 2003. Parliamentary Debates, Col 407, Hansard. Accessed 2 October 2016. www. parliament.the-stationery-office.co.uk/pa/cm200203/cmhansrd/vo030702/debtext/30702-10.htm.

Huete, Raquel, Alejandro Mantecón and Jesús Estévez. 2013. Challenges in lifestyle migration research: Reflections and findings about the Spanish crisis. *Mobilities* 8(3): 331–348. doi:10.1080/17450101.2013.814236.

Jansen, K., and S. Vellema. 2011. What is technography? *NJAS – Wageningen Journal of Life Sciences* 57(3–4): 169–177.

Jensen, Ole B., Mimi Sheller and Simon Wind. 2014. Together and apart: Affective ambiences and negotiation in families' everyday life and mobility. *Mobilities* (10)3: 1–20.

Jessop, Bob. 1999. The changing governance of welfare: Recent trends in its primary functions, scale, and modes of coordination. *Social Policy & Administration* 33(4): 348–359.

Katz, C. 1994. Textures of global change: Eroding ecologies of childhood in New York and Sudan. *Childhood* 2(1–2): 103–110.

Kazig, Rainer, and Peter Weichhart. 2009. Die Neuthematisierung der materiellen Welt in der Humangeographie. *Berichte zur Deutschen Landeskunde* 83(2): 109–128.

Kien, Grant. 2008. Technography = technology + ethnography: An introduction. *Qualitative Inquiry* 14(7): 1101–1109.

Kohlmorgen, Lars. 2004. *Regulation, Klasse, Geschlecht: Die Konstituierung der Sozialstruktur im Fordismus und Postfordismus.* Münster: Westfälisches Dampfboot.

Kuhm, Klaus. 1997. *Moderne und Asphalt: Die Automobilisierung als Prozeß technologischer Integration und sozialer Vernetzung.* Pfaffenweiler: Centaurus.

Kuhn, Thomas S. 1962. *The Structure of Scientific Revolutions.* Chicago: University of Chicago Press.

Larsen, Jonas, Kay W. Axhausen and John Urry. 2006. Geographies of social networks: Meetings, travel and communications. *Mobilities* 1(2): 261–283.

Larsen, Jonas, and Michael Hviid Jacobsen. 2009. Metaphors of Mobility – Inequality on the Move. In *Mobilities and Inequality*, edited by Timo Ohnmacht, Hanja Maksim and Manfred Max Bergman, 75–96. Aldershot: Ashgate.

Larsen, Jonas, John Urry and Kay W. Axhausen. 2006. *Mobilities, Networks, Geographies.* Farnham: Ashgate.

Latour, Bruno. 2005. *Reassembling the Social: An Introduction to Actor-Network-Theory.* Oxford: Oxford University Press.

Law, John. 2002. Objects and spaces. *Theory Culture Society* 19(5–6): 91–105.

Law, John, and John Urry. 2004. Enacting the social. *Economy and Society* 33(3): 390–410.

Lemke, Thomas. 2002. Foucault, governmentality and critique. *Rethinking Marxism: A Journal of Economics, Culture & Society* 14(3): 49–64.

Malkki, Liisa. 1992. National Geographic: The rooting of peoples and the territorialization of national identity among scholars and refugees. *Cultural Anthropology* 7(1): 24–44.

Manderscheid, Katharina. 2012. Automobilität als raumkonstituierendes Dispositiv der Moderne. In *Die Ordnung der Räume*, edited by Henning Füller and Boris Michel, 145–178. Münster: Westfälisches Dampfboot.

———. 2014a. The movement problem, the car and post-Fordist mobility: Automobility as dispositif and mode of regulation. *Mobilities, Special Issue: Foucault and Mobilities Research* 4(9): 604–626.

———. 2014b. Criticising the solitary mobile subject: Researching relational mobilities and reflecting on mobile methods. *Mobilities* 9(2): 188–219.

Manderscheid, Katharina, and Tim Richardson. 2011. Planning inequality: Social and economic spaces in national spatial planning. *European Planning Studies* 19(10): 1797–1815.

McShane, Clay. 1994. *Down the Asphalt Path: The Automobile and the American City*. New York: Columbia University Press.

Merriman, Peter. 2013. Rethinking mobile methods. *Mobilities* 9(2): 1–21.

Meißner, Hanna. 2011. Totalität und Vielfalt – Gesellschaftliche Wirklichkeit als multidimensionaler Zusammenhang. *PROKLA* 165(4): 543–560.

Mikkelsen, Miguel Romero, and Pia Christensen. 2009. Is children's independent mobility really independent? A study of children's mobility combining ethnography and gps/mobile phone technologies 1. *Mobilities* 4(1): 37–58.

Miller, Daniel. 2001. *Car Cultures: Materializing Culture*. Oxford: Berg.

Miller, Peter, and Nikolas Rose. 2009. *Governing the Present: Administering Economic, Social and Personal Life*. Cambridge: Polity.

Murdoch, Jonathan. 2001. Ecologising sociology: Actor-Network theory, co-construction and the problem of human exemptionalism. *Sociology* 35(1): 111–133.

O'Brian, Margaret, Deborah Jones, David Sloan and Michael Rustin. 2000. Children's independent spatial mobility in the urban public realm. *Childhood* 7(3): 257–277.

Otto, Marcus. 2014. *Der Wille zum Subjekt: Zur Genealogie politischer Inklusion in Frankreich (16.–20. Jahrhundert)*. Bielefeld: Transcript.

Packer, Jeremy. 2003. Disciplining Mobility: Governing and Safety. In *Foucault, Cultural Studies and Governmentality*, edited by Jack Z. Bratich, Jeremy Packer and Cameron McCarthy, 135–161. Albany, NY: SUNY Press.

———. 2008a. *Mobility without Mayhem: Safety, Cars, and Citizenship*. Durham, NC, London: Duke University Press.

———. 2008b. Automobility and the Driving Force of Warfare: From Public Safety to National Security. In *The Ethics of Mobilities: Rethinking Place, Exclusion, Freedom and Environment*, edited by Sigurd Bergmann and Tore Sager, 39–64. Aldershot: Ashgate.

Paterson, Matthew. 2007. *Automobile Politics: Ecology and Cultural Political Economy*. Cambridge: Cambridge University Press.

Paterson, Matthew, and Johannes Stripple. 2010. My space: Governing individuals' carbon emissions. *Environment and Planning D: Society and Space* 28(2): 341–362.

Pel, Bonno. 2014. Interactive metal fatigue: A conceptual contribution to social critique in mobilities research. *Mobilities* 1–19.

Pooley, Colin, Jean Turnbull and Mags Adams. 2005. *A Mobile Century? Changes in Everyday Mobility in Britain in the Twentieth Century*. Farnham: Ashgate.

Povinelli, Elizabeth A., and George Chauncey. 1999. Thinking sexuality transnationally. *GLQ: A Journal of Gay and Lesbian Studies* 5(4): 439–449.

Rajan, S. C. 2006. Automobility and the liberal disposition. *Sociological Review* 54: 113–129.

Rammert, Werner, and Cornelius Schubert. 2006. *Technographie: Zur Mikrosoziologie der Technik*. Frankfurt am Main: Campus.

Reckwitz, Andreas. 2006. *Das hybride Subjekt: Eine Theorie der Subjektkulturen von der bürgerlichen Moderne zur Postmoderne*. Göttingen: Velbrück Wissenschaft.

———. 2008. *Subjekt: Einsichten*. Bielefeld: Transcript.

Rose, Nikolas. 1996. The death of the social? Refiguring the territory of government. *Economy and Society* 25(3): 327–356.

———. 1999. *Powers of Freedom: Reframing Political Thought*. Cambridge: Cambridge University Press.

Ross, Kristin. 1995. *Fast Cars, Clean Bodies: Decolonization and the Reordering of French Culture*. Cambridge, MA, London: MIT Press.

Savage, Mike, Evelyn Ruppert and John Law. 2010. *Digital devices: Nine theses*. CRESC Working Paper Series 44 (86), Milton Keynes, Manchester.

Schad, Helmut, and Cédric Duchêne-Lacroix. 2013. Multilokales Wohnen als hybride Praxis – Implikationen der 'Mobilities Studies' und der Akteur-Netzwerk-Theorie. In *Mobilitäten und Immobilitäten: Menschen – Ideen – Dinge – Kulturen – Kapital*, edited by Joachim Scheiner, Hans-Heinrich Blotevogel, Susanne Frank, Christian Holz-Rau and Nina Schuster, 259–374. Essen: Klartext.

Schneider, Norbert F., Ruth Limmer and Kerstin Ruckdeschel. 2002. *Mobil, flexibel, gebunden: Familie und Beruf in der mobilen Gesellschaft*. Frankfurt am Main, New York: Campus.

Schwanen, Tim, and Karen Lucas. 2011. Understanding Auto Motives. In *Auto Motives. Understanding Car Use Behaviours*, edited by Karen Lucas, Evelyn Blumenberg and Rachel Weinberger, 3–38. Bradford: Emerald.

Schwanen, Tim, and Mei-Po Kwan. 2009. 'Doing' critical geographies with numbers. *The Professional Geographer* 61(4): 459–464.

Seiler, Cotton. 2008. *Republic of Drivers: A Cultural History of Automobility in America*. Chicago, London: University of Chicago Press.

Shaw, Ben, Ben Watson, Bjorn Frauendienst, Andreas Redecker, Tim Jones and Mayer Hillman. 2013. *Children's Independent Mobility: A Comparative Study in England and Germany (1971–2010)*. London: Policy Studies Institute.

Sheller, Mimi, and John Urry. 2000. The city and the car. *International Journal of Urban & Regional Research* 24(4): 737.

———. 2006. The new mobilities paradigm. *Environment and Planning A* 38(2): 207–226.

Sheppard, Eric. 2001. Quantitative geography: Representations, practices, and possibilities. *Environment and Planning D: Society and Space* 19(5): 535–554.

Taipale, Skari. 2014. The dimensions of mobilities: The spatial relationships between corporeal and digital mobilities. *Social Science Research* 43(1): 157–167.

Urry, John. 2000. *Sociology beyond Societies: Mobilities for the Twenty-First Century*. New York: Routledge.

———. 2003. Social networks, travel and talk. *The British Journal of Sociology* 54(2): 155–175.

———. 2004. The 'system' of automobility. *Theory, Culture & Society* 21(4/5): 25–39.

————. 2007. *Mobilities*. Cambridge: Polity.

Van Acker, Veronique, Bert Van Wee and Frank Witlox. 2010. When transport geography meets social psychology: Toward a conceptual model of travel behaviour. *Transport Reviews* 30(2): 219–240.

Vannini, Phillip, and April Vannini. 2008. Of walking shoes, boats, golf carts, bicycles, and a slow technoculture: A technography of movement and embodied media on Protection Island. *Qualitative Inquiry* 14(7): 1272–1301.

Weiss, Anja. 2005. The transnationalization of social inequality: Conceptualizing social positions on a world scale. *Current Sociology* 53(4): 707–728.

Wikipedia. 2014. *List of countries by vehicles per capita*. Accessed 27 July 2014. http://en.wikipedia.org/wiki/List_of_countries_by_vehicles_per_capita.

Wolff, Janet. 1993. On the road again: Metaphors of travel in cultural criticism. *Cultural Studies* 7(2): 224–239.

Worldbank. 2014. *Passenger cars (per 1,000 people)*. Accessed 24 July 2014. http://data.worldbank.org/indicator/IS.VEH.PCAR.P3.

Zeiher, Helga. 1990. Organisation des Lebensraum bei Großstadtkindern – Einheitlichkeit oder Verinselung? In *Lebenslauf und Raumerfahrung*, edited by Lothar Bertels and Ulfert Herlyn, 35–57. Opladen: Springer.

6   Passengers without havens?

Discourses on the hypermobile subject and self-conceptions of frequent travellers

Marcel Endres

The career of the 'mobile subject' in the social sciences and the humanities is both unprecedented and suspicious. It has yet become almost formulaic to note that mobility is a key element of social change, both propelling and driven by technological change, spatial shifts of culture and economical transformations on a global level. In the last two decades, social theory has disclosed an incontestable historical trend towards a normalisation, familiarisation and habitualisation of frequent travel, commuting and residential mobility. If indeed 'the paradigmatic modern experience is that of rapid mobility often across long distances' (Lash and Urry 1994, 253) and mobility can be identified as a 'cipher for what subjectivity is supposed to be in the twenty-first century' (Jochum and Voß 2013, 4), such representations imply a deep relation between ideas about *mobile society* at large and the everyday related *appropriation and internalisation of mobility* on the individual level.

In other words, the *mobile subject* has become an object of knowledge in the social sciences, a conceptual blueprint that may be helpful and plausible for grasping the suchness of social actors in a mobilised world. Many authors have discussed the conceptual history and epitomic nature of mobility in relation to the discursive construction of subject formations (Cresswell 2002; Richardson and Jensen 2000; Varney 2005). However, the substantial role of contemporary academic discourses in constructing certain templates of mobile subjectivity has not yet been fully displayed. All too often, the general observation that 'the globalisation of mobility extends into the core of the self'(Elliott and Urry 2010, 3) is not further scrutinised by detailed qualitative analyses of those instanced to be the hypermobile protagonists of these new kind of subjectivities.

As a label for 'the maximisation of physical movement' (Khisty and Zeitler 2001, 598), hypermobility has been tackled in several works on the geography of globalisation and the relation of aviation and sustainability (Adams 2000; Whitelegg 1993) and in quantitative studies about the travel patterns, socioeconomic characteristics and primary reasons of the hypermobile (Gossling et al. 2009).

The aim of this chapter is to confront current academic discourses on mobile subjectivity with a more socio-phenomenological and actor-centred view of hypermobile lifestyles. It follows the assumption that there are significant discrepancies between representations of the mobile subject in social scientific discourses and the empirical self-constitution of professional frequent travellers. The core thesis is that the self-concepts of individuals who share a radicalised experience and practice of mobility do not simply reflect a logic of fluidity, detachment and social escapism but moreover evince a specific importance of definable place attachments, durable personal relationships and solid biographical orientations. Furthermore, it shall be shown that issues of fixity and permanency act as significant conditions for leading a hypermobile life in the long term. To substantiate this core argument, I will first outline some central aspects of mobile subjectivity shaped by a broad interdisciplinary discourse across sociology, geography, social history and postmodern philosophy. I argue that discourses about mobile subjects in academic debates are interfused by diverse prepossessions concerning the rationalisation and internalisation of mobility in empirical lives. In the second part, I will focus on the self-constitutive strategies, tactics and world views through which highly mobile individuals manage and consolidate the 'seepage' of mobility into their daily lives and personal biographies. To do so, I refer to an interview-based corpus of subjective narratives, valuations and lifestyle-related self-concepts provided by frequent travellers with different professional and private backgrounds. I will finally discuss how academic discourses of mobile subjectivity are suitable for capturing (or even fail to capture) the micro social level of personal tactics, strategies and viewpoints of highly mobile individuals.

The discursive construction of mobile subjectivity

Ideas about mobile subjectivity have a rather long tradition. Since 'global mobility is etched in human behaviour since humanity began' (Carr 2010, 1), travelling individuals have long been eyed with suspicion and fascination, both as a disturbance of consisting social orders or as lively promises of social change to come (Cresswell 2006, 25–53). Correspondingly, discursive conceptions of mobile subjects, whether idealising or generalising, romanticising or stigmatising, are rooted in ambivalent sets of motives, intentions, features and purposes ascribed to those on the move. 'Mobility is both centre and margin – the lifeblood of modernity and the virus that threatens to hasten its downfall' (Cresswell 2006, 21).

After almost three decades of empirical research and theory production, the new mobility paradigm has inseparably coalesced with the issue to signify the human subject in connection with mobility. Along these lines, the self-imposed objective of the new mobility paradigm involves the challenge to disclose the relation between the systemic and powerful structure of diverse mobilities and the traits within empirical social life and the social character of individuals.

Regarding the term subject, I follow Reckwitz, who understands it as a 'bundle of dispositions' composed of a variable, more or less fragile set of cultural codes (Reckwitz 2006, 33). These codes mainly consist of three interacting fields: the material culture of (technical) artefacts, aesthetic movements and humanities discourses, yet with flowing boundaries between scientific, political and popular discourses about the subject (Reckwitz 2006, 90). With a view to the current relation of the individual and social system, these discourses tend to overdetermine and idealise an entrepreneurial and creative concept of a mobilised self:

> The . . . working subject is guided by a semantics of innovative fluidity and mobility, of a permanent dissolution of structures into pure, open, disordered activity (based on the leading figures of the "flexible" and "mobile"), of a search for novelty for the sake of novelty. . . . This kind of mobility is without any specific goal, but moreover acknowledged . . . as a pure process of movement: the mobility of new products, a change of job and place ("nomadism"), "mental mobility", global market conditions, new projects.
>
> (Reckwitz 2006, 508, own translation)

In this sense, it is crucial to stress the ambiguity of what it means to be 'guided', which implies that the subject is both an effect of hegemonic discourses that constitute a field of possible action *and* an entity whose power to act is based on a certain self-will (Graefe 2010). Regarding the concept of a mobile subject, the implication of such a double sense – of subjection and the capability to act – is helpful for emphasising tensions and contradictions between ideas about mobile subjectivity and empirical mobile subjects.

Polarisations of mobility and place

Here, I will reconstruct some general aspects of discourses on the relation of mobility and subjectivity in the humanities and social sciences. First, it is crucial to note that sociology and humanities have passed on ascriptions of sustaining ambivalences between notions of place and the essence of mobility in terms of stability and fluidity. As Cresswell emphasises, '[S]tasis and mobility, fixity and flow, are the subjects of deep knowledge that inform any number of ways of seeing the world' (Cresswell 2006, 22). Concepts of mobility refer strongly to a topological dualism of point and line, uniqueness and ubiquity, stillness and fluidity, or more generally, to a bipolar constellation of place and mobility (Malkki 1996; Massey 1999). Despite the critical reformulation of place-mobility relations in recent social theory, the dualistic character of fixities and flows remains vital even with a view to the constitution of mobile subjectivity.

To retrace this polarity, it is useful to refer to Simmel's considerations on social rationalisation and the mental life of modern subjects (Simmel et al. 2009). Drawing on 'a deeply grounded relationship . . . between the movement in space and the differentiation of social and personal contents of existence' (589), he derives opposing social types of mobile subjectivity, particularly idealised in the urban character and the vagrant. 'It is the typical contrast of social activities: whether they involve simply a striving outwards from the spatially and objectively given, . . . or whether they rotate around fixed points' (560). Simmel's demarcation between the spatially fixed character of the urban subject and the unattached, footloose orientation of the vagrant subject is based on the idea of an irreconcilable polarity between mobile and placed life, as 'this difference in formal spatial behaviour becomes the vehicle, instrument and growth-factor of an otherwise already existing latent or open opposition' (597).

Simmel's work is paradigmatic for analysing a fundamental conflict about the prerogative to interpret the socio-spatial constitution of the human subject at the beginning of the 20th century. I argue that such contradictions of mobile and placed social life are still present in current theoretical debates, though under reverse signs. Key therefore are theoretical models of a reflexive or liquid modernity, underpinning the fluid, blurring and disembedding character of current societies (Bauman 2000; Beck 1992; Beck et al. 1994; Giddens 1991). Mobility is inextricably linked to concepts of freedom, emancipation, flexibility and 'the modern', while place has been understood as a fixed entity mainly characterised in terms of stability, constraint and preservation. Concerning the contradictory classification of mobility and place, both sets of relational terms are, for their part, discursively loaded. In accordance with these oppositional intentions, the domestication of mobility and acceleration is suggested to work as a 'condenser of identity' by promoting a trend towards an increasing disembedding of individuals from temporal and spatial fixes (Beck and Bonss 2001; Giddens 1994; Rosa 2006), Following this argument, mobilities and places seem to produce conflictual constellations in (and between) different lifestyles and everyday situations of individuals.

This question of compatibility is laid out, for instance, in research schemes on professional mobility and family lives (Lück and Schneider 2010; Schneider et al. 2002). A peculiar aspect of these studies is that mobility is mainly inhibitory to or at least defers family development, while conversely the decision to start a family requires a drop in mobility, though with strong gender-specific differences. The hypothesis that mobility challenges family functionality refers to a concept that considers reproduction and co-presence of members as a given condition. 'It is thus frequently taken for granted that members of a nuclear, non-divorced family all share the same domestic space' (Bonnet et al. 2008, 144). Such definitions imply that family is an institution that is mainly placed because 'in cohabiting with others, self-regulation is only possible when coexisting in one and the same space' (Singly and Boukaïa 2000, 27; cited in Bonnet et al. 2008, 145). Based on these theoretical implications, the opposition of fixity and flow is reproduced prior to any empirical investigation into the relation between family and mobility. In consequence, family coherence is considered deficient even when one or several members are highly mobile. It is therefore remarkable that 'living forms, such as long distance relationships, shuttles or job nomads, were hardly studied' (Viry and Lück 2006, 214). Another way to adopt polar constellations of fixity and flow may be found in studies on mobilities of highly skilled workers and wealthy entrepreneurs. The advantages of a literal 'life in the fast lane' are often emphasised as the most salient feature of these exclusive milieus. 'Elite mobilities inform cultures of luxury, success and "the good life" and enforce a self-stylisation of global elitism founded on hypermobility, meritocracy and entrepreneurial heroism. In the present liquid era, nothing in this styling can stay still for long, neither money nor a regionally fixed identity' (Birtchnell and Caletrío 2014, 1). This interpretation may be largely true with regard to the expressive representation of elitist lifestyles. However, it categorically factors out the potential role of stabilities and permanencies in terms of intimate friendships and relationships, as well as durable place- and context-related senses of belonging that might still be active in the personal background of hypermobile lives. These elements might be concealed and weakened by the radiant fluidity of frequent flying, project-based workflows and the ephemeral nature of meetings and acquaintances. However, it does not necessarily justify declarations of their negligibility based on the assumption that 'the mobilities lived by globals today seem more rootless' (Elliott 2014, 36), solely because in-depth information about personal spheres, family affairs and private networks at the upstage of hypermobile lives is difficult to collect. These examples indicate how dichotomies of mobility and place run the risk of being reproduced, often against a stated intent to overcome conceptual borders between fixed and moving entities.

Epitomising mobility

The second crucial thing to note is that the social and symbolic power of mobility is strongly linked to certain material artefacts, social contexts and ideas about the 'good life' that act as epitomes of mobility (Brög et al. 2000, 47; Vannini 2009, 7). In connection with the foregone, it is therefore crucial to clarify various shifts in the normative status of mobility. Cars, Blackberries and iPhones, airport lounges, luxury hotels, glamorous lifestyles in the fast lane and coveted jobs on the global stage seem to symbolise the certainty that 'mobility is liberating and empowering' (Adams 2000, 1). It has been outlined that the 'mobile subject' is, to a certain extent, a product of vivid imaginations (Jensen and Richardson 2007), evoked not only in politics and the media, but also in scientific concepts and theories. I argue that current academic discourses on mobile subjectivity are, carefully spoken, not necessarily free of the problem of recapitulating such connotations, albeit or even because mobility recently appears to be considered in a more rationalised and reflexive manner (Cresswell 2010, 18–19). From this viewpoint, the relational fabric of mobilities and ideas about the mobile subject are not simply a field to be disclosed but an essential trait of scientific concepts that 'systematically constitute the objects of which they speak' (Foucault 2002, 54). By converting empirical observations of extreme forms of mobility into concepts of a super mobile social reality, critical mobility research runs the risk of transposing certain facts of social reality into certain fetishes of theoretical plausibility and of ending the questioning of the reasoning behind them along the way 'from matters of fact to matters of concern' (Latour 2004, 225). In consequence, theoretical concepts about a social world tend to overemphasise and overgeneralise the logic of both subjectification and subjection to mobility by the epitomic use of objects and ideas.

In very simplified terms, one can discern two dominant epitomising connotations of mobility in the history of the social sciences. On the one hand, anti-mobile ontologies against the moving masses or certain social groups have supported a characterisation of the mobile subject as a symbol of crisis, irritation and alien-ation regarding the respective present (Gerhard 1998). For instance, anti-Semitism and anti-Ziganism are probably the prime examples of the scientific equation of alleged penchants for mobility with a social spectre of an unstable and parasitic nature. Diasporic and itinerant life has been freighted over the long run with a stain of estrangement and unnaturalness, not only in public discourses in politics and the media but even through the scientification of 'spatial behaviour' in early 20th-century geography, sociology and anthropology. On the other hand, mobile subjects have been viewed positively in terms of transfiguration – in both senses of the word. Whether promising or romanticising, mobility has frequently been oversubscribed by an idealised image of the travelling mind as the progressive incarnation of freedom and independence and the embodied potentiality of self-conceptualisation, unleashed by the interplay of mobilising technologies and the blurring of spatial boundaries (Cresswell 2006, 22–55). Cases in point for such epitomisations include concepts of neo-nomadism and drifter culture supporting a sublimation of self-extension by travel and the permanent experience of other-ness (D'Andrea 2007), as well as models of cosmopolitanism and the globalised subject as idealised images of translocal self-figuration and multiple belonging (Beck and Cronin 2014). Here, mobility is positively laden with terms related to freedom and independence.

The point I want to stress is that a large part of current theoretical debates still work with a semantics that situates the mobile subject in a contradictory field of emancipation and estrangement. Depending on the social context in which physical movement is situated, mobile subjects are thought to be either immedi-ately exposed to effects of disruption, drifting, deracination and disorientation or to profiteers, unleashing independence, freedom and boundlessness. Moreover, conceptions of such mobile identities as dispersed, stretched, fragmented and expanded show an exhaustive use of attributes originating from spatio-temporal state descriptions in the physical sciences. By evoking weighty epitomes derived from a certain 'nature' of movement, some research understands human subjectiv-ity as a mere embodiment of 'invariable shifts' of mobility.

Isomorphism of system and subject

My third point is that recent debates on the nexus of mobility and identity stress that changes in social systems and technical infrastructures challenge and pro-pel analogical or resemblant shifts in mobile subjectivity. 'One of the distinctive features of modernity, in fact, is the increasing interconnections between the two "extremes" of extensionality and intentionality: globalising influences on the one hand and personal dispositions on the other' (Giddens 1991, 1).

From this point of view, the interaction of individualisation, globalisation and risk seems to constitute subjects that embody an isomorphic relation between sys-temic dynamics and practical knowledge in daily life – between the essence of mobility regimes and individual attitudes, feelings and expectations. However, these considerations imply firm congruency between concepts of a mobilised world at large and ideas about mobile subjects raised by substantial critics of globalisation theories.

> A troubling aspect of the literature on globalisation is its tendency to read social life . . . without any model of subjective mediation. In other words, globalisation studies often proceed . . . as if an accurate map of the space and time of post-Fordist accumulation could provide an accurate map of the subject and her embodiment and desires.
>
> (Povinelli and Chauncey 1999, 445)

The general problem I want to emphasise here is that mappings of the subject often work as a self-referential argument – an ontological signpost resulting from the transfer of findings about fragmentation, decentralisation and dissipation (derived from the macro level of systems) into ideas about the very nature of the mobile subject (applied on the micro level). 'Systems come first and serve to augment the otherwise rather puny powers of individual human subjects. Those subjects are brought together and serve to develop extraordinary powers only because of the assemblages that implicate them, and especially those that move them, or their ideas, or information or various objects' (Elliott and Urry 2010, 15).

However, mobility researchers have conceded that individuals act reflexively and inventively, sometimes irrationally and unpredictably, when struggling and juggling with the various conditions, constraints and potentials of mobility-driven systems (Hildebrandt and Dick 2009; Kesselring 2006; Poppitz 2009). Such analyses help to clarify that mobile subjects cannot be conceptualised solely as systemic and discursive effects, for these highly mobile subjects themselves act and behave in ways that interfere, deflect and transform the various impacts of mobility systems in their daily lives. The point here is not to claim a neo-Cartesian existence of an essential and indeterminable 'core' of the subject or to disregard the obviously subjecting power of mobility regimes. It is rather to make clear that the mobile subject cannot be conceptualised as a result of a dialectic initiated by systems but rather must be considered a powerful element of the dialectic itself. This applies to scientific discourses on mobilities as well: there is no 'outside' from where mobility regimes could be observed by adopting a purely moderate or somehow neutral position. Whatever kind of mobility discourse is launched becomes a component of the regime itself. However, to the extent that such dialectics are adopted and reproduced, the project of rationalising mobility collides with the erratic fluidity of people, objects and thoughts. Harvey's statement that 'flexibility and geographical mobility, once acquired, become harder to control' (Harvey 1989, 187) is therefore true in a circular sense. Mobility, as a systemic effect, simultaneously produces conditions on which it relies in order to evolve exuberantly, but it also raises many inconsistencies and ambiguities not inherent in the system itself.

I shall briefly illustrate this inconsistent relationship between system and subject through two examples. One is the relationship between automobile behaviour and congestion development. It has been shown that the emergence of traffic congestion is not only reducible to asymmetries between sheer traffic volume and the capacities of streets and guidance systems, while the driver subject is reducible to a model of individual rational action. Moreover, congestion has to be considered as a social product of very heterogeneous choices, behaviours and responses on the individual level. A good example are the 'flocking effects' of bypassing recommendations in navigation systems, which can lead to additional congestion on low-capacity deviations once a critical mass of drivers prefer to take alternative routes (Lee and Kattowitz 2014; Thrift 2008, 109). It is therefore not possible to avoid traffic congestion dynamics exhaustively through traffic guidance and surveillance systems. Instead, it is crucial 'to understand car culture in a deeper context of affective and embodied relations between people, machines and spaces of mobility and dwelling, in which emotions and the senses play a key part' (Sheller 2004, 3). Thus, the car system not only 'seems to provide the solution to the problems of congestion that it itself generates' (Kingsley and Urry 2009, 249) but moreover clashes with a whole panoply of individual 'wrongdoings' that can always bring the self-regulating configurations to their limits once again.

Another example is the relation between mobility imperatives and emerging discourses on deceleration. Nearly every thrust in the development of transportation technologies is accompanied by calls for a containment of the alleged social consequences of mobility. 'Many examples of contemporary social deceleration can be inextricably linked to fundamental processes of acceleration; the relation between social speed and slowness turns out to be dialectical in character' (Rosa and Scheuerman 2009, 7). This is not only true for large, often anti-modern or technology-sceptical social movements but also for modern discourses on the individual need for stillness, recreation and 'demobilisation'. A large part of the leisure economy – sectors like recreational tourism, the lifestyle industry, self-help literature, life coaching and the meditation business – is deeply engaged with enhanced individual needs of deceleration. Apart from the suspicion that only such 'limited or temporary forms of deceleration . . . aim at preserving the capacity to function and further accelerate within acceleratory systems' (Rosa 2009, 95), they still mark a blind spot in illustrations of hypermobile subjectivity. This biased image in consideration of the 'globals' firmly emphasises the pure will to be mobile, whereas the role of counter-capacities, addressed by the potential *not* to be mobile, is rarely questioned. In this sense, viewing mobile lives though the lens of isomorphic relations with social regimes of mobility does not fully match the discursive self-reliance and negotiation practices by which even mobile lifestyles might be constituted.

Idealisations of hypermobile subjectivity

Fourthly, I want to refer to the 'hypermobile subject' as a problematic (and often exaggerated) ideal figure emerging from the normative power of mobility together with new existential conditions in people's daily lives and biographies. Academic debates on the effects of mobility touch upon a broad range of basic concepts enquiring into the constitution of the human 'ego'. Terms like global subjects, mobile self, translocal identity, network individuality and portable personhood not only reflect the emphasis of far-reaching impacts of mobility on personal lives, but they also generally shift the perspective of what human subjects are thought to be 'made of' in an ever mobilised world. The concept of a hypermobile subject serves as an ideal type located in 'a continuum of mobile postmodern subjecthood that is becoming the mark of both "postmodernity" and "globalisation" ' (Cresswell and Merriman 2010, 250). Thus, we are confronted with a heterogeneous pallet of modes deemed to be the pioneering force behind a more comprehensive negotiation of subjectivity in late modern societies. Framings like business travellers, mobile elites, global tourists and lifestyle migrants not only express a strong conviction about movement and displacement to be the outweighing experience, intention and lived practice but also reflect the purpose to unravel the complexity of individual mobilities into certain mobility-driven ways of existence.

One of these figures is the 'nomad' as part of a broader ontological concept of human subjectivity, which is, however, inextricably linked to thinking on mobility far across the borders of academic writing, public media and literature (Cresswell 1997). Developed as an antithetical and subversive character against the 'sedentary' structure of thought, the metaphor of the nomad has exerted powerful fascination in theoretical writings about 'mobility as a means for achieving a more adequate representation of ourselves' (Braidotti 1994, 256). Vilém Flusser suggests the nomad as a precursor of a looming 'end of the Neolithic' (Flusser 1990, 27) that is to replace a temporary, atypical era of human sedentariness with a new kind of mobile existence driven by the 'discovery of human dignity in uprootedness' (Flusser et al. 2003, 85). Similarly, travelling and transmigration are considered important formations towards a nomadic existence on a global scale, which sustainably 'delegitimates the state as arbiter of identity and citizenship' (Joseph 1999, 22). Regarding the spatio-temporal constitution of identity, the global nomad has been conceptualised as a 'liminal' personality: strictly detached, place-independent and flux-oriented (Iyer 2001; Richards and Wilson 2004; Schaetti 2000). Meanwhile, in terms of cultural relations, the signification of 'hypermobility as a rising global condition that reshapes identity and subjectivity forms' seems to suggest 'a theory of neo-nomadism as an ideal-type of postidentitarian mobility' (D'Andrea 2007, 24).

It is hardly possible to survey or even discuss the entire interrelation of the figure of the nomad and the use of the term in relation to concepts of physical mobility. Instead, I prefer to briefly outline some essential arguments specifically against adopting, generalising and idealising the term to describe empirical lifestyles. A basic objection refers to the misguided equation of the imaginary of an alternative, nomadic thought in postmodern philosophy with an empirical practice of fluid and frictionless travel as a way of being-in-the-world. While it has been regularly noted that traditional nomadism is linked to the social weight of definite places, belongings and continuities, models of nomadic mobility imply 'a subject position that offers an idealised model of movement based on perpetual displacement' (Kaplan 1996, 66). There is a 'formalist, post-modern tendency to over-generalise the global currency of the so-called nomadic, fragmented and deterritorialised subjectivity' (Ang 2001, 24). In this vein, the main problem in the use of the nomadic subject as an ideal type is the tendency to translate far-flung patterns and multilocal structures of personal mobilities into concepts about a certain quality of mobile lives.

Another important frame of reference involves concepts of a 'networked' subject that concern the role of connectivity as both a result and a trigger of spatial movements. Networks have been conceptualised to transfer certain inner structures and coherences of groups and communities into a more general theory of interpersonal relationships (Milgram 1967; Mitchell 1969; Watts 2003). Subsequently, reciprocal impacts of geographic mobility and social networks have gained increasing importance in holistic theories of a network society (Castells 2006). An essential argument is the theoretical conceptualisation of a spiral effect between the growth of regular and long-distance mobility and the delocalisation of networks and spaces of action, producing an 'increasing distance between globalisation and identity, between the Net and the self' (Castells 2006, 22). The prime concept of the new network subject is a hypermobile and nearly placeless elite, detached from any local liabilities and living in a symbolic, standardised and ahistorical space embodied by an inclusive web of air hubs, lounges, hotels, leisure sites and office complexes (Gottdiener 2001). These elites appear to represent the blueprints of a network subject, derived from a mechanical relation of connectivity and travel that promotes loose social networks, detachment from place and evermore personal mobility on the individual level. Touching on Castells' holistic theory together with ideas of network individualism and connectionism (Boltanski and Chiapello 2005; Wellman 2001), the ideal type of a networked self has been further developed particularly in the recent sociology of business mobilities. The general idea here is that 'networked transport, information and communication infrastructures are not just becoming an essential part of everyday life but also shaping identities and the emotional repertoire through which individuals encounter, define and respond to others and the world' (Caletrio 2012, 143). It has been rightly argued that 'mobile society reshapes the self' (Elliott and Urry 2010, 3) accompanying calls for a 'sustained consideration of the "experiential texture" of the lives of globals' (Elliott and Urry 2010, 67).

However, the empirical basis for the lives of hypermobile people may be too thin to diagnose certain subjective strategies for adapting the effects of mobility into an ephemeral, detached and escapist existence in opposition to a rather tightly tied, place-related lifestyle (Elliott and Urry 2010, 65–84). Recent works have shown that extending personal mobilities does not necessarily entail a weakening or broadening of social ties but moreover interacts with a multiple set of individual factors (Kesselring 2004; Ohnmacht et al. 2008; Viry 2012). It has also been stated that some highly mobile groups and individuals live and maintain local orientations and relatively fixed personal and professional networks (Gustafson 2009; Hartmann 2011). Even hypermobile travellers as a group are probably much more heterogeneous and inconsistent than the emphasis on an elitist circle of mobile globals suggests.

Altogether, the focus on subjects and types implies a forceful academic urge to establish a social ontology of mobility as a principle of being-in-the-world. Again, this is not to deny that to be 'driven by' and to be 'made of' mobilities is not a essential part of individual lives. Moreover, my question is whether such an ontology is exhaustive enough to embrace the complexity of subject formations, even when they are deeply embedded in hypermobile social environments and biographical backgrounds infused throughout the experience of migration, travel and everyday mobility.

A socio-phenomenological approach to hypermobile lifestyles

The following results are based on analysis and interpretation of 38 interviews held from 2009 to 2012. The scope of the study is deliberately cross-sectional and mainly involves German frequent travellers from very different professional sectors, such as trade, consulting, the pharmaceutical industry, finance management, planning and architecture, media and journalism, aid and development work, music and the arts, NGO work and politics, the university and tourism. The sample therefore consists of individuals engaged and working in the context of international business travel (Beaverstock et al. 2010) and therefore reflects social milieus that have recently been termed the 'highly mobile upper middle-class' (Andreotti et al. 2014, 30) and partially a wealthy group of global travellers subsumed under the 'mobile elite' (Birtchnell and Caletrio 2014).

Interviewees were recruited via various channels: by direct inquiries to companies and institutions, online traveller and flyer forums and personal recommendations. To ensure both consistency and variability within the sample, care was taken to recruit only individuals with a considerable amount of mobility by a minimum of either the total yearly time spent abroad from their current main residence (>100 days), the yearly number of overnight return trips (>30), covered yearly distances (>50,000 kilometres/year) or the number of different destinations (>10/year). The sample shows a slight over-representation (65 per cent) of male interviewees as well as a predominance (70 per cent) of people aged 40 to 60, whereas the proportion of male and female respondents is nearly equal in the group of younger travellers (20 to 40). The mobility of nearly all respondents is mainly professional, while combinations of private and professional purposes play a considerable role as well. A vast majority (90 per cent) states that their mobility consists in regular international and intercontinental travel. Regarding their socioeconomic status, nearly all respondents report high income levels, and some mention various forms of private hedging. About half are permanent employees of private companies or cross-sectoral institutions, while more than a third report being self-employed or working in a business co-partnership. Only a few interviewees say they work in the civil service or under fixed-term contracts.

The interview method consists of the triangulation of several instruments: firstly, an open and flexible interview guide based on a problem-centred perspective (PCI) of the observations and valuations. The PCI model combines a substantial openness and impartiality towards the interviewed person with a topical focus on pre-structured core questions. Secondly, a strong alignment towards narration stimuli helps to trace mobility-related self-assessments, opinions and 'world views', as well as biographical and lifestyle-related details. Narrative interview techniques can be extraordinary useful for recording individual contexts between personal socialisation and mobility-related decisions. Thirdly, 'ego-centred maps' were used as a tool during the interviews. These maps were generated by the interviewees during the talk to designate their various trips and abodes. They serve as a very useful tool for affirming completeness with regard to meanings of the different abodes and destinations, to the various place-relations of self-conceptions and to the consistency of mobility biographies.

The triangulation of interview methods is inspired by a socio-phenomenological approach that regards 'person and world as intimately part and parcel' (Seamon 2000, 161). A socio-phenomenology of mobility is based on the assumption that mobile life-worlds are not simply determined by the external impacts of systems, discourses, norms or environments but rather are co-constructed as individual realities that are neither true or false but 'subjectively meaningful . . . as a coherent world' (Berger and Luckmann 1989, 33; see also Schutz 1972, 241–249). In line with this radical empiricism, the aim of these qualitative talks was to gain a closer picture of the individual self-conceptions and the world views of frequent travellers, regardless of the various difficulties in bringing them to a level of comparability. Thus, mobile subjects are seen as a complex set of constructions, realisations, reflections and social performances. Since the narrative character of the material prevents it from being organised along a rigid scheme, my aim is not to develop another typology of mobile lives between different socio-spatial or mobility-related extremes. Rather, I wish to differentiate the most conspicuous results in three exploratory fields of particular importance within mobile lives. Our first aim is to show how continuous extreme mobility is sensed, perceived and experienced. What are the characteristic interactions between human senses and the environment, both steadily and on the move? Our second aim is to figure out how individuals deal with ever increasing mobility in their daily lives and how they transform specific experiences into specific practices. What kinds of routines and habits are emerging from a permanent implementation of extreme mobility in our everyday lives? Finally, I want to show the extent to which mobility relates to biographical contexts of subjective life-course-related orientations and strategies. What are the tangible process-related and strategic characteristics of mobility-in-a-lifetime? Above all, we aim to illustrate some essential ambivalences and contradictions in empirical lives that do not fit in the overall discursive conception of hypermobile subjects.

Senses of hypermobility: perception, experience, appropriation, habituation

The first level concerns the relation between the moving individual and the environment it is moved by, moving through and moving in. There are two important scopes in connection with a phenomenological perspective of the conceptual framing of hypermobile subjects. The first one focuses the change of immediate and particularly environmental perception, by which the experience of mobility is accompanied. In this regard, sociologists have underpinned a shift towards a more kinetic and mobilised perception of environments (Armitage 2001; Bissell 2009; Larsen 2001; Schivelbusch 1986, 66). To be mobile includes a sense of being part of the mobile environment itself, as transport technologies enable mobility both *of and across* the human senses. Depending on specific modes and frequencies of mobility, human subjects become successively familiar with a sense of 'dwelling-in-transit' and 'dwelling-in-motion' (Urry 2007, 37, 152).

The second perspective highlights the hybridisation of mobile environments and human actors. As already demonstrated for car cultures, technical objects and human subjects can coalesce through deep 'emotive bonds' (Sheller 2004, 17). The relation between consumer and vehicle is therefore not one of pure expedience but is rather shaped by affection, sensation and aestheticisation. This has also been seen in the use of mobile information and communication technologies (ICTs) with regard to daily experiences and practices of virtual and communicative travel (Lasen 2010; Sheller 2004). If it is true that movers and surroundings melt together by 'technogenic and impure identification' (Kronlid 2008), there might be similar relationships in the lives of hypermobile individuals.

To follow these linkages in human perception, moving environments and mobilising technologies, I refer initially to some basic self-observations of frequent travellers.

In general, nearly all respondents note that their perception of mobility has changed remarkably over time, depending on a change in travel modes and the frequency of trips, described as a long-term shift from a notion of impressiveness and enhanced attention towards a sense of indifference and insensibility. Together with the emergent sensual indistinctness of motion states, a subtle transgression from mobile vision towards a 'tunnel effect' is depicted. The latter is not applied exclusively to visibility but more generally to a sense of holistic bodily involvement, as shown in the following statement:[1]

> In the beginning, . . . it was pretty exciting for me – kind of like being a Chosen One . . . a feeling of the sublime. . . . But sometimes . . ., after a certain point, well, I unwillingly stopped having any sense of motion. I stopped noticing that I was moving at all. I mean, sometimes the difference between moving and waiting dissolved completely. You forget about whether you ever travel, and where, and how fast. Maybe other people travelling less have the same experience, but to me the habituation effect is all the stronger, no matter how tight my trip schedules are. Sure, I still know and feel the difference between motion and standstill, but sometimes it simply slips my mind. It doesn't depend on my mental condition.
>
> (48, m, project management)

On the other hand, advanced sensual familiarisation with the mobile surroundings and the kinaesthetic cues and stimuli of permanent travel can certainly be observed. In this sense, mobile spaces affect social perception by constituting a specific context of material envelopment (Frers 2007). The permanent intimacy with the infrastructural, technological and topological organisation of mobile space corresponds both to the extension of autonomy and to the external control of individual mobility. However, this reflection, to become part of a mobile sphere by a 'dialectics of navigability' (Jochum and Voß 2013, 11), is expressed both in terms of mastering and subjection to mobility:

> I really enjoy all these trips: the airport atmosphere, the priority stuff, even because I know exactly what I do need with me and how to move and where to go. It's fun to slip through the crowd. . . . It is like dancing, most of the time. But . . . there are situations . . . when I just feel like a particle dragged along a stream. . . . That is, as if to be placed under disability. You have no time for anything except your business trip and all the things connected to it. Hotel, quick lunch, taxi, next meeting: then I virtually lose sight of the places and people around me. It can be really arduous . . ., just pure stress. . . . You're just a little blowfly shooed around.
>
> (38, f, media and PR management)

Hypermobile professional travel revolves tightly around a complex set of material micro settings, behavioural precepts and daily choreographies built on schedules, swift procedures and personal responsibilities. Many interviewees emphasise the importance of carefully ensuring smoothness and of coping with the mobile environments as effortlessly as possible. Frequent global mobility obviously affects the appropriation of abilities to traverse transportation space. However, the dense scheduling of mobile time can collide with personal and social contexts outside the highly mobile business-as-usual:

> Maybe one of the biggest problems is tuning out, slowing down, not only when I am abroad, but especially when I come back home from somewhere. It's like coming back from another planet: I am still psyched by the trip and busy with entirely different things than my folks and family. They say 'stop rushing', but I can't do so on command; they ask me 'how was your trip?', but I am still not really able to tell. . . . You live in two different worlds: one full of rapid impressions, which is incredibly important, . . . and . . . another that seems to be endlessly slow and trivial. Of course, I know that's not true at all, but it's not easy to switch back and forth.
>
> (53, m, policy and development consultancy)

The appropriation of hypermobility generally entails a subtle arrangement of routinised and ritualised procedures concerning activity and recreation. This applies particularly to practices during travel time, which is no means viewed as dead time from A to B, but rather internalised and performed towards a habitualisation of dwelling in mobility. Time on the move plays an integral role in organising professional and private life. While mobile environments are principally employed as workplaces just like any other, many respondents attach importance to 'bits' of privacy despite their systematic limitation in the semi-public bustle of travel space. Even though travel activity plays a large role in self-organisation, mobility is strictly coordinated in accordance with habitual practices of reconciling phases of work and leisure:

> Of course it is a big difference if you work at a fixed place or in a train. But for me, these stations and rides are part of my toolkit. Do I have a choice? It has become just ordinary to use them like that, . . . and to use the time and the opportunities . . . I do a lot of work on the way, like others who sit in their office. . . . It does not disturb my daily routines to travel, no. It is simply implemented. . . . For example, when I have evening flights . . . overseas, I always go to sleep at first and then I wake up two or three hours before arriving. . . . I have to trick the jet lag. . . . Well, you settle into the situation when you travel so much.
>
> (36, f, film actor)

Another crucial context in the daily experience of highly mobile lives can be characterised as a specific nexus of anonymity and social proximity. Daily mobility routines are regularly involved in a sphere of tried-and-true communication practices and rituals between co-travellers, a space of superficial intersubjectivity, 'slick' and 'shallow' chats about the usual standards and issues of steady mobility. On the other hand, it is emphasised that even situations of temporary encasement and 'thrownness' in foreign social contexts are predestined to enable particular forms of interpersonal encounters of both informative and intimate natures.

> What is special is . . . that unique combination of usual aloofness . . . and very interesting acquaintances. People are stand-offish most of the time when on the move . . . and . . . so am I. . . . There is no reason to get to know each other only because you are boxed in together. This is actually . . . funny, the more so as . . . we are sociable animals [laughs] . . . Well, on flights I've also had a lot of thrilling talks though . . . with total strangers . . . about private or professional stuff both. It's another kind of social control, maybe somehow weaker. I do need these exchanges. . . . That is why my job has to do with travelling. . . . And it even happens when I . . . have after-work meetings, which are terribly boring. So who cares? Just find the right moment to leave and get chummy with the TV or the mini bar. Then again local partners invite me and I am totally surprised by the hospitality. . . . It's a big contrast I'm drawing on.
>
> (29, f, project management)

While these explanations disclose the very ambivalence of subjective perceptions in terms of detachment and social richness, they also touch upon a broader connection between highly mobile lifestyles and the field of intercultural relations. Without discussing the extensive conceptual range of interculturalism and transculturalism here, I want to address at least a few specific features dominating the empirical self-conceptions of hypermobile travellers.

Firstly, the convergence of cultures on a global scale is reflected in terms of enrichment and estrangement. On the one hand, the meeting and exchange of cultural knowledge is a highly appreciated element and a felt advantage of global mobility. On the other hand, it can switch completely into frustration and inadequacy even when asymmetric relations and limits of intercultural communication surface:

> I would say clearly . . . I've learned a lot about or from other cultures, even after years of living abroad. But I will never be able to catch on to everything. There is no patent remedy or global codex on how to behave correctly in every situation. . . . All the concepts of intercultural competence are fairly limited, especially in meetings with local people.
>
> (46, m, industrial planning and development)

> Some people are over-motivated. They . . . jump into work, then fail to care for themselves, their thinking becomes gloomy, they become alienated from society, often unnoticed. The main danger is to mistake the wrong idea of disowning your origins . . . with openness towards others. . . . Then they scare people off, feel dissatisfied. . . . Some are virtually going to seed mentally . . .
>
> (47, m, foreign emergency operations)

Secondly, global mobility seems to have contradictory consequences for personal cultural awareness. On the one hand, a certain mental flexibility is seen as an essential condition for appropriate intercultural competence. On the other hand, ideas of cosmopolitanism and transnationalism are definitely evaluated with a critical eye by underpinning that even personal cultural backgrounds are important prerequisites for dealing with global challenges.

Thirdly, many interviewees stress that their trips allow them to get in touch with local cultures only superficially due to travel or security restrictions, the segregating effects of travel space and a certain predestination of professional interculturality. In this vein, global travellers emphasise that their abilities to adopt cross-cultural suppleness and malleability depend strongly on an enhanced awareness of limitations in identity transformation, that is to say the significant knowledge of one's cultural ignorance:

> I cannot allege to understand, let's say, Japanese or even [US] American culture. . . . Well, large parts of it, but not entirely. On the contrary, I know better now what I do not grasp fully, because . . . I've developed a certain sense for these fine lines that can't be crossed or to avoid offending your partner . . . in business negotiations. After reaching this point, I had to admit the limits of adaptability. But there is no turning back as well. Moreover, you learn a lot about your own background. . . . The way we tend to look at others, well, you get a bird's-eye view of people and things to which you relate. It . . .

may sound weird, but I have moved away from my culture, and coevally I approached it ever more. . . . You both get alienated from your own people and grow fond of them at the same time.

(61, m, wholesale management, shareholding)

Hypermobility is therefore not simply attributable to a 'liquefied' character of personal sensation and experience but involves serious ambivalences between emphatic (and sometimes euphoric forms of identifying with the mode of restless travel, a pronounced habitualisation of practices and attitudes towards mobility and a recurring sense of estrangement and exposure).

Place attachment and social networks

Following these accounts, I want to focus on the subjective valuation of two central elements of social life and their relationship in highly mobile lives: place attachment and social networks.

Place attachment is one of the key topics of mobility research. Meanings of place for personal lives are often heuristically associated with terms like (residential) home, (local) belonging, (physical) presence and (fixed) bonds, whereas mobility is often considered to affect such attachments to place by physical absence and a decreasing affiliation to local bonds and personal relationships (Relph 1976; Tuan 1998). Recent research holds that place attachment involves multiple strategies for producing and substantiating personal belonging. Place attachments can therefore be developed and upheld by individuals often regardless of their spatio-temporal presence and local participation (Gustafson 2001, 2009; Lewicka 2011). Furthermore, assignments of meanings like home and belonging are not necessarily tantamount to the residential status of a place. In addition, travel itself establishes a mobile texture of places, by which attachments are not necessarily unsettled or erased but rather become reformulated, reallocated and restored. In other words, place attachment is transformed and becomes 'manoeuvrable' under conditions of mobility (Casakin and Kreitler 2008; Christensen and Jensen 2011).

Most respondents define home as a central category of subjective belonging associated with a certain geographic determinability stretching from the immediate terrain of one's residential area and neighbourhood to whole cities or regions. In most cases, locations termed home are identical, either locally or regionally consistent with the places of residence, while less, even younger interviewees indicate residences not geographically congruent with areas called homes. In contrast, only a few interviewees describe home as a feeling of belonging that is geographically irrelevant or indecisive, despite reporting that they indeed have one or more permanent residences. Furthermore, some of those with a geographically definable home cite additional belongings without geographical specification, while those without a nameable home location state that homemaking decisions are, in a sense, postponed to a later stage of their lives. Generally, expressions of 'location-less belonging' are either attributed as ego-centred ('wherever I am'), material ('where my things are') or related to family members and social networks ('where my folks are').

In conjunction with these diverse interrelations of homes, belongings and places of residence, several strategies for linking place attachment, residential and regular professional mobility can be noted. More than half the interviewees practice a strategy of 'consolidation', with a single main residence as the place where the sense of emotional belonging and home is situated. A main reason for this amalgamation of home and residence is the intent to establish a point of stability in view of an otherwise hypermobile lifestyle. Adversely, the avoidance of residential mobility is considered to relieve or even guarantee the long-term organisation of professional mobility.

> I have travelled a lot in my lifetime. These days, I am sometimes abroad several weeks and months, . . . but changed my place only one single time from my parents' to my own house. . . . This has been the base camp for us, it is close to our children's families and the local associations. Without that, my mobility would at least be harder to live with. I don't know anyone who manages this travelling circus devoid of any kind of fixed pivotal point.
>
> (60, m, geotechnics, building engineering)

A different important kind of dealing with place attachment and mobility consists of various strategies of 'branching out' one's belongings and 'distributing' their home over more than a single place. A main trigger behind these changes in place-related identity is a shift of orientations or new opportunities in professional careers, which encourage or enforce a supra-regional move of residence or the decision to migrate. As a consequence, the diachronic meshing of residential moves and continuing affiliations with certain locations results in a strategy of 'philopatry' towards a certain place:

> Of course, it makes a big difference if you have to decide mentally to change place or not, I mean, to move your private life completely elsewhere. Especially combinations of travel and professional changes . . . are really bad, because you are not only abroad for a couple of days, but you move partially . . . to the place of your new job. This is the reason why I always kept my old flat . . . and I tend to be there as much as possible, because it has become my favourite place by and by. . . . But my work is elsewhere, so . . . giving up (the flat) would not only mean to lose my life centre, but also my ability to do all these changing jobs. They somehow . . . depend on each other.
>
> (49, f, international cultural management)

Another kind of event concerns the displacement of global business relations, changing fields of competence or places of action and often accompanies the establishment of temporary or long-term second homes. In this vein, multisited mobility may release dynamics of gradual 'fission' of personal place attachments.

> I'm not able to reduce my home to a single locality, because I have moved to at least five cities in the past, . . . and now I currently have several centres of

life in three different cities: my house in F., my office with a granny flat in D. and a service apartment in H., each with a circle of activities, friends and colleagues. . . . Well, how do I assess it? You know, in principle, it's always one of these, depending on where I am, but together it is more than the sum of all parts. . . . One can say my home consists of several stations, but . . . of course they all exist at the same time and they won't become meaningless only because I'm not there for a while.

(53, m, international legal consultancy)

Finally, a minority of interviewees reports to be 'homeless' in a sense of local attachment by following a 'mnemonic' strategy supported by information technology and the media but strongly associated with places, circles of friends and shared experiences:

What is important to me is . . . a sort of personal itinerary, impressions and memories, data, audio files, photos and texts, gathered or shared with friends and mates, or just ideas and some crap I can share with myself, no matter where I am . . . This is to say, I taught my home to walk . . . by leaving my own trails. . . . . Strictly speaking, it's a . . . wearable memory, . . . sort of a personal 'snail shell' I'm dragging around with me. . . . Without that I would be really messed up [laughs], . . . really lost, because that's my line to all the places and people that belong to me.

(33, f, musician, producer)

The production of 'home' as a place of subjective belonging is therefore an integral element of hypermobile lives, not less important but rather 'stored', unlike strictly local attachment. To feel attached or emotionally related to one or more defined places therefore seems more of a bedrock than an obstacle for achieving a hypermobile life. This is additionally supported by the fact that all interviewees describe clear hierarchical structures and strong associative differences concerning the meaning of 'good' and 'bad' places as parts of their professional and private travel lives. Many places are met with an attitude of indifference regardless of the duration of stay, while less frequented places may be of even higher value from the personal point of view. What makes places meaningful in hypermobile lives is therefore not directly affected by patterns of presence as part of the mobile profession but moreover by diverse aesthetic, cultural and particularly social qualities.

This leads to my second point concerning the relationship between hypermobility and the individual structures (and meanings) of *social networks*. Mobility has been seen as having far-reaching consequences for spatial structures and dimensions of friend and family networks. An extension of personal mobility seems to effect rather large, dispersed, transient and loose individual networks, both in the spatial and the social dimensions (Axhausen 2007; Larsen et al. 2006). Conversely, spatially extended networks must be maintained by enhanced communication and mobility to keep them alive, as they constitute a 'compulsion for proximity' (Boden and Molotch 1994; Urry 2002, 263). Thus, hypermobility appears to be both a producer and, in turn, a product of spacious social networks.

One of the main findings is a predominance of strong, durable and 'dense' cores of social networks. At least all interviewees depict a very stable essential sphere of relationships composed of family members, cohabitants and close friends, together with a small set of long-term relationships to workmates, fellow students or school-mates. There is also a broader circle of mainly work-related acquaintances and partnerships, though these differ from case to case in size, geographic extension and strength. In addition, primary and secondary networks are often kept strictly separate, though these boundaries are not necessarily congruent with a separation of private and business life. Furthermore, both structural characteristics and delim-itations vary strongly, depending on the nature of the business and profession.

> To meet a lot of people and to keep in touch . . . is simply a part of work . . . and these contacts change quite a lot over time. However there is a small bot-tom of mates and locals, with which I have to do time and again. . . . I would clearly distinguish an inner circle of very important friends, my partner and some family members that is . . . at most ten people. . . . None of these rela-tionships are new or loose . . . or cooled down, and looking back . . . ten or fifteen years, I can say nothing has changed at all, although none of them always knows where I'm roving.
>
> (46, f, travel journalism, advertisement consultancy)

The last remark refers to the problem of keeping relationships and friendships, which may be the more complex if private networks increasingly dispersed in the past, especially when members of it have moved elsewhere. Hypermobile lifestyles thus require considerable effort to coordinate meetings in the private sphere. Even members' flexible schedules must be brought into accordance by arranging time slots for meetings well in advance. What is more, a great readiness to link work-related trips with opportunities to share private time is emphasised.

> [A] small part of my friendships and family is just round the corner, some elsewhere . . . some travelling a lot as well. We have to wangle it anew every time. [This] . . . is not easy. But we developed a certain routine to manage when, how and where we meet. Sometimes I do a whistle stop to meet a friend, or stay for a night when I am around where they live. Sometimes even my partner travels with me or joins me where I am, for example in case of a work stay followed by a weekend. Over time, you become somewhat inven-tive to get it straight, anyhow.
>
> (32, m, music, audio engineering)

Apart from spatio-temporal coordination, sustaining personal networks is said to require a high tolerance towards one's mobility. In order to prevent the sever-ing of contact, many interviewees reportedly rely on the engagement of their life partners and families and a willingness to accept curtailments. In this respect, mobility produces a notable tension between traditional role models and the search for alternate models of partnership.

> It has been a difficult to arrange. My wife suffered for some time as a single parent. It went better when she was going to be successful in associations and her work. To be honest, my career and steady absence prevents her from doing the same. It is . . . as it were, a sophisticated form of mutual bribery. She can hold a part-time job, because I'm earning enough. And by taking care of household issues and the family, she allowed me to pursue my professional career. The one is not conceivable without the other.
>
> (57, m, marine geology)

> My husband is not mobile at all. . . . [A]nd we had to learn to cope with the situation, such like when you arrive at home in a mood that is on a quite different level of speed and rhythm. It was not easy to manage our colliding worlds, because he is very rooted. . . . That is what I call private resources, something that gives you moral support and runs things at home. Some say it is a conservative model, but it is also . . . an infinite process of learning . . .
>
> (45, f, management consultancy)

While these explanations show a significant entanglement of resilient networks and permanent mobility, a few interviewees consider the tension between mobile and location-based lives to be a tensile test for friendships and partnerships.

> My last partner and my friendships are still very local, . . . but I moved elsewhere, mentally. . . . Now I look around and see kids, houses, parents. . . . But I also wish to share my experiences. . . . Okay, I tell someone, but I cannot experience them together. . . . I can get the blues at a hotel bar with someone who knows exactly what's up with me, but . . . we'll be gone later, so I can't really share either. . . . It makes me lonesome in some respects, doing something special without sharing it . . . could be a tightrope for friendships.
>
> (34, f, architecture and planning, project management)

One striking point about these problems is the tendency of experiences to drift apart in a relationship with pronounced mobility and to culminate into the paradoxical situation 'that it lends itself to tremendous fluidity and yet breeds a craving for lasting satisfactions' (Elliott and Urry 2010, 103). However, the contradictory constellation of longing for intimate relationships and friendships and the need to share mobile existence with others is not indissoluble. This can be seen in cases where a certain watershed of mobile lives has been passed either by reconfiguring personal networks and family work towards mutual agreement or by means of an intensification and concentration of private life in certain periods and situations reserved for familiar intimacy and shared experiences.

> At times you have to sort the wheat from the chaff, I have a handful of heartfelt friendships . . . and apart from my partner and the children, I can go months

without seeing them. It takes a little coordination, but we keep in sight of each other and never let it tail off. But it is definitely no question of frequency, because they say what I am doing is okay. . . . And we catch up on this . . . by arranging a shared weekend when all are free to come. It is kind of self-sustaining, . . . because everybody takes part to make sure that it works . . . So, even though our . . . meetings are fewer, they're much more intense.

(61, m, wholesale management, shareholding)

Biographical aspects of hypermobile life

Touching upon the relation of social networks, cross-cultural experience and questions of identity, hypermobile individuals express themselves as patchworks, sometimes partially fragmented, but at least unique identities as a result of the various intercultural encounters, personal involvements and social confrontations released by their travel activities. Many of the answers given show a high-level reflexivity about each of these aspects of mobile identity. In a nutshell, leading a hypermobile life consists in ongoing identity work but without the need to invent everything anew. Even long-term mobile interviewees emphasise that assurance of one's own social, intellectual and cultural origin should stay on a par with curiosity for the next personal challenge and travel experience. This is why individual experiences, practices and valuations of stable place relations and durable social networks are of high importance within the biographical directions and self-concepts of hypermobile subjects. To lead a life on the move involves the ability to cope with the resistances and contradictions between the socio-spatial 'aeriality' of professional travel and the dense context of personal relations and networks. This includes several life-course-related consequences.

Firstly, there are remarkable age-dependent differences in the structure and organisation of mobile lives between young starters and long-term business travellers. Though some career starters may have prior experience with frequent travel by growing up with highly mobile parents, they increasingly report engagement with the demand to balance their restless feet with the need to stay attached and socially rooted. Against the background of this general tension, highly mobile lives often reach a decisive tipping point or 'mobile life crisis' in connection with family formation, the search for identity and the reconstruction of social environments. Thus, the decision to continue depends on whether the harmonisation of professional mobility and private affairs is successful. Even interviewees at a later stage of professional life often say that many imponderables and conflicts concerning the coordination of occupational mobility and the personal design of family and social relationships have been surmounted. This is not only due to a lessening of private responsibilities, for example by children reaching adulthood and decreasing family work, but moreover to a consolidation and perpetuation of local and personal relations, financial security and home-building and provision issues. Remarkably, the steadiness of attachments and relationships is indicated as a decisive reason why late-stage professionals still hold onto travel intensely or in some cases more than before, even though they could take the opportunity to do more location-based work. In contrast, a permanent weakening of social ties and place attachments appears to have a rather disintegrating effect on highly mobile careers over the long term and makes them more likely to be abandoned or slowed down. This might also be the reason why some travellers describe their mobile lives as rather footloose in terms of relationships and attachments, though they still deal with the question of social roots and place relations as a future personal issue. In short, there is little evidence of an increasing penchant for escapism, detachment and distance from locality as an irreversible trend in hypermobile lives but rather a growing demand to safeguard social and local affiliations.

Secondly, the socio-phenomenological nature of the hypermobile life stems to a certain extent from requirements and conditions within each specific professional context, including different modes, rhythms and frequencies of mobility, the way and depth of involvement in ICT-based media environments and communication practices, as well as corporate culture and business conduct. The strength of intersections between professional and private networks varies strongly, depending on the possibility and aspiration to merge the respective self-conception with the expected or desired development of the occupational career. While a high acceptance of mobility is conditional from the very beginning in many careers, for instance in considerable parts of the trade and finance sector, it is rather a consequence of professional advancement in other areas, for example in the arts, sports and journalism. In connection with the dynamic involvement of personal mobility, a more or less sudden thrust and pressure on life organisation released by changing mobility requirements may then provoke short-term deprivation of socio-spatial relations or otherwise allow rather gradual adaptations. As a rule, hypermobility implies dramatic displacements and relocations inside personal networks, consisting of ambivalent effects that cause it (or parts of it) to shrink, harden, expand and dilute. Therefore, a more qualitative analysis reveals a considerable heterogeneity arising from the complex engagement of subjects with their social origins, biographical stage and personal planning horizons. However, it is indeed difficult to recognise a unique devotion of hypermobile subjects to fluidity and unrelatedness, though there is a strong desire to get their self-locations and relationship networks in tune with the urge and obligation to be on the move.

Thirdly, I will address the deep ambivalence of perceptions and representations concerning the fluid character of mobile environments in relation to the socio-spatial embedding and resilience of hypermobile lives. Subjective discourses about traversing hypermobile space are engaged in a field of conflicting strands. While many interviewees explicitly refer to the symbolic role of stylisation, self-staging and the privilege of mobility, they all the more display a high degree of reflexivity about their lifestyles by exposing a certain social artificiality concerning the relational arrangements of work, mobility and status. However, the prefab 'numbness and dumbness' in intersubjective relations is regularly broken up by the wealth of memorable experience and 'unsophisticated' encounters. It seems that even because hypermobile lives are to a large extent enshrouded into a social world of ephemeral intensity, restrained conversation and sterile sensation, the counterpart of attention is expressively directed to topics of shared authenticity and social closeness. Rather than feeling like part of an elitist circle ready to sacrifice fixity and intimacy for a luxurious life in the fast lane, mobile professionals grapple with the reciprocal integration of mobile livelihood, identity work and planning a consistent biography. In demonstrating awareness of the danger to become drifted-in-mobility and yet implicitly intending to keep on the move over the long run, frequent travellers apparently reflect a radical internalisation of the basic contradiction of exposure and self-determinability in relation to their mobile lives.

Conclusion

Returning to my initial considerations, I will finally tackle these results with the specific construction of a hypermobile subject as discussed in the first part of the chapter.

Hypermobile subjects are undeniably entangled in the wake of sociotechnical change and globalised economies. This implies that social action and individual existence becomes mobilised in being kept even more on the leading strings of a flexible logic utilising labour, knowledge, creativity and innovation. Furthermore, flexibility and change suggests releasing human subjects from the patronising corset of social belonging and place attachment by suggesting a self that is thrown back on its own with the mission of redefining its individual role as a social being. None of these arguments can be pursued in isolation, which is the genuine reason for the paradoxical relation of mobility, freedom and subjectivity.

For the same reason, conceptions of the 'nomadic self' or 'networked self' are problematic, since they each overexpose certain aspects of mobility behaviour. Once poured into a mould, these leading (or tragic) figures often tend to be worn out by the attribution to all whose mobility appears exceptional enough to be drawn into the metaphorical spotlight. This is particularly evident in the face of hypermobile lives, which can be epitomised only insufficiently, if at all, by a narrative of nomadic or network subjectivity, especially in a socio-phenomenological perspective. There is not even an unambiguously 'cold, detached pleasure . . . of global roaming' while 'fixed social relations . . ., by comparison, are drab' (Elliott and Urry 2010, 74), but rather a steady contrast of social solitude and social intensity. This is true both for senses of mobility in daily life and for the practices and values concerning attachment to place and the reconfiguration of personal networks. Hypermobile subjects therefore neither celebrate a network identity of a pronounced spatial escapism and social detachment based on far-flung, loose and ephemeral ties, nor can they be understood as nomadic beings in the postmodern sense of a pure, itinerant practice that infiltrates and levers place bonds and forms of social closeness.

Furthermore, circular relations of mobility and place are addressed. Hypermobile lives cannot fully be understood based on the background of an antithetical constellation of place and mobility. Practices and experiences of radical lifestyle mobility are closely concatenated with certain meanings of places as they obviously involve not so much an absorption as a permanent re-anchorage of 'critical fluidity'. Accordingly, the socio-spatial constitution of hypermobile lifestyles cannot be clearly identified in a theoretical continuum of fixity and flow but rather must be considered a negotiation and alignment of different paces, rhythms, distances and states, in both the social and spatial senses. Though ideas of networked selves and global nomads might be attractive metaphors to frame and contextualise transformations of place and mobility, they ultimately prove rather unsuitable to the idiosyncratic and ambivalent constitution of hypermobile lives.

Finally, I want to underpin the importance of a more socio-phenomenological and ego-centred view of mobile lives, a coupling of in-depth research with social structure analysis and a critical stocktaking of discourses in the social sciences regarding the interaction of systems and subjects. Even the impression that mobility, among other things, promotes the emergence of a more fragile, decentralised and plural subject calls for more insights precisely where the reshaping originally takes place. This places the micro level of self-conceptions and biographical reconstructions in a more prominent place than in recent mobility research.

Note

1 Most of the interviews were conducted in German. Apart from idioms or phrases, care was taken to translate the quotations as literally as possible. The brackets include the respondents' age, gender and professional field.

References

Adams, John. 2000. The social implications of hypermobility. *Prospect. The Leading Magazine of Ideas* March 2000, 1–10.

Andreotti, Alberta, Le Galès and Francisco J. Fuentes. 2014. Local and Transnational Everyday Practices in Four European Cities: Are New Barbarians on the Road? In *Mobilities and Neighbourhood Belonging in Cities and Suburbs*, edited by Paul Watt and Peer Smets, 23–41. Basingstoke: Palgrave Macmillan.

Ang, Ien. 2001. *On Not Speaking Chinese: Living between Asia and the West*. London: Routledge.

Armitage, John. 2001. Projectiles of hypermobile organization. *Ephemera* 2(1): 131–148.

Axhausen, K. W. 2007. *Moving through Nets: The Physical and Social Dimensions of Travel: Selected Papers from the 10th International Conference on Travel Behaviour Research*. Amsterdam, Boston: Elsevier.

Bauman, Zygmunt. 2000. *Liquid Modernity*. Cambridge: Polity.

Beaverstock, Jonathan V., Ben Derudder, James Faulconbridge and Frank Witlox. 2010. International Business Travel and the Global Economy: Setting the Context. In *International Business Travel in the Global Economy*, edited by Jonathan V. Beaverstock, Ben Derudder, James Faulconbridge and Frank Witlox, 1–7. Farnham: Ashgate.

Beck, Ulrich. 1992. *Risk Society: Towards a New Modernity*. London, Newbury Park, CA: Sage.

Beck, Ulrich, Anthony Giddens and Scott Lash. 1994. *Reflexive Modernization: Politics, Tradition and Aesthetics in the Modern Social Order*. Stanford, CA: Stanford University Press.

Beck, Ulrich, and Ciaran Cronin. 2014. *Cosmopolitan Vision*. Cambridge: Polity.

Beck, Ulrich, and Wolfgang Bonss. 2001. *Die Modernisierung der Moderne.* Frankfurt am Main: Suhrkamp.

Berger, Peter L., and Thomas Luckmann. 1989. *The Social Construction of Reality: A Treatise in the Sociology of Knowledge.* New York: Doubleday.

Birtchnell, Thomas, and Javier Caletrío. Eds. 2014a. *Elite Mobilities.* London: Routledge.

———. 2014b. Introduction. The Movement of the Few. In *Elite Mobilities,* edited by Thomas Birtchnell and Javier Caletrío, 1–19. London: Routledge.

Bissell, David. 2009. Visualising everyday geographies: Practices of vision through travel-time. In *Transactions of the Institute of British Geographers* 34(1): 42–60.

Boden, Deidre, and Harvey Molotch. 1994. The Compulsion to Proximity. In *NowHere: Space, Time and Modernity,* edited by Deirdre Boden and Roger Friedland, 257–285. Berkeley: University of California Press.

Boltanski, Luc, and Ève Chiapello. 2005. *The New Spirit of Capitalism.* London: Verso.

Bonnet, Estelle, Beate Collet and Béatrice Maurines. 2008. Working away from Home: Juggling Private and Professional Lives. In *Tracing Mobilities: Towards a Cosmopolitan Perspective,* edited by Weert Canzler, Vincent Kaufmann and Sven Kesselring, 141–162. Aldershot, Burlington, VT: Ashgate.

Braidotti, Rosi. 1994. *Nomadic Subjects: Embodiment and Sexual Difference in Contemporary Feminist Theory.* New York: Columbia University Press.

Brög, Werner, Erhard Erl and Birgit Glorius. 2000. Introductory Reports: Germany. In *Transport and Ageing of the Population: Report of the Hundred and Twelfth Round Table on Transport Economics,* edited by Economic Research Gate, 43–141. Paris: European Conference of Ministers of Transport.

Caletrio, Javier. 2012. Global elites, privilege and mobilities in post-organized capitalism. *Theory, Culture & Society* 29(2): 135–149.

Carr, Stewart S. 2010. *The Psychology of Global Mobility.* New York, Dordrecht, Heidelberg, London: Springer Science+Business Media.

Casakin, H. P., and S. Kreitler. 2008. Place attachment as a function of meaning assignment. *Open Environmental Sciences* 2: 80–87.

Castells, Manuel. 2006. *The Rise of the Network Society.* Malden, MA: Blackwell.

Christensen, Ann-Dorte, and Sune Jensen. 2011. Roots and routes. *Nordic Journal of Migration Research* 1(3): 146–155.

Cresswell, Tim. 1997. Imagining the Nomad: Mobility and the Postmodern Primitive. In *Space and Social Theory: Interpreting Modernity and Postmodernity,* edited by Georges Benko and Ulf Strohmayer, 360–379. Oxford, Malden, MA: Blackwell.

———. 2002. Theorizing Place. In *Mobilizing Place, Placing Mobility: The Politics of Representation in a Globalised World,* edited by Ginette Verstraete and Tim Cresswell, 11–32. Amsterdam: Rodopi.

———. 2006. *On the Move: Mobility in the Modern Western World.* New York: Routledge.

———. 2010. Toward a politics of mobility. *Environment and Planning D: Society and Space* 28: 17–31.

Cresswell, Tim, and Peter Merriman. 2010. *Geographies of Mobilities: Practices, Spaces, Subjects.* Farnham, Burlington, VT: Ashgate.

D'Andrea, Anthony. 2007. *Global Nomads: Techno and New Age as Transnational Countercultures in Ibiza and Goa.* Abingdon, New York: Routledge.

Elliott, Anthony. 2014. Elsewhere: Tracking the Mobile Lives of the Globals. In *Elite Mobilities,* edited by Thomas Birtchnell and Javier Caletrío, 21–40. London: Routledge.

Elliott, Anthony, and John Urry. 2010. *Mobile Lives: Self, Excess and Nature.* London, New York: Routledge.

Flusser, Vilem. 1990. Nomaden. In *Herbstbuch eins: Auf, und, davon: Eine Nomadologie der Neunziger*, edited by Horst G. Haberl, 13–41. Graz: Droschl.

Flusser, Vilém, Kenneth Kronenberg and Anke K. Finger. 2003. *The Freedom of the Migrant: Objections to Nationalism*. Urbana: University of Illinois Press.

Foucault, Michel. 2002. *The Archaeology of Knowledge*. London: Routledge.

Frers, Lars. 2007. Perception, Aesthetics and Envelopment: Encountering Space and Materiality. In *Encountering Urban Places: Visual and Material Performances in the City*, edited by Lars Frers and Lars Meier, 25–45. Aldershot, Burlington, VT: Ashgate.

Gerhard, Ute. 1998. *Nomadische Bewegungen und die Symbolik der Krise: Flucht und Wanderung in der Weimarer Republik*. Opladen: Westdeutscher.

Giddens, Anthony. 1991. *Modernity and Self-identity: Self and Society in the Late Modern Age*. Stanford, CA: Stanford University Press.

———. 1994. *The Consequences of Modernity*. Cambridge: Polity.

Gossling, Stefan, Jean-Paul Ceron, Ghislain Dubois and Michael C. Hall. 2009. Hypermobile Travellers. In *Climate Change and Aviation: Issues, Challenges and Solutions*, edited by Stefan Gössling and Paul Upham, 132–150. London: Earthscan.

Gottdiener, Mark. Ed. 2001. *Life in the Air: Surviving the New Culture of Air Travel*. Lanham, MD: Rowman & Littlefield.

Graefe, Stefanie. 2010. Effekt, Stützpunkt, Überzähliges? Subjektivität zwischen hegemonialer Rationalität und Eigensinn. In *Diskursanalyse meets Gouvernementalitätsforschung: Perspektiven auf das Verhältnis von Subjekt, Sprache, Macht und Wissen*, edited by Johannes Angermüller, 289–313. Frankfurt am Main: Campus.

Gustafson, Per. 2009. More cosmopolitan, no less local. *European Societies* 11(1): 25–47.

———. 2001. Roots and routes. *Environment and Behaviour* 33(5): 667–686.

Hartmann, Michael. 2011. Die transnationale Klasse – Mythos oder Realität? In *Nachrichten aus den Innenwelten des Kapitalismus*, edited by Cornelia Koppetsch, 79–98. Wiesbaden: VS Verlag für Sozialwissenschaften.

Harvey, David. 1989. *The Condition of Postmodernity: An Enquiry into the Origins of Cultural Change*. Oxford: Blackwell.

Hildebrandt, Nikolaus, and Michael Dick. 2009. Die hierarchischen Ebenen menschlicher Mobilität: Eine empirische Exploration der subjektiven Erfahrungs- und Deutungshorizonte. In *Mobilität als Tätigkeit: Individuelle Expansion – alltägliche Logistik – kulturelle Kapazität*, edited by Michael Dick, 27–43. Lengerich: Pabst Science.

Iyer, Pico. 2001. *The Global Soul: Jet Lag, Shopping Malls and the Search for Home*. London: Bloomsbury.

Jensen, Anne, and Tim Richardson. 2007. New region, new story: Imagining mobile subjects in transnational space. *Space and Polity* 11(2): 137–150.

Jochum, Georg, and Günther Voß. 2013. Piloten und andere Steuerleute: Zur Navigationskunst des mobilen Subjekts. In *Transnationale Vergesellschaftungen: Verhandlungen des 35: Kongresses der Deutschen Gesellschaft für Soziologie in Frankfurt am Main 2010*, edited by Hans-Georg Soeffner. Wiesbaden: Springer.

Joseph, May. 1999. *Nomadic Identities: The Performance of Citizenship*. Minneapolis: University of Minnesota Press.

Kaplan, Caren. 1996. *Questions of Travel: Postmodern Discourses of Displacement*. Durham, NC: Duke University Press.

Kesselring, Sven. 2004. Society on the Move: Mobilitätspioniere in der Zweiten Moderne. In *Entgrenzung und Entscheidung: Was ist neu an der Theorie reflexiver Modernisierung?*, edited by Ulrich Beck and Christoph Lau, 258–280. Frankfurt am Main: Suhrkamp.

————. 2006. 'Pioneering mobilities: New patterns of movement and motility in a mobile world in a mobile world. *Environment and Planning A* 38: 269–280.

Khisty, C. J., and U. Zeitler. 2001. Is hypermobility a challenge for transport ethics and systemicity? *Systemic Practice and Action Research* 14: 597–613.

Kingsley, Dennis, and John Urry. 2009. Post-Car Mobilities. In *Car Troubles: Critical Studies of Automobility*, edited by Jim Conley and Arlene T. McLaren, 235–252. Farnham, Burlington, VT: Ashgate.

Kronlid, David. 2008. What Modes of Moving Do to Me: Reflections on Technogenic Processes of Identification. In *Spaces of Mobility: Essays on the Planning, Ethics, Engineering and Religion of Human Motion*, edited by Sigurd Bergmann, Thomas Hoff and Tore Sager, 125–154. London, Oakville, CT: Equinox.

Larsen, Jonas. 2001. Tourism mobilities and the travel glance: Experiences of being on the move. *Scandinavian Journal of Hospitality and Tourism* 2: 80–98.

Larsen, Jonas, John Urry and K. W. Axhausen. 2006. *Mobilities, Networks, Geographies*. Aldershot, Burlington, VT: Ashgate.

Lasen, Amparo. 2010. Mobile Culture and Subjectivities: An Example of Shared Agency between People and Technology. In *Interacting with Broadband Society*, edited by Leopoldina Fortunati, 109–124. Frankfurt: Peter Lang.

Lash, Scott, and John Urry. 1994. *Economies of Signs and Space*. London: Sage.

Latour, Bruno. 2004. Why has critique run out of steam? From matters of fact to matters of concern. *Critical Inquiry. Special Issue on the Future of Critique* 30(2): 225–248.

Lee, John D., and Barry H. Kattowitz. 2014. Perceptual and Cognitive Aspects of Intelligent Transportation Systems. In *Human Factors in Intelligent Transportations Systems*, edited by Woodrow Barfield and Thomas A. Dingus, 55–93. New York: Psychology Press.

Lewicka, Maria. 2011. Place attachment: How far have we come in the last 40 years? *Journal of Environmental Psychology* 31(3): 207–230.

Lück, Detlev, and Norbert F. Schneider. 2010. Introduction to the special issue on mobility and family. increasing job mobility – Changing family lives. *Zeitschrift für Familienforschung* 22(2): 135–148.

Malkki, Liisa. 1996. National Geographic: The Rooting of Peoples and the Territorialization of National Identity among Scholars and Refugees. In *Becoming National: A Reader*, edited by Geoff Eley and Ronal Grigor Suny, 434–453. New York: Oxford University Press.

Massey, Doreen. 1999. *Power-Geometries and the Politics of Space–time*. Heidelberg: University of Heidelberg, Institute of Geography.

Milgram, Stanley. 1967. The "small world" problem. *Psychology Today* 1(1): 60–67.

Mitchell, Clyde J. Ed. 1969. *Social Networks in Urban Situations: Analyses of Personal Relationships in Central African Towns*. Manchester: Manchester University Press.

Ohnmacht, Timo, Andreas Frei and Kai Axhausen. 2008. Mobility biography and network geography: Whose social relations are spatially dispersed? *Swiss Journal of Sociology* 34: 131–164.

Poppitz, Angela. 2009. Work and Ride – Mobiles Arbeiten im Zwischen(zeit)raum Bahnfahrt. In *Mobilität als Tätigkeit: Individuelle Expansion – alltägliche Logistik – kulturelle Kapazität*, edited by Michael Dick, 236–251. Lengerich: Pabst Science.

Povinelli, Elizabeth A., and George Chauncey. 1999. Thinking sexuality transnationally. *GLQ: A Journal of Gay and Lesbian Studies* 5(4): 439–449.

Reckwitz, Andreas. 2006. *Das hybride Subjekt: Eine Theorie der Subjektkulturen von der bürgerlichen Moderne zur Postmoderne*. Weilerswist: Velbrück Wiss.

Relph, Edward. 1976. *Place and Placelessness*. London: Pion.

Richards, Greg, and Julie Wilson. 2004. *The Global Nomad: Backpacker Travel in Theory and Practice*. Clevedon, Buffalo, NY: Channel View.

Richardson, Tim, and Ole Jensen. 2000. Discourses of mobility and polycentric development: A contested view of European spatial planning. *European Planning Studies* 4(8): 503–520.

Rosa, Hartmut. 2006. *Beschleunigung: Die Veränderung der Zeitstrukturen in der Moderne*. Frankfurt am Main: Suhrkamp.

———. 2009. Social Acceleration: Ethical and Political Consequences of a Desynchronized High-Speed Society. In *High-speed Society: Social Acceleration, Power and Modernity*, edited by Hartmut Rosa and William E. Scheuerman, 77–111. University Park: Pennsylvania State University Press.

Rosa, Hartmut, and William E. Scheuerman. 2009. Introduction. In *High-speed Society: Social Acceleration, Power and Modernity*, edited by Hartmut Rosa and William E. Scheuerman, 1–29. University Park: Pennsylvania State University Press.

Schaetti, Barbara F. 2000. *Global Nomad Identity: Hypothesizing a Developmental Model*. Cincinnati, OH: Graduate College of the Union Institute.

Schivelbusch, Wolfgang. 1986. *The Railway Journey: The Industrialization of Time and Space in the 19th century*. Leamington Spa, Hamburg: Berg.

Schneider, Norbert F., Ruth Limmer and Kerstin Ruckdeschel. 2002. *Mobil, flexibel, gebunden: Familie und Beruf in der mobilen Gesellschaft*. Frankfurt am Main: Campus.

Schutz, Alfred. 1972. *The Phenomenology of the Social World*. Evanston, IL: Northwestern University Press.

Seamon, David. 2000. A Way of Seeing People and Place. In *Theoretical Perspectives in Environment-Behavior Research*, edited by Seymour Wapner, 157–178. New York: Springer Science+Business.

Sheller, Mimi. 2004. Automotive emotions: Feeling the car. *Theory, Culture & Society* 21(4–5): 221–242.

Simmel, Georg, Anthony J. Blasi, Anton K. Jacobs and Mathew J. Kanjirathinkal. 2009. *Sociology: Inquiries into the Construction of Social Forms*. Leiden, Boston: Brill.

Singly, François D., and Claire-Anne Boukaïa. 2000. *Libres ensemble: L'individualisme dans la vie commune*. Paris: Nathan.

Thrift, Nigel. 2008. Re-animating the Place of Thought: Transformations of Spatial and Temporal Description in the Twenty-First Century. In *Community, Economic Creativity and Organization*, edited by Ash Amin and Joanne Roberts, 90–119. Oxford: Oxford University Press.

Tuan, Yi-fu. 1998. *Escapism*. Baltimore, MD: Johns Hopkins University Press.

Urry, John. 2002. Mobility and proximity. *Sociology* 36(2): 255–274.

———. 2007. *Mobilities*. Cambridge: Polity.

Vannini, Phillip. 2009. The Cultures of Alternative Mobilities. In *The Cultures of Alternative Mobilities: Routes Less Travelled*, edited by Phillip Vannini, 1–20. Farnham, Burlington, VT: Ashgate.

Varney, Denise. 2005. Transit Heimat: Translation, transnational subjectivity and mobility in German theatre. *TRANSIT* 2(1). Accessed 20 January 2016. www.escholarship.org/uc/item/9jz180fs.

Viry, Gil. 2012. Residential mobility and the spatial dispersion of personal networks. *Social Networks in Urban Situations: Analyses of Personal Relationships in Central African Towns* 34: 59–72.

Viry, Gil, and Detlev Lück. 2006. Conclusion: Chapter XI. In *State-of-the-Art of Mobility Research: A Literature Analysis for Eight Countries*, edited by E. Widmer and Norbert F. Schneider, 205–222. Job Mobilities Working Paper No. 2006-01.

Watts, Duncan J. 2003. *Six Degrees: The Science of a Connected Age*. New York: Norton.

Wellman, Barry. 2001. Physical place and cyberplace: The rise of personalized networking. *International Journal of Urban and Regional Research* 25(2): 227–252.

Whitelegg, J. 1993. *Transport for a Sustainable Future: The Case for Europe*. London: Belhaven.

7 'Inappropriate' Europeans

On fear, space and Roma mobility

Birgitta Frello

An earlier version of this chapter was published in Danish as Frello (2011) in *Academic Quarter*.

Introduction

In the early summer of 2010, news stories about groups of foreigners who came to Denmark and committed various crimes were rampant in Danish media. Attention focused quickly on a few small groups that had settled illegally in an abandoned post office on the outskirts of Copenhagen and on Amager fælled (Amager Commons), a public green near Copenhagen. In this chapter, I refer to both groups simply as the Roma on the commons.

The presence of these small groups of Roma was perceived as bothersome for the surroundings partly because of the waste they left and partly because their presence was associated with increased incidences of theft from a nearby allotment association. At first, the media referred to these disturbing campers as Roma, as Gypsies or, more generally, as Eastern Europeans. Soon, however, they were established to be Roma from Romania, and this was the term used apart from the tabloids' occasional use of the derogatory term Gypsy.

A few weeks after their arrival, the social democratic Mayor of Copenhagen, Frank Jensen, followed up on the media coverage with demands for action, supported by the conservative Minister of Justice Lars Barfoed (Thomsen 2010). The next day, 7 July, 23 individuals were arrested for violating the sanctity of privacy and for illegal camping. The Immigration Service made the quick decision to deport all of them and ban their re-entry to Denmark for two years.[1] The deportation was substantiated by reference to 'considerations of public order and health' – that is, with reference to their illegal type of residence, not to their alleged criminal activities, such as theft from the allotment gardens (Pressemeddelelse 2010).

The moral panic that preceded the deportations was basically initiated by a few newspapers, backed by popular resentment and by politicians from a broad political spectrum – from the Social Democratic Party to the nationalist Danish People's Party.[2] The majority of the national media approached the issue in a broad journalistic manner, which also involved questioning stereotypes about Gypsies and Roma. Part of the press, however, tended to cover the problems of theft and illegal lodging in terms of a 'Gypsy problem' (Sigona 2005), as in this headline from the national-conservative newspaper, *Jyllands-Posten*. 'The police warn against Gypsies. Currently, Gypsies are ravaging in several places in the country where they are trying to cheat people and committing petty crime' (Westh and Ellegaard 2010a).[3] The same newspaper identified the EU as part of the problem. 'The Gypsies cannot be sent home. Despite suspicion of several cases of petty crime, the police cannot curb the many Gypsies and East Europeans, who are currently in Denmark. The rules of free movement in the EU prevent it' (Westh and Ellegaard 2010b).[4]

Although supported by a broad spectrum of Danish political parties, the debate about the deportation of the 23 Roma also included critical voices. The deportation was criticised for being discriminatory and based on racism, and it was followed up by an increased media focus on the poverty that brought the Roma to Denmark and the problems they encountered in Denmark in terms of prejudice and exclusion from local shelters and reception centres for homeless people. Judged from this perspective, the reference to the illegal residence appeared as an attempt to gloss over the real purpose of getting rid of people belonging to a group that is and historically has been unwelcome and discriminated against throughout Europe. The European Roma Rights Centre (ERRC) filed appeals on behalf of 10 of the deported, arguing that the deportation amounted to collective expulsion [European Roma Rights Centre (ERRC) 2010]. The following year, the Ministry of Integration cancelled the decision in 14 cases after a verdict from the Danish Supreme Court in which the deportation in two cases were deemed illegal due to the triviality of the offenses (nyidanmark.dk 2011).

In August and September 2010, the focus of the Danish media broadened to a general coverage of the situation of Roma in the EU, following the French deportation of thousands of Romanian and Bulgarian Roma in August. These massive deportations sparked a debate across Europe on discrimination and racism (cf. Commissioner for Human Rights 2012). The debate involved among others the vice president of the European Commission responsible for Justice, Fundamental Rights and Citizenship, Viviane Reding, who in a press release stated that:

> I personally have been appalled by a situation which gave the impression that people are being removed from a Member State of the European Union just because they belong to a certain ethnic minority. This is a situation I had thought Europe would not have to witness again after the Second World War.
>
> (Reding 2010)

While the French deportations were widely registered and criticised, the Danish went largely unnoticed. This is perhaps understandable, considering the limited number of people involved – compared to the thousands that were expelled from France. I will argue, however, that the fact that the group in Denmark was so small makes the deportation and the moral panic that preceded it particularly apt for analysis, since it points to the fact that what was at stake here was not just a question of self-defence against a criminal group.[5] No one accused the 23 Roma of worse crimes than disturbing the peace, petty theft and illegal lodging. So why the fuss? The answer, I contend, should be found in the public image of Roma – and particularly of Roma mobility – rather than in their actual behaviour. Therefore, the moral panic in Denmark after the arrival of the 23 Roma in 2010 can shed light on how notions of mobility are not only dependent on the 'act' itself or on material and legal conditions, such as economy or citizenship. They are equally dependent on broader cultural conventions and discourses that regulate the normativity surrounding the understanding of mobility, rendering some forms of mobility recognisable and legitimate, while others – although formally legal – are rendered dubious if not downright threatening. Understanding how 23 poor, temporary migrants can trigger a reaction like the one in Denmark in 2010 involves analysing how relations among fear, space and mobility are produced.

The analysis is based on the overall coverage of the incident by conventional Danish media (national newspapers, including their web versions, and public service TV and radio) in the period from the first emergence of stories about illegal lodgers in May 2010 until the slowdown on media reactions to the Danish and French deportations around the end of September 2010.

I will outline some central problems related to the situation of European Roma, followed by a brief outline of historically constituted images of Roma, which position them as 'internal outsiders' in Europe (despite their long European history) and as nomads (despite their often sedentary life). Then I turn to the Danish case and analyse the banalisation of the relevance of Roma as an ethnic category and of nomadism as characteristic of Roma culture. Following this, I analyse how the Roma on Amager Commons were positioned in the debate as deviant not only in relation to sedentarism but also in relation to perceptions of appropriate mobility. This analysis is followed by a discussion of the securitisation of the Roma presence through the racialisation of space. I conclude by addressing the seeming paradox that possibly the most pan-European of all European people are routinely rendered as 'inappropriate Europeans'.

European Roma

'We don't all have the same access to the road', Janet Wolff claimed in an oft cited passage (Wolff 1993, 253) – and rightly so. Obstacles to mobility are plenty. Furthermore, while *access* to mobility is often considered a scarce resource, this is only one aspect of a more general problem of social inequalities related to mobility that also include involuntary mobility related to natural disasters, war and persecution. Thus, the decisive difference may not be the question of *access* to mobility but rather the question to whom the possibility of *mastering* their own mobility is granted. Roma who are temporarily or permanently settled on the outskirts of Western European cities and who have been subject to deportations on a larger scale constitute textbook examples of Zygmunt Bauman's argument that globalisation produces two essentially different mobile classes: on the one hand, the 'tourists', who move freely across borders, and, on the other hand, a class of redundant and unwelcome migrants – of 'vagabonds' who travel not because they want to but because *'they have no other bearable choice'* (Bauman 1998, 93, emphasis in original). They are tossed around in their attempt to create a better life and must grasp the opportunities that they can find, but they cannot themselves determine the conditions for their travel.

This distinction between different categories of movers needs to be further pinned down, however. The borders of the EU constitute a first line of separation between welcome and unwelcome migrants, enabling the EU member states to ignore – at least to certain extent – the suffering and aspirations of those who are unwelcome, as long as they do not manage to cross the heavily guarded external borders of the EU. Once these borders are crossed, however, movement is relatively easy, due to the Schengen and to the principle of free movement of labour. The passport is, of course, a major factor in this social structuring of mobility. Despite their sometimes fragile legal status and the consequences that ensue in terms of lacking identity papers and citizenship (Bancroft 2005; Cahn 2012; Commissioner for Human Rights 2012), European Roma nevertheless have a legal existence that opens doors of opportunities that are blocked to non-European migrants.[6]

While the financial crisis and the subsequent fear of 'welfare tourism' in the richest parts of the EU indicate social cleavages within the EU that positions not only Roma but also larger groups of Southern and Eastern Europeans as unwelcome 'vagabonds', Roma still occupy a special position in this hierarchy of migrants. Their position involves images of different categories of migrants that meld into each other: on the one hand, the image of the culturally recognisable EU citizen who is expected to possess skills that make him/her attractive in the labour market and, on the other hand, the image of the poor, culturally alien and unwelcome third world migrant. The Roma emerge as 'inappropriate' Europeans in the sense that they are positioned in the interstice between these images.

Most Roma migrants within the EU come from Romania and Bulgaria, where there are relatively large Roma minorities who are and historically were subject to widespread contempt and discrimination. This discrimination has changed form but did not disappear after the fall of communism (Bancroft 2005). While discrimination against Roma minorities in Eastern Europe has been the subject of attention and critique from a Western European point of view, as well as that of specific demands in relation to prospective EU membership, the situation for Roma in Western Europe has attracted less attention. However, while the situation for Roma is different in Eastern and in Western Europe, discrimination and prejudice against Roma – including overt anti-Gypsyism – can be found all over Europe (Bancroft 2005; Commissioner for Human Rights 2012; Fekete 2014; O'Nions 2014; Sigona and Trehan 2009; Thornton 2014).

Like other ethnic categories, the category Roma is flexible, and to the extent that Roma today perceive themselves as an ethnic group (which they do not always do) and are perceived as such by others, contemporary categorisations and identifications are more important than origin. The estimated number of Roma in Europe is 10–12 million (Pietarinen 2011). However, official numbers and estimates given by Roma organisations often differ. Furthermore, since many European countries – including Denmark – do not register people in terms of ethnicity, the estimated number of Roma in some European countries varies depending on the context and on the consequences of assuming an identity as Roma in the specific context (Rövid 2011; cf. Willems 1997). The Council of Europe estimates the number of Roma in Denmark to be between 1,500 and 10,000 persons (The Ministry of Foreign Affairs of Denmark 2013, 51). Most of them came to Denmark as migrant workers in the 1960s and 1970s or have descended from these immigrants.[7]

Historically, Roma are a persecuted minority in Europe and in this context the idea of a shared ethnic identity constitutes a double-edged sword (cf. Bancroft 2005; Mayall 2004; Rövid 2011). The heterogeneity of the Roma population in Europe makes the question of the legitimate representation of their interests extremely complicated (McGarry 2010; Pantea 2014). And while the idea that the Roma constitute a people with a common culture and origin – regardless of its accuracy – is an important element in the struggle for minority rights, the downside is that the reference to 'culture' as an argument for minority rights helps maintain cultural stereotypes that may be discriminatory.[8]

Roma images

Why was it pertinent to mention that the illegal lodgers on Amager Commons were Roma rather than Romanians? The answer lies, I will suggest, in the historical positioning of Roma.

Like minority studies in general, Gypsy and Roma studies have also undergone major transformations in recent decades, as previous conceptualisations of culture and ethnicity have changed in favour of a more constructivist understanding.[9] This has led to questioning on much of the established knowledge about Gypsies and Roma – including the idea that they are one people with a common origin, language and culture (cf. Willems 1997) – and to an enhanced sensitivity towards the individual Roma's shifting strategies of self-definition (cf. Pantea 2014). While some scholars stress the complexity and ambiguity of the referent of the term 'Gypsy' (cf. Mayall 2004), others distinguish between Roma and Gypsy travellers, arguing that the term Roma refers to groups who speak various dialects of the Romani language, who are mostly based in Central and Eastern Europe and who usually live a sedentary life. Gypsy travellers, on the other hand, are mostly based in Western Europe, some are of Romani origin, but many of them are not, and not all of them live a nomadic life. Angus Bancroft (2005) employs this distinction but also emphasises its artificiality and inappropriateness with regard to the complexities of the practices, relationships and identities of the peoples in question.

Wim Willems (1997) points out that the term Gypsy has historically been employed as a name for various groups of people who have made a living in ways that involve an itinerant lifestyle. The actual groups that were covered by the term varied depending on the circumstances, but despite the vagueness of the group definition, the popular ideas about what characterises it have been quite stable through time. Historically, the sedentary majority has perceived Gypsies with a mixture of fear and fascination – as uncivilised, half-criminal beggars but also as an exotic and creative people (cf. Willems 1997). This ambivalence continues to this day. Willems in particular emphasises the role of the German historian Heinrich Grellmann, who in 1783 published the book *Die Zigeuner*, in which he gathered the contemporary knowledge about different travelling people under the name Gypsy and endowed the group with a collective history (see also Lee 2000; Lucassen et al. 1998). Willems argues that not only popular knowledge but also scholarly and semi-scholarly work, notably the work by members of the Gypsy Lore Society, have reproduced Grellmann's account, for instance by taking the oriental origin and itinerant lifestyle of Gypsies for granted.

Due to the persistence of the narratives of the itinerant people and the Oriental origin, Roma challenge the national idea of a correspondence between identity and place. Not only are they perceived as nomads, they have also committed what Zygmunt Bauman calls 'the unforgettable and hence unforgivable sin of the late entry' (Bauman 1991, 59). In Bauman's discussion of Georg Simmel's notion of the stranger as 'the person who comes today and stays tomorrow' (Simmel 1964, 402), he emphasises the importance of the notion of the 'beginning': 'Being an event in history, having a beginning, the presence of the stranger always carries the potential of an end' (Bauman 1991, 59f).[10] When the nation is based on a narrative of ageless existence, itinerant people constitute a challenge and a threat to the very foundation of the nation. Liisa Malkki argues that a consequence of the sedentarist metaphysics involved in the idea of the nation is the pathologisation of people who do not fit into the picture – such as refugees and nomads. They are perceived as deviant – at best as psychologically fragile, at worst as a threat (Malkki 1992, 32). This perception influences the living conditions of Roma in terms of both national and local policies, public attitudes towards them and, more fundamentally, in the sense that Europe is characterised by a nationally defined landscape in which an unequivocal national belonging is a normative requirement (cf. Kabachnik 2009, 2010; Sigona 2003, 2005; Tileagă 2006). In such a landscape, the (perceived) nomad represents a 'threat to spatial order' (Bancroft 2005, 109).

David Mayall notes that 'Gypsies cross at least two mental maps: as foreigners or aliens, and as travellers or nomads' (Mayall 2004, 276). Thus he directs attention to the fact that they challenge the national idea of belonging – because they are perceived as outsiders – and they challenge the notion that a sedentary lifestyle is the normal way of life – because they are perceived as nomads. Mayall's distinction provides a good starting point for analysing the complex images of the Roma on Amager Commons. Both of the 'mental maps', however, turn out to involve ambivalence and paradox.

The image of the Roma as *foreigners* situates them ambivalently in relation to Europe. On the one hand, they not only live in Europe, they are also the most pan-European of all European people in the sense that they are scattered across borders without claiming a specific national territory or belonging as a group. On the other hand, they are perceived as foreigners who immigrated to Europe from

India and who are 'excluded from the ideological and geographical "place" of Europe' (Bancroft 2005, 2) and treated as 'internal outsiders', not only in terms of public opinion towards domestic Roma minorities in individual EU member states but also in terms of images of Europe and of internal migration in the EU.

Inspired by Edward Said's work on Orientalism, Ken Lee argues that Gypsylorism constituted the Roma as both outsiders and insiders in relation to Europe: 'Whilst Orientalism is the discursive construction of the exotic Other *outside* Europe, Gypsylorism is the construction of the exotic Other *within* Europe – Romanies are the Orientals within' (Lee 2000, 132, emphasis in original). Inspired by Lee, I will use the term Gypsylorism as a reference to the construction of Roma as internal Others, characterised by cultural stereotypes about Gypsies. Roma constitute a 'troubled' category of movers in the sense that on the one hand they constitute an *internal* minority, who as residents of an EU country enjoy equal formal rights with other citizens of the EU, including the right to free movement anywhere in the EU. On the other hand, they are widely conceived as illegitimate intruders. As stated by MEP for the Danish People's Party, Morten Messerschmidt: 'We have an internal market for workers, we do not have a single market for people who want to beg or for bands of thieves and that kind of thing' (DR 2010).[11]

The image of Roma as *nomads* is paradoxical – not only in view of the fact that many are sedentary. Their – perceived or practised – mobility falls uneasily between two seemingly contradicting discourses that offer basic interpretative frameworks for understanding issues of legitimacy, human dignity, identity, culture and belonging. They fall between the discourse of *sedentarism* as the natural state of things and the discourse of *mobility* as a central feature of a cosmopolitan outlook – and as an important aspect of the EU in terms of the principle of free movement of labour. There is an obvious tension between these two discourses because the celebration of mobility challenges the naturalness of the sedentary lifestyle. Roma, however, challenge both, and they do so – not necessarily because of their specific patterns of migration and strategies for survival, which differ depending on factors such as gender, economy and local opportunities (cf. Grill 2012; Pantea 2012, 2013) – but because their actions are widely interpreted through the Gypsylorist narrative of the exotic nomadic people who turn their back on society and live by theft, fortune telling and conning.

Sedentarism and the naturalisation of the national order of things can have serious consequences for people who are conceived to be in the 'wrong' place (Cresswell 2006; Malkki 1992). However, the problem not only concerns people whose location deviates from the national norm. Noel B. Salazar argues that some people are perceived as immobile when they are in fact mobile (Salazar 2011). I will argue that the opposite is also the case and with equally important social consequences. While the idea of natives as 'incarcerated in bounded geographical spaces, immobile and untouched yet paradoxically available to the mobile outsider' (Narayan, 1993, 676; cited in Salazar 2011, 582. See also Appadurai 1988, 37) has been widely criticised, my point is that images of the Other's relation to place concerns more than ideas of the 'bounded native'. Ideas of the 'mobile Other' can also be restraining. Thus, part of the problems faced by European Roma is related to their imagined lack of boundedness: to the fact that notwithstanding their actual practice – be it sedentary or mobile – they are widely conceived to be an 'itinerant people' (Lucassen et al. 1998), a group characterised by forms of mobility that evade the norms that other migrants move by – norms that are recognisable as legitimate by local majorities. The problematic position of Roma in European historical and cultural imagination renders their mobility suspicious in the public eye and renders them 'inappropriate' Europeans despite their legal status.

Banal ethnicisation and nomadicisation

Roma, Gypsy, Romanian, Eastern European – in the Danish context, differing terms are used to designate unwelcome travellers of European origin who make a living (or who are believed to make a living) by illegal activities. Moreover, the meanings of these terms rub off on one another. Even when the term Eastern European is applied in order to avoid accusations of ethnic prejudice, the connotations follow suit. The terms function as 'sticky' signs, in the sense explored by Sara Ahmed:

> To use a sticky sign is to evoke other words, which have become intrinsic to the sign through past forms of association. . . . The association between words that generates meanings is concealed: *it is this concealment of such associations that allows such signs to accumulate value.* I am describing this accumulation of affective value as a form of stickiness, or as "sticky signs".
>
> (Ahmed 2004, 92, emphasis in original)

I will argue that Roma is constituted as such a 'sticky' sign through the persistent narrative of the deviant lifestyle and that the negative connotations that stick to the sign Gypsy are pinned to the sign Roma through association as well. This is also how the negative connotations can increasingly stick to other terms that were previously not associated with Gypsies, such as Romanian or Eastern European. Thus, in the debate about the Roma on Amager Commons, the 'inappropriateness' of their mobile practice was not only linked to the question of lack of skills and illegal residence. The Gypsylorist images had a huge influence on the debate.

From the perspective of those advocating the deportation of the 23 Roma, this was a necessary provision in order to prevent other unwelcome foreigners from following their example: 'If we do not make sure to send them home, we show that Denmark is a place where you can just camp here and there in parks and abandoned buildings' (Minister of Justice, Lars Barfoed, quoted in Information 2010b).[12] This argument rests on an established narrative about Denmark as a welfare paradise that attracts the 'wrong' kind of immigrants (cf. Koefoed and Simonsen 2007). It was, however, accompanied by a sometimes subtle, sometimes overt cultural Othering – the latter being found for example in the web version of the tabloid newspaper, *Ekstrabladet*'s video clip featuring a journalist who must push through the bushes in order to find camps that repeatedly prove to be abandoned, leaving only filth and rubbish (Wallberg 2010). Such reports position the Roma as the primitive Other by mimicking the action of the white explorer, and they reflect the mythological representation of a people who cannot be detained and who live and move according to their own rules. Such overt processes of cultural Othering can probably be expected from the tabloid press. Images of the cultural Other were, however, also produced in sometimes more subtle and perhaps less intentionally derogative ways, such as when a member of the Copenhagen City Council for the Social Liberal Party, Manu Sareen, criticised the government policy of excluding non-Danes from shelters for homeless people by arguing: '[l]isten. These are fellow human beings. Even though they behave completely insanely' (Danmarks Radio 2010).[13]

Inspired by Michael Billig's concept of 'banal nationalism' (Billig 1995), I will use the term banal ethnicisation in order to highlight the fact that Romani ethnicity not only was made relevant in such explicit references to a specific Roma or Gypsy culture or mentality, it was also treated as part of the basic narrative about the nature of the problem in the sense that it appeared as an unremarkable statement of fact in mainstream news reporting. Usually foreign visitors, be they tourists, immigrants, temporary workers or homeless people, are referred to in terms of their country of origin. Ethnic categories are rarely made relevant unless ethnicity is ascribed a particular relevance. Then why was it relevant to mention that the unwelcome visitors were Roma, and what difference did it make in terms of the reactions they met?

The narrative of the itinerant people was also banalised. On the one hand, it was explicitly employed in support of the deportation, such as in the case Kim Andersen (MP for the Liberal Party), who argued that 'they are a nomadic people. They do not have national sense of self like most Europeans have after all' (Danmarks Radio 2010). On the other hand, the prevalence of this narrative becomes manifest from the fact that it was also employed by critics of the deportation, as when the editorial in *Politiken*, a leading liberal newspaper, referred to the nomadic lifestyle as an argument for tolerance: '[t]he Roma way of life is different. They are nomads, and there is less and less room for them and other travelling people in our closed and well groomed welfare society' (Politiken 2010).

Apart from such direct references to the believed nomadism of the Roma, the narrative of the itinerant people also functioned in a more indirect way – as a banal nomadicisation that did not serve as part of an argument for or against deportation. This was found for instance in the newspapers' 'fact sheets' where it was frequently noted – without any reflection on the relevance of the information – that the Roma are or originally were a nomadic people who emigrated to Europe from India.[14] Thus, the reference to nomadism did not necessarily serve as an explanation of today's problems. At times it was even directly rejected by way of pointing out that most Roma today are settled. However, nomadism was made relevant as background information in line with the information that the Roma were persecuted in Europe for centuries and that hundreds of thousands were murdered in Nazi concentration camps.

Why is a group of people who has been rooted in Europe for hundreds of years routinely characterised in terms of their alleged non-European origin? The decisive point here is not whether the information is *true* (which it seems to be only partly).[15] The most important question is which *work* it performs when reiterated over and over again. Both the ethnicisation and the nomadicisation are 'banal' in the sense that they were mentioned repeatedly as unremarkable and uncontroversial facts that did not serve a specific political argument. This very 'banality' contributes to the 'stickiness' of the derogative connotations of the ethnic label.

Moral geographies

The perseverance of the narrative of an itinerant people positions the Roma in a conflict with the sedentarist idea of a natural link between identity and place. Thus it serves as a legitimation for the refusal to treat them as ordinary work migrants. Kim Andersen defended the deportation by arguing that the case in point concerned:

> a people who came here . . . many many years ago . . . and who have Indian blood in their veins, and who of course are a nomadic people, and who very much live at night, and who are not interested in adjusting to a welfare society and to the norms of a community governed by law. . . . [E]ven if we offered them various courses and labour market training and what do I know, they would of course not be interested.
>
> (Danmarks Radio 2010)

Here, the attitude and interests of the 23 Roma on the Commons – and all the other potential Roma migrants who may arrive in Denmark – appear to be 'known' in advance – a knowledge that, in Andersen's rendition, limited the range of possible and meaningful action on the part of the Danish authorities. Being nomads, Roma migrants 'would of course not be interested' in any integration initiatives. The fact that only a small proportion of the Roma are or have been nomads and that the nomadic life is not necessarily an expression of cultural propensity but sometimes forced on them by local majorities does not itself reduce the strength of the narrative of the itinerant people. When belonging to a place appears natural and when non-belonging appears to be the central characteristic of Roma existence, then the Roma are identified as a problem even prior to their actions.

However, analysing the aversion to the perceived nomadic practice of Roma solely in terms of sedentarism is too reductive. To focus exclusively on sedentarism as a norm does not sit well with the celebration of mobility as a central element of the EU. Tim Cresswell argues that mobility is a '*root metaphor* for contemporary understandings of the world of culture and society' (Cresswell 2006, 25, emphasis in original). This does not, however, imply that privileging a nomadic point of view automatically provides a viable alternative to sedentarism (For a discussion, see Adey 2010; Cresswell 2006; Faist 2013). Rather, sedentarism and nomadism are two 'moral geographies', both of them involving 'hidden politics' (Cresswell 2006, 55).

At the crossroads between nomadism and sedentarism, the mobility of the 23 Roma on Amager Commons emerged as a problem to the Danish public because they fell between recognisable and legitimate positions. The problem was not their mobility but their 'undecidability' in terms of their position in this moral geographical landscape. Roma mobility emerged as a problem in advance of their actions by virtue of the preconceptions that they were met with in terms of the construction of their position as in-between European and non-European and in terms of their alleged preference for a nomadic lifestyle and self-imposed non-belonging. This is how it made sense when Nikolaj Bang, a Parliamentary candidate for the Conservative Party, ridiculed the idea of recognising the Roma as a national minority because 'a community with its own culture and norms, which literally prides itself on *not* being a part of a country or a society, which apparently does not at all want to be citizens, perhaps they do not fall under the term "national minority"' (Bang 2010).[16]

Securitisation and the racialisation of space

The representation of Roma migrants as a threat to the recipient Western European countries is not limited to the Danish case. Owen Parker argues that the Roma who were expelled from France in 2010 were the object of a securitisation process in the sense that they were presented as a 'threat to the integrity of state and, in particular, France's republican way of life' (Parker 2012, 478; see also Nacu 2012) and therefore that they called for urgent measures, such as deportation.

The fact that the presence of 23 Roma were sufficient to spark a similar reaction in Denmark supports this argument: the amount of trouble they made was incommensurable with the spurred reaction. Nevertheless, their very modest 'camps' were enough to create an image of an emergency situation that required special measures. Even though the problems experienced in the Danish case were limited to some rubbish and some alleged petty theft, these problems were 'securitised' in the sense that the presence of the 23 Roma was articulated as a security issue that justified a particularly resolute action. The Gypsylorist tale of the self-selected marginal existence, the nomadic and fleeting life in unsanitary camps that is also associated with crime and other dubious behaviour thus contributes to making the Roma the object of a physical exclusion and of a discursive Othering. This can easily be radicalised into representing them as a threat to society and thus serve as an argument for special measures of self-defence: '[t]here must be no softness' as Minister of Justice Lars Barfoed put it before the deportations (quoted in Thomsen 2010).[17]

The securitisation argument rests on an understanding of threats as dependent on social construction. Rather than being simply a reflection of factual threats, 'security' is a speech act that creates what it names (Wæver 1995). Sara Ahmed argues in a similar vein that the language of fear *creates* fear rather than being a reflection of an already existing fear. It creates a 'distinction between those who are "under threat" and those who threaten' (Ahmed 2004, 72). The uneven distribution of fear regulates the movement of bodies in space, since 'fear works to align bodily and social space: it works to enable some bodies to inhabit and move in public space through restricting the mobility of other bodies to spaces that are enclosed or contained' (Ahmed 2004, 70).

Some bodies are allowed to extend into space in the sense that spaces welcome certain bodies while others are blocked or rendered problematic in spaces that are otherwise conceived as generally accessible. Historically, this unequal distribution of the accessibility of space is produced not just through physical and legal/administrative measures but also through the reiteration of narratives about those who fit in and those who do not. Thus, while unauthorised camping on Amager Commons is illegal for everybody, such practice is conceived very differently by the majority population if it is conducted by a group of Romanian Roma or by, say, a group of Swedish youngsters who want to hang around Copenhagen without paying for housing. The latter may be considered a problem for the neighbours, but they would hardly become a major media concern or give rise to comments from the Minister of Justice, not to mention being sanctioned by deportations and banned from re-entering the country.

Sara Ahmed connects the argument of the social construction of threats to race, space and mobility, arguing that racism 'works as a way of orientating bodies in specific directions, thereby affecting how they "take up" space. We "become" racialised in how we occupy space, just as space is, as it were, already occupied as an effect of racialisation' (Ahmed 2006, 24). I argue that the Roma are racialised in Ahmed's sense of the term and that this racialisation is pivotal for the constitution of the conditions for their mobility and for the ways in which it is sanctioned. Ironically, while the Roma are widely believed to be nomads, what characterises their mobility maybe more than anything else is that it is heavily pre-constituted as deviant, often securitised and thus constrained and blocked by local majorities and authorities or, as an editorial in the liberal newspaper *Information* puts it, '[A]pparently [the Roma] are expected to display a very particular type of mobility: Away from the place where the rest of us are (*Information* 2010a).[18]

Conclusion: inappropriate Europeans

The moral panic that rose when a small group of Roma put up their camps on the usually more or less deserted recreational space of Amager Commons can serve as a mundane example of how relations among fear, space and mobility are produced. The Roma on Amager Commons may not have been deported *because* they were Roma, but the reference to the fact that they were was neither innocent nor neutral. The Roma on the Commons were conceived as mobile not only in the obvious sense that they travelled the distance between Romania and Denmark but also and most importantly in the sense that they were believed to embody a specific type of mobility, that is, a mobility that is widely considered to be connected to problematic forms of nomadism. This 'inappropriate mobility' of the 23 deported Romanian citizens was produced through a Gypsylorist image that provided a cultural explanation through which the interpretation of the specific problems of poverty, exclusion, homelessness and crime was filtered. The analysis shows the ways in which the narrative of the 'itinerant people' was given explanatory power regardless of whether it was supported by the way of life of the affected individuals. This narrative positioned the Roma in an ambivalent position both vis-à-vis Europe (through the reiteration of the narrative of their Indian origin) and vis-à-vis the idea of national belonging (through the reiteration of the narrative of nomadism and self-exclusion). Thus, the problems that Roma migrants face involve not only overt anti-Gypsyism but also the banalisation of narratives that support their exclusion from the idea of the 'appropriate' European.

Mobility is sometimes equated with openness and willingness to engage with the Other. In this respect, the concept is part of a family of concepts that celebrate transgression as a positive, critical and potentially liberating endeavour involving some kind of cosmopolitan attitude – a family of concepts that also includes concepts such as 'hybridity' and 'transculture' (for a discussion, see Frello 2008, 2015). In social science and social philosophy, such an attitude is sometimes particularly connected to Europe and the EU – as a hope, an obligation or a potential (cf. Beck and Grande 2007; Delanty 2005).

Roma may be the most pan-European of all European people, and from an optimistic perspective one could say that, by virtue of this position, they carry the potential of embodying the vision of a cosmopolitan Europe. The potential displacement of the naturalised (nationalised) connection among culture, territory and identity the Roma represent by virtue of their pan-European existence is, however, rarely interpreted along these lines. Rather than granting them a special position as citizens of the EU, their positioning reflects the contours of the ideal EU citizen in constituting the *counter image* of this citizen. Their pan-European existence is transformed into an image of a cultural Otherness bordering on hereditary cultural deviance. Likewise, their alleged nomadic lifestyle is brought to support the image of cultural deviance, rather than feeding into a generalised celebration of mobility. Thus, the Europeanness of Roma is constantly questioned because the question of origin is routinely – albeit indirectly – made relevant, and thus the perception of them as 'late arrivers' is reproduced. In sum, rather than emerging as 'quintessential' Europeans, they are rendered 'inappropriate' Europeans.

Roma are often mentioned as an example of a people that challenge sedentarism by their way of life. However, the case of the Roma on the Commons suggests that maybe the image of the nomadic people works to constitute them as collectively deviant prior to their actual actions. Regardless of what they do, they are *produced* as a certain type of mobile people. In other words, the 'problem' not only concerns the unequal access to and control over mobility, it also concerns the specific construction of the mobile subject and the historical and cultural imageries that such constructions depend on (cf. Franquesa 2011; Frello 2008).

While the turn towards mobility rather than stability, routes rather than roots, nomadism rather than sedentarism in the social sciences has provided a much needed critical gaze on certain conventional truths and methodologies (Urry 2000), the social implications and political usages of the celebration of mobility need to be studied in their specificities. Rather than mobility being either deviant (in relation to a sedentary norm) or a norm itself, we should analyse it as a discursive construct that is given meaning dependent on the specific situation, power relations, and point of view.

Notes

1 The Immigration Service (*Udlændingeservice*) is an agency under the Ministry of Justice.
2 According to a survey made by *Rambøll Analyse, Danmark* for the newspaper *Jyllands-Posten* after the debate about the Roma on the Commons in 2010, 62 per cent of the respondents believed that the presence of Roma in Denmark constituted a problem (Broberg and Borg 2010).
3 'Politiet advarer mod sigøjnere. I øjeblikket huserer sigøjnere flere steder i landet, hvor de forsøger at snyde folk og begår småkriminalitet.'
4 'Sigøjnere kan ikke sendes hjem. På trods af mistanke om masser af småkriminalitet, kan politiet ikke dæmme op for de mange sigøjnere og østeuropæere, der i øjeblikket er i Danmark. Det forhindrer reglerne om fri bevægelighed i EU.'
5 To be met with reactions that are out of proportion to the number of Roma arriving seems to be a characteristic of Roma mobility. See Bancroft (2005, chapter 6).
6 However, although the EU membership opened the borders of the EU for Romanians and Bulgarians, the principle of free movement of labour did not apply fully to the citizens of the two countries until 2014.
7 Roma do not have the status of a national minority in Denmark. The reason given is the 'lack of continuous historical presence in Denmark of persons with a Roma background' (The Ministry of Foreign Affairs of Denmark 2013, 51).
8 For discussions of the validity and consequences of (de)constructions of Roma/Gypsy ethnicity and origin, see Bancroft (2005); Willems (1997). For a defence of the argument for a shared Roma culture, see Tavani (2012).
9 For a research overview, see Stewart (2013).
10 For a discussion of Simmel's notion of the 'stranger' in relation to European Roma, see Bancroft (2005, 165–169).
11 'Vi har et indre marked for arbejdstagere, vi har jo ikke et indre marked for folk der vil tigge eller tyvebander og den slags ting'.
12 'Hvis vi ikke sørger for at sende dem hjem, viser vi, at Danmark er et sted, hvor man bare kan campere rundt omkring i parker og forladte bygninger.'
13 'Prøv at høre: det er også vores medmennesker. Selvom de opfører sig fuldstændig vanvittigt.'
14 E.g. Bostrup (2010); Frese (2010); Kongstad (2010); Ruby (2010).
15 (Lucassen et al. 1998; cf. Willems 1997). For a defense of the theory of the Indian origin, see Iovita and Schurr (2004).
16 'En befolkningsgruppe med egen kultur og normer, som ligefrem bryster sig af *ikke* at være en del af et land eller et samfund, og som tilsyneladende slet ikke ønsker at være statsborgere, måske nok ikke falder ind under betegnelsen "nationalt mindretal"'.
17 'Der skal ikke være nogen blødsødenhed'.
18 '. . . tilsyneladende forventes [de] at udvise en helt særlig bevægelighed: Væk fra der, hvor vi andre er'.

References

Adey, Peter. 2010. *Mobility: Key Ideas in Geography*. London: Routledge.
Ahmed, Sara. 2004. *The Cultural Politics of Emotion*. Edinburgh: Edinburgh University Press.
———. 2006. *Queer Phenomenology: Orientations, Objects, Others*. Durham, NC: Duke University Press.
Appadurai, Arjun. 1988. Putting hierarchy in its place. *Cultural Anthropology* 3(1): 36–49.
Bancroft, Angus. 2005. *Roma and Gypsy-Travellers in Europe: Modernity, Race, Space and Exclusion*. Research in Migration and Ethnic Relations Series. Aldershot: Ashgate.

Bang, Nikolaj. 2010. *Romaer*. http://x-bang.dk/.

Bauman, Zygmunt. 1991. *Modernity and Ambivalence*. Cambridge: Polity.

———. 1998. *Globalization: The Human Consequences*. Cambridge: Polity.

Beck, Ulrich, and Edgar Grande. 2007. *Cosmopolitan Europe*. Cambridge: Polity.

Billig, Michael. 1995. *Banal Nationalism*. London: Sage.

Bostrup, Jens. 2010. Når romaerne kommer ind på en skole, flygter de andre – hvis de kan. *Politiken* section 1 (24 October): 10.

Broberg, Mads Bonde and Orla Borg. 2010. Flertal: Nej til romaer. *Jyllands-Posten* section 1 (21 August): 8–9.

Cahn, Claude. 2012. Minorities, citizenship and statelessness in Europe. *European Journal of Migration and Law* 14(3): 297–316.

Commissioner for Human Rights. 2012. *Human Rights of Roma and Travellers in Europe*. Human Rights Writings. Strasbourg: Council of Europe.

Cresswell, Tim. 2006. *On the Move: Mobility in the Modern Western World*. London: Routledge.

Danmarks Radio. 2010. P1 Debat. *P1 Debat* (8 July). Danmarks Radio P1.

Delanty, Gerard. 2005. The idea of a cosmopolitan Europe: On the cultural significance of Europeanization. *International Review of Sociology – Revue Internationale de Sociologie* 15(3): 405–421.

DR. 2010. Deadline (8 July). *Deadline 22.30*. DR2.

European Roma Rights Centre (ERRC). 2010. *ERRC Challenges Danish Expulsion of EU Roma*. Errc.org. www.errc.org/cikk.php?cikk=3675.

Faist, Thomas. 2013. The mobility turn: A new paradigm for the social sciences? *Ethnic and Racial Studies* 36(11): 1637–1646.

Fekete, Liz. 2014. Europe against the Roma. *Race & Class* 55(3): 60–70.

Franquesa, Jaume. 2011. We've lost our bearings: Place, tourism, and the limits of the mobility turn. *Antipode* 43(4): 1012–1033.

Frello, Birgitta. 2008. Towards a discursive analytics of movement: On the making and unmaking of movement as an object of knowledge. *Mobilities* 3(1): 25–50.

———. 2011. Romaerne På Fælleden: Om at Krydse Globale Fortællinger. *Akademisk Kvarter: Tidsskrift for Humanistisk Forskning* 2(2): 102–116.

———. 2015. On Legitimate and Illegitimate Blendings: Towards an Analytics of Hybridity. In *Researching Identity and Interculturality*, edited by Fred Dervin and Karen Risager, 193–210. London: Routledge.

Frese, Mads. 2010. Minoritetsdebat: Fransk roma-politik får hård kritik. *Information* section 1 (19 August): 5.

Grill, Jan. 2012. 'Going up to England': Exploring mobilities among Roma from Eastern Slovakia. *Journal of Ethnic and Migration Studies* 38(8): 1269–1287.

Information. 2010a. Ledende Artikel: Se hvor ulækkert vi opfører os 9 July.

———. 2010b. Ledende Artikel: Lakmusprøven for civiliserede samfund. *Information* section 1 (19 August): 5.

Iovita, Radu P., and Theodore G. Schurr. 2004. Reconstructing the origins and migrations of diasporic populations: The case of the European gypsies. *American Anthropologist* 106(2): 267–281.

Kabachnik, Peter. 2009. To choose, fix, or ignore culture? The cultural politics of gypsy and traveler mobility in England. *Social & Cultural Geography* 10(4): 461–479.

———. 2010. Place invaders: Constructing the Nomadic threat in England. *Geographical Review* 100(1): 90–108.

Koefoed, Lasse, and Kirsten Simonsen. 2007. The price of goodness: Everyday nationalist narratives in Denmark. *Antipode* 39(2): 310–330.

Kongstad, Jesper. 2010. Romaer er uønskede i EU-lande. *Jyllands-Posten* section 1 (July 31): 13.

Lee, Ken. 2000. Orientalism and gypsylorism. *Social Analysis* 44(2): 129–156.

Lucassen, Leo, Wim Willems and Annemarie Cottaar. Eds. 1998. *Gypsies and Other Itinerant Groups: A Socio-Historical Approach*. Basingstoke: Macmillan.

Malkki, Liisa. 1992. National Geographic: The rooting of peoples and the territorialization of national identity among scholars and refugees. *Cultural Anthropology* 7(1): 24–44.

Mayall, David. 2004. *Gypsy Identities, 1500–2000: From Egyptians and Moon-Men to Ethnic Romany*. London: Routledge.

McGarry, Aidan. 2010. *Who Speaks for Roma? Political Representation of a Transnational Minority Community*. New York: Continuum.

The Ministry of Foreign Affairs of Denmark. 2013. *Twentieth and Twenty-First Periodic Report of Denmark Concerning the International Convention on the Elimination of All Forms of Racial Discrimination*. Copenhagen: Author.

Nacu, Alexandra. 2012. From silent marginality to spotlight scapegoating? A brief case study of France's policy towards the Roma. *Journal of Ethnic and Migration Studies* 38(8): 1323–1328.

ny i danmark.dk. 2011. Pressemeddelelse: Intergrationsministeren: EU-borgere risikerer fortsat udvisning, hvis de begår kriminalitet. *Nyidanmark.dk*. www.nyidanmark.dk/da-dk/Nyheder/Pressemeddelelser/Integrationsministeriet/2011/April/integrationsministeren_euborgere_risikerer_fortsat_udvisning.htm.

O'Nions, Helen. 2014. Some Europeans are more equal than others. *People, Place & Policy Online* 8(1): 4–18.

Pantea, Maria-Carmen. 2012. From 'making a living' to 'getting ahead': Roma women's experiences of migration. *Journal of Ethnic and Migration Studies* 38(8): 1251–1268.

———. 2013. Social ties at work: Roma migrants and the community dynamics. *Ethnic and Racial Studies* 36(11): 1726–1744.

———. 2014. On pride, shame, passing and avoidance: An inquiry into Roma young people's relationship with their ethnicity. *Identities* 21(5): 604–622.

Parker, Owen. 2012. Roma and the politics of EU citizenship in France: Everyday security and resistance*. *JCMS: Journal of Common Market Studies* 50(3): 475–491.

Pietarinen, Kati. 2011. Green voices for inclusion. In *Roma and Traveller Inclusion in Europe. Green Questions and Answers*, edited by Kati Pietarinen, 7–10. Brussels: Green European Foundation.

Politiken. 2010. Ledende Artikel: Politiken mener: Orden. *Politiken* section 1 (9 July): 1.

Pressemeddelelse. 2010. *Udlændingeservice*. nyidanmark.dk. 2010. Udlændingeservice. Pressemeddelelse. www.nyidanmark.dk/da-dk/nyheder/nyheder/udlaendingeservice/2010/juli/us-afviser-23-romaer.htm.

Reding, Vivane. 2010. *Statement on the Latest Developments on the Roma Situation*. Speech/10/428. European Commission. http://europa.eu/rapid/press-release_SPEECH-10-428_en.htm.

Rövid, Márton. 2011. One-size-fits-all Roma? On the normative dilemmas of the emerging European Roma Policy. *Romani Studies* 21(1): 1–22.

Ruby, Jørn Uz. 2010. Folket ingen vil have. *Jyllands-Posten* section 1 (4 September): 14.

Salazar, Noel B. 2011. The power of imagination in transnational mobilities. *Identities: Global Studies in Culture and Power* 18(6): 576–598.

Sigona, Nando. 2003. How can a 'nomad' be a 'refugee'? Kosovo Roma and labelling policy in Italy. *Sociology* 37(1): 69–79.

———. 2005. Locating 'the Gypsy problem': The Roma in Italy: Stereotyping, labelling and 'nomad camps.' *Journal of Ethnic and Migration Studies* 31(4): 741–756.

Sigona, Nando, and Nidhi Trehan. 2009. Introduction: Romani Politics in Neoliberal Europe. In *Romani Politics in Contemporary Europe: Poverty, Ethnic Mobilisation, and the Neoliberal Order*, edited by Nando Sigona and Nidhi Trehan, 1–20. Basingstoke: Palgrave Macmillan.

Simmel, Georg. 1964. The Stranger. In *The Sociology of Georg Simmel*, 1, edited by Kurt H. Wolff. Free Press paperback edition, 402–408. New York: Free Press.

Stewart, Michael. 2013. Roma and Gypsy 'ethnicity' as a subject of anthropological inquiry. *Annual Review of Anthropology* 42: 415–432.

Tavani, Claudia. 2012. *Collective Rights and the Cultural Identity of the Roma: A Case Study of Italy*. Studies in International Minority and Group Rights, 3. Leiden: Brill.

Thomsen, Claus Blok. 2010. København vil af med romaerne. *Politiken* section 1 (6 July): 1.

Thornton, Gabriela Marin. 2014. The outsiders: Power differentials between Roma and Non-Roma in Europe. *Perspectives on European Politics and Society* 15(1): 106–119.

Tileagă, Cristian. 2006. Representing the 'other': A discursive analysis of prejudice and moral exclusion in talk about Romanies. *Journal of Community & Applied Social Psychology* 16(1): 19–41.

Urry, John. 2000. *Sociology beyond Societies: Mobilities for the Next Century*. International Library of Sociology. London: Routledge.

Wallberg, Filip. 2010. Kommunen: Vi kan hegne fælleden ind. *Ekstrabladet.dk*. http://ekstrabladet.dk/112/article1349496.ece.

Wæver, Ole. 1995. Securitization and Desecuritization. In *On Security*, edited by R. D. Lipschutz, 46–85. New York: Columbia University Press.

Westh, Asger, and Carsten Ellegaard. 2010a. Politiet advarer mod sigøjnere. *Jyllands-Posten* 30 May.

———. 2010b. Sigøjnere kan ikke sendes hjem. *Jyllands-Posten* Section 1 (30 May): 1.

Willems, Wim. 1951–1997. *In Search of the True Gypsy: From Enlightenment to Final Solution*. London: Frank Cass.

Wolff, Janet. 1993. On the road again: Metaphors of travel in cultural criticism. *Cultural Studies* 7(2): 224–239.

Part III

Mobilised infrastructures

8 For the power, against the power

The political discourses of high-speed rail in Europe, the United States and China

Ander Audikana and Zenhua Chen

There's no reason why we can't do this. This is America.

President Barack Obama (16 April 2009, Washington DC)

The public has had many questions regarding the cause and handling of the crash. I think that we should listen to the public and seriously address their questions and provide responsible answers.

Premier Wen Jiabao (28 July 2011, Wenzhou)

We are all *No TAV*.[1]

Beppe Grillo (14 February 2013, Susa)

Introduction

The development of mobility infrastructures has traditionally been subject to political considerations in order to assure national security, strengthen territorial integration and build national markets (Button 2006). More recently, other arguments in terms of economic competitiveness and sustainability have been adopted by public authorities. Mobility infrastructures, as a particular type of sociotechnical networks, can be considered as 'Machiavellian instruments of power' (Summerton 1999, 94) or as apparatuses of security in order to ensure that 'things are always in movement' but 'in such a way that the inherent dangers of this circulation are cancelled out' (Foucault 2007, 65). They structure social and territorial configurations, and their significance varies over space and time.

High-speed rail (HSR) systems represent major mobility infrastructures of contemporary network society. From the early 1960s, several countries have promoted the construction of HSR systems. In some countries, HSR networks have already been developed while other countries are planning to have HSR systems in the next decades. All these developments, which involve a large amount of capital investment and have important territorial impacts, have been extensively studied by economists, engineers and geographers whereas the political significance of HSR projects has not been systematically considered.

This chapter proposes a comparative analysis of the political discourses related to the development of HSR in Europe, the US and China. HSR is at different stages of development in these three contexts. In Europe, HSR has been established for many years, while in the US, HSR projects are expected to be launched in the future. China possesses the world's largest HSR network. Our analysis focuses on how HSR systems can be subject to different political significances. It is necessary to understand how these mobility infrastructures are continuously (re)conceptualised in political discourses. Following Latour (2013, 338), the political discourse refers to 'how to connect beings to others so that the collective holds together', since 'the political has to allow beings to pass through and come back while tracing an *envelope* that defines, for a time, the "we", the group in the process of self-production'. Under this perspective, we form the hypothesis that political discourses on HSR have played a role in shaping different groups, collectives or subjects. Two research questions are addressed. First, what different types of political subjects can be identified in relation to HSR systems? We assume that three different political subjects can be considered by following Foucault's theory, namely, the population, the public and the people. Second, what are the differences and similarities between the three empirical contexts analysed in relation to each political subject? Our study shows that while HSR systems have been presented in a relatively similar way in relation to the functional demands of the population, there are fundamental differences in the way the public and the people have been politically shaped in different contexts.

This chapter is based on empirical research[2] and a literature review of studies from the perspectives of sociology and political science. We analyse the meaning and function of the HSR issue in political discourses. How has HSR been politically enounced (meaning)? In which context and through what strategies (function)? The approach is partially inspired by a Foucauldian methodological intuition: 'what interests me in discourse is that someone has said something at a given time. I am not investigating the meaning but the function attributable to the fact that something was said at that particular moment' (Foucault 2001, 467). Nevertheless, it is not our objective to look 'behind the curtain', since – as affirmed by Deleuze, 'that everything is always said in every age is perhaps Foucault's greatest historical principle' – 'politics hides nothing' (1988, 54). By describing 'what has been said' on HSR 'by someone at a given time', we explore complementarily the meaning attributed and the strategies associated to HSR systems. Admittedly, the corpus of political discourses on HSR (including speeches, governmental reports, interviews, charters, public comments, Internet opinions, etc.) is vast. In order to avoid possible misinterpretations, the analysis and results provided by other researches remain critical.

The discussion is organised as follows. In the next two sections, the analytical framework is introduced by discussing how mobility studies have conceptualised the interplay between mobility and power. Then, the analytical distinction between the three types of political subjects is presented. Based on this triple distinction, the three subsequent sections empirically illustrate how, through the discourses on HSR, different political subjects are shaped in Europe, the US and China.

The interplay between mobility and power

Although much attention has been focused on analysing the practices and representations of mobility, the 'new mobilities paradigm' seems not to have systematically investigated the political significance of mobility. Sheller and Urry (2006, 211) suggest that 'it is not a question of privileging a "mobile subjectivity", but rather of tracking the power of discourses and practices of mobility in creating both movement and stasis'. However, it is significant to note that these authors do not mention scientific fields such as political science, international relations or public policy analysis as contributors to the formation of the 'new mobilities paradigm'.[3] Some scholars admit that 'the role of power in mobility' is 'still [a] very open question' (Jensen 2011, 255). Söderström et al. (2013, 10) have recently considered that in order to explore the 'critical potential of mobility studies', it is necessary to 'address explicitly the interplay of mobility and power'. Bærenholdt (2013, 20–21) affirms that there is a 'dominating interest in, if not even fascination with, the micro-sociology and phenomenology of mobile practices rather than macro issues' and concludes that 'when dealing with issues of power, hegemony and social order, mobility studies are rather vague'. This seems especially true from a state-centred perspective, since the new mobilities paradigm has not yet made a contribution to political theory.

It is probably Cresswell (2010) who has conceptualised this interplay better through his article on the politics of mobility. Considering mobility as an entanglement of movement, representation, and practice, he seeks to understand how and to what extent mobility can be 'powerfully political'. The author goes beyond the research on inequalities of mobility (Kaufmann et al. 2004; Ohnmacht et al. 2009) and addresses the question of 'how mobility becomes political'. While the analytical framework proposed by Cresswell is useful to better understand how mobility becomes a political issue, it does not provide insights on the *effects* of this evolution in terms of political mobilisation.

The literature on technical networks and infrastructures is more relevant to understand the political *effects* of mobility issues analysing both how power is exercise through infrastructures of mobility, and how these are eventually contested. Graham and Marvin (2001, 392) show that although the 'technological mobilities' may contribute to the 'secession' or 'partition' of metropolitan space, 'strategies of resisting' urban splintering can also be constructed. They follow Swyngedouw (1993, 195) when this author suggests that 'the changed mobility' 'associated with the installation of new mobility commodities and infrastructure may negatively affect the control over place of some while extending the control and power of others'. Oosterlynck and Swyngedouw (2010) show how a controversy around air traffic management at Brussels Airport was followed by strong local opposition that cancelled the consensual management strategy led by the administration. In this example, a controversy around air traffic management becomes an issue for 'proper political engagement' seeking to rebalance the inequalities related to the production and consumption of mobility. Equally, Jensen and Richardson (2004, 238), when they introduce the term of monotopia – defined as one-dimensional discourse of space through which the construction of seamless networks is promoted – also consider the 'possibilities for new resistance counter-understandings of place'.

These interrelated dynamics of domination and resistance around mobility issues have been theoretically mentioned by some scholars based on Foucauldian analytical perspectives. Jensen (2011, 268) notes that 'as power is always joined by resistance', subjects participate in shaping and making mobility and mobile practices 'from below'. When investigating the construction of the transnational mobile subjects, Jensen and Richardson (2007, 148) suggests that such a strategy 'should not be read as a full account of the politics of mobility' 'but one part of the story of the contested production of future transnational mobility' where 'local struggles and resistances play a part'. Inspired by the concept of governmentality, Bærenholdt (2013, 29) develops the concept of governmobility that refers to 'a situation where the regulation of mobilities are internalised in people's mobile practices'. In this view, the dynamics of domination and resistance seem completely associated, even inseparable.

From this literature review, two elements must be retained for further investigation. First, we propose to focus on the effects of mobility in terms of political mobilisation: how do mobility and mobility infrastructures influence power relationships? Second, in order to understand how mobility affects power relationships, it is necessary to consider the dynamics both of domination and resistance. In order to do so, we propose to turn our attention to the way mobility issues shape political subjects.

Discourses on political subjects: the population, the public, the people

Since Machiavelli, much political theory has focused on political means or instruments. The concept of governmentality itself developed by Foucault emphasises the importance of considering the modern State 'as a practice' (Foucault 2007, 277), which refers to the idea of apparatus. The concept of apparatus has been adapted into public policy analysis through the concept of policy instrument (Halpern et al. 2014). An apparatus is 'a notion of generative social technologies, which combines words and things in installing certain dispositions' (Bærenholdt 2013, 24). Moreover, when we consider HSR projects as apparatuses of security, we also refer to the activity of 'arranging things in order to lead them', 'it is not a matter of imposing a law on men, but of the disposition of things' (Foucault 2007, 99). We assume that an apparatus is a tool-setting patterns of conducts. More precisely, from a spatial point of view, the apparatuses of security seek to plan a 'milieu' defined as 'that in which circulation is carried out' (ibid., 21). Foucault considers circulation as 'movement', 'change of place', but also as 'freedom' (ibid., 48–49). These apparatuses are not supposed to control the territory but to maximise the possibilities of mobility/freedom. That is why we propose to understand HSR projects as concrete means in order to ensure circulation in contemporary societies:

> Freedom is nothing else but the correlative of the deployment of apparatuses of security. An apparatus of security . . . cannot operate well except on

condition that it is given freedom, in the modern sense [the word] acquires in the eighteenth century: no longer the exemptions and privileges attached to a person, but the possibility of movement, change of place, and processes of circulation of both people and things. I think it is this freedom of circulation, in the broad sense of the term, it is in terms of this option of circulation, that we should understand the word freedom, and understand it as one of the facets, aspects, or dimensions of the deployment of apparatuses of security.

(ibid., 48–49)

However, if politics is essentially considered as an activity of creating collectives (Latour 2013), one should consider which types of groups, collectives or subjects can emerge as a consequence of the implementation of these particular apparatuses of security. Depending on how they are enounced, these apparatuses would contribute to creating or consolidating different political subjects. The objective is to shift our attention from the political means to the political subjects. We assume that apparatuses of security are conceptualised in discourses in relation to some particular political subjects. Specifically, by adapting Foucault's theory, it can be hypothesised that the apparatuses of security need to be considered in relation to three different political 'personages' or 'subjects': the population, the public and the people. (See Figure 8.1.) We will briefly discuss each of them.

According to Foucault, the population is the very central collective subject of the modern apparatuses of security. The population is at the same time an object and a subject: it is an object 'on which and towards which mechanisms are directed in order to have a particular effect on'. It is also a subject 'since it is called upon to conduct itself in such and such a fashion' (Foucault 2007, 43). The population is considered as a phenomenon of nature and a set of elements that 'form part of the general system of living beings' (ibid., 366). As a biological entity, the population has one mainspring of action: desire. Foucault indicates that

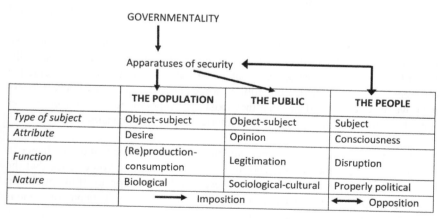

GOVERNMENTALITY

Apparatuses of security

	THE POPULATION	THE PUBLIC	THE PEOPLE
Type of subject	Object-subject	Object-subject	Subject
Attribute	Desire	Opinion	Consciousness
Function	(Re)production-consumption	Legitimation	Disruption
Nature	Biological	Sociological-cultural	Properly political
	Imposition		Opposition

Figure 8.1 Foucault's concept of governmentality (Source: Diagram by authors.)

since 'every individual acts out of desire' and 'one can do nothing against desire' (ibid., 72), the problem 'is how to say yes to this desire' and 'concerns rather everything that stimulates and encourages this self-esteem' (ibid., 73). Foucault concludes that 'we have a population whose nature is such that the sovereign must deploy reflected procedures of government within this nature, with the help of it, and with regard to it' (ibid., 75).

Although in some cases, the public is considered as one aspect of the population, we propose to establish an analytical distinction between these two entities. The public is the 'population seen under the aspect of its opinions, ways of doing things, forms of behaviour, customs, fears, prejudices, and requirements; it is what one gets a hold on through education, campaigns, and convictions' (ibid., 75). The public goes beyond the idea of biological entity. When Foucault deals with the concept of the public, he refers to opinions or representations. He presents the public 'as subject-object of a knowledge': subject of a knowledge that express an 'opinion' and object of a knowledge since the State seeks to 'modify opinion' and, along with opinion, the 'way of doing things', the 'way of acting', the 'behaviour as economic subjects, and as political subjects' (ibid., 275). Unlike the population, the public is not moved by desire but rather by its opinions. The public is supposed to provide legitimation to the governmental structures.

The third political personage considered by Foucault is the people. The people is conceived as a force of resistance or contestation on the part of those who do not accept to be part of the population. We consider the people a conscious autonomous subject that makes opposition to the apparatuses of security implemented under a dynamic of governmentality. It is characterised by the disruptive effects of its action:

> The people comprises those who conduct themselves in relation to the management of the population, at the level of the population, as if they were not part of the population as a collective subject-object, as if they put themselves outside of it, and consequently the people is those who, refusing to be the population, disrupt the system.
>
> (Foucault 2007, 43–44)

Although the people is to some extent considered in opposition to previous ones, these three political subjects are closely related to one another. They represent different forms of political collectives that have been conceived and have emerged in different historical contexts in relation to some particular exercise of power. However, we make the hypothesis that they exist contemporaneously and overlap over time. Foucault suggests such a mutual interrelation, when he states that:

> When one speaks of obedience, and the fundamental element of obedience in government is the people who may engage in sedition, you can see that the notion of 'population' is virtually present. When one speaks of the public on whose opinion one must act in such a way as to modify its behaviour, one is already very close to the population.
>
> (Foucault 2007, 277)

This chapter considers HSR systems as apparatuses of security that contribute to shape these three political subjects. HSR systems contribute to the formation of the population, considered as a biological entity, but they also act through education, campaigns, convictions in order to transform the public's attitudes, ways of doing things or ways of living. In addition, the implementation of HSR systems may lead to disruptive situations or even revolts carried out by the people, the group that enounces HSR systems in a different manner. The following sections empirically illustrate how these three political subjects are conceptualised and shaped in relation to HSR systems in Europe, the US and China.

The population as the target object-subject of a convergent political discourse

In the three empirical contexts, we assume that HSR systems have been primarily considered as instruments to create, increase and maintain mobility while eliminating its dangers or negative impacts. Under such a hypothesis, the principal target of these instruments is the population. HSR systems aim to 'stimulate' and 'encourage' the self-esteem and the desire of mobility of the population but at the same time to guarantee the 'security of the population', neutralising the perverse effects or risks related to the development of mobility.

In Europe, it is notably based on the idea of the European HSR network, considered as a continental underground, that HSR systems have been presented as instruments to act upon population. The European authorities garnered no interest in HSR until the Paris-Lyon HSR line was achieved in France during the early 1980s. The commercial success of the HSR service attracted much attention from other European countries including the United Kingdom, Belgium, the Netherlands and Germany. Led by France, these countries worked together in the hope to develop an international HSR network (Hughes 1988). During the same time, the Community of European Railways submitted a proposal for building a continental HSR network to the European authorities for approval (CER 1989). This proposal was later approved and became a part of the contemporary European transportation policy (Fragola 2007). It also served as an instrument of a more ambitious cohesion strategy and a factor to maximise benefits of the single market (CEC 1990).

The idea of a European HSR network further facilitates the formation of the Trans-European Networks (TEN) programme. The Treaty of Maastricht stated that to achieve the objective of internal market and economic and social cohesion, 'the Community shall contribute to the establishment and development' of TEN in the areas of transportation, telecommunications and energy infrastructures. Since then, the European authorities have promoted the construction of the European HSR network as a part of the TEN programme. During the same time, the initial motivations have been progressively completed by new arguments such as sustainability and security. The commissioner in charge of mobility and transportation stated in 2010 that the development of future HSR connections 'remains a key priority of several European programmes' and the 'completion of these projects will soon give the Union and its citizens a true HSR network' that will 'allow its users to travel in conditions of improved comfort and safety while at the same time reducing their impacts on the environment' (EC 2010, 1). The 2011 'White Paper on a Single European Transport Area', known as the road map 'towards a competitive and resource efficient transport system', plans to complete the European high-speed rail network by the year of 2050 (EC 2011).

The HSR systems are in this context part of the 'seamless networks' intended to ensure 'frictionless functionality of the EU territory' (Jensen and Richardson 2004, 234). They seek to promote mobility, while dealing with frictions such as those related to comfort, sustainability and security. Although the European spatial policy can also be understood as a contribution to European identity (Jensen and Richardson 2004, 247), we consider that the functional aspects, especially now, are predominant over those associated with identity. The HSR systems are hence essentially elaborated within a discourse of the Europe of flows that is primarily oriented to market integration and competitiveness (Hajer 2000, 138). Equally, the 'mobile subjects' of the European transnational space must be considered as the advantaged individuals of the population who 'desire particular forms of mobility' and whose 'movements are motivated and can be shaped through economic incentives' (Jensen 2013, 42). Given this perspective, HSR systems contribute to stimulating a new highly mobile fraction of the population. It is not by accident that Favell (2008, 10–11) employs the term of population to refer to the 'pioneers of the European integration' ('this population – the *Eurostars* as I call them'): 'the key population heralding the building of a new Europe beyond the nation-state'.

In the US, the HSR programme announced by the Obama administration in 2009 was part of the American Recovery and Reinvestment Act of 2009 and was supposed to contribute to economic recovery through job creation. The programme identified 11 HSR corridors across the country. The development of HSR was presented as a way to deal with the economic crisis as it was supposed to further the transition strategy towards the development of green transportation industries, promoting green growth and economic competitiveness. Considering the transportation system as the lifeblood of the economy, the construction of a rail network is expected to 'help serve the needs of national and regional commerce in a cost-effective, resource-efficient manner, by offering travellers and freight convenient access to economic centers' (DOT 2009, 3). Other objectives also considered refer to the risks of collapse and friction related to the American mobility system. Then Secretary of Transportation Ray LaHood, stated that 'we face a complex set of challenges in the 21st century building a robust, green economy, gaining energy independence, reversing global climate change, and fostering more liveable, connected communities' (ibid., no page). At the presentation of the new programme, Vice President Joe Biden, stressed the importance of the HSR programme as an instrument to ensure mobility and to cope with 'congestion' and 'suffocation':

> With high-speed rail system, we're going to be able to pull people off the road, lowering our dependence on foreign oil, lowering the bill for our gas in

our gas tanks. We're going to loosen the congestion that also has great impact on productivity, I might add, the people sitting at stop lights right now in overcrowded streets and cities. We're also going to deal with the suffocation that's taking place in our major metropolitan areas as a consequence of that congestion.

(White House 2009, no page)

The HSR programme in the US is presented explicitly as the infrastructure of mobility that will support the development of a new economic model, avoiding the collapse of the system. Minn (2013, 189) considers the HSR programme as a rational Keynesian response that 'would annihilate space by time and render a spatial or mobility fix to the crisis' and 'facilitate circulation of labor and consumers'. For Minn, HSR is a 'medium for the production of space to meet the needs of capitalism'. In sum, a new spatial arrangement is proposed in order to ensure that 'things' will be again rapidly put in movement.

In China, the HSR programme must be considered not as a response to a situation of crisis but as part of the economic development strategy carried out over recent years in that country. After a decade of investment and construction, China has become the country with the highest HSR mileage in the world. With the rapid growth of its economy, the existing passenger rail service was not able to meet the exponential increase in travel demand. One of the objectives of developing HSR infrastructure is to provide fast and convenient passenger rail services to satisfy the need of the increasing travel demand. Another objective for developing HSR in China is to reduce regional disparity. In 2004, the State Council approved China's first Mid- to Long-Term Railway Network Development Plan, which proposed to build four north-south and four east-west HSR lines to connect major economic centres. In July 2011, during the Beijing-Shanghai high-speed railway launch ceremony, the former Chinese Premier Wen Jiabao stated: 'the construction of Beijing-Shanghai High-speed Railway is an important decision made by the Communist Party of China Central Committee and State Council. It has great significance in improving the modern Chinese transportation system and promoting economic and social development and meeting people's demand for travel' (Wen 2011).

The Chinese HSR policy seems less related to the problems of mobility in terms of security, environmental problems and comfort, and it is designed to provide the population an alternative way to move faster and farther. Indeed, while in Europe and the US, HSR policies have been implemented in response to problems such as roadway and air traffic congestion, the Chinese HSR projects have been launched in parallel to the development of motorisation and air traffic. In this view, the Chinese HSR systems seem to provide a necessary spatial arrangement to the 'new population' currently emerging as a consequence of economic development.

When considering HSR systems in relation to the population as target political subject, we note a relative convergence in the political discourses of HSR. In the three cases considered, the question raised is how things can be kept in movement while avoiding dangers. Although HSR policies in Europe, the US and China have emerged and developed in different historical contexts, they all seem to have been associated with a universal conception of the population. The same apparatuses are applied everywhere by governments in order to stimulate or accompany the demand or the desire for mobility among the population. Equally, except in China where dealing with the dangers and problems related to mobility is not a major priority, HSR systems are presented as solutions to respond to the problems of security, environmental impacts and comfort. Alternative spatial arrangements are not considered, and any different type of development to offer the population is excluded.

The construction of different publics: specific governmental discourses on HSR

The population is not the only target subject that governments consider when implementing HSR systems. We make the hypothesis that HSR projects are also apparatuses through which opinions, attitudes and ways of doing things can be transformed, and in so doing, the public can be shaped. While we suggest that the population is a universal subject that is present in the three cases analysed, in this section we show that the public is specifically shaped in each case. This specificity results from the diversity of discourses and conceptualisations elaborated locally by governments in relation to HSR projects.

Without denying that HSR was originally presented by European authorities as an instrument to promote the integration process (Ross 1994), we argue that the discourses on HSR targeting the public have been primarily elaborated at national and regional levels. Indeed, the political significance of HSR varies among European countries. While HSR has been a prevalent issue in some national political arenas, it attracts less attention in other countries. In small countries, such as Belgium, the Netherlands, Denmark and Switzerland, since HSR systems are not crucial from the internal transportation perspective, the political significance of HSR is low. In countries where more incremental rail modernisation strategies have been adopted, such as in Sweden and, to some extent, Germany (Perl 2002), HSR systems have carried less political significance. In contrast, HSR has been a major political issue in countries such as France, Italy, Spain, Portugal and, more recently, the United Kingdom. While in France and Spain, HSR policy is traditionally based on national consensus, in Italy, Portugal and the United Kingdom, it is a matter of controversy.

In France, the national railway industrial agents have played a major role in the evolution of HSR policy during its conception and initial implementation (Fourniau 1995). The French government has subsequently decided to extend the network based on territorial considerations and in response to local demand. The TGV (Train à Grande Vitesse) is seen as the result of the French state-based policy-making style (Dobbin 2001) representing the 'French grandeur'. Former President Nicolas Sarkozy stated, in this regard, that 'the TGV, it's France' (VRT 2011), while Jean-Marie Le Pen, France's former far-right leader, remembered that 'the TGV, it's France and not Europe' (LNO 2007). In Spain, HSR has become a major political object at both the national and the local levels and represents, in the words of former president of government, José Luis Rodríguez Zapatero, a 'governmental continuity' (Audikana 2012, 319). In Spain, where the HSR services have been denominated 'Spanish HSR' or AVE (Alta Velocidad Española), the development of this mobility infrastructure has been directly linked to territorial integration. Regional authorities have considered HSR projects as instruments to reinforce internal identity, especially in Catalonia, the Basque Country and Andalusia. Bel (2010) has shown that different Spanish governments have planned and implemented a radial railway network to reinforce political centralisation. Indeed, one of the ideas inspiring Spanish strategy is to connect Madrid with all provincial capitals. This strategy has partially involved Portugal where the plans to connect Lisbon with Madrid were strongly criticised by the political opposition before being abandoned. In Italy, where Silvio Berlusconi frequently presents himself as the major advocate for HSR (Berlusconi 2013), and in Germany (Albalate and Bel 2012), HSR has been presented as a national cohesion policy to solve issues of territorial disparities, respectively between the north and south, and the west and the east.

The preceding brief overview summarises the diversity of political significances associated with HSR development, which vary depending on different contexts and political traditions. European national and regional authorities have weakened the functional conceptualization in terms of market merge and have reinforced instead the identities of the publics through the implementation of HSR projects. In some cases, the idea of a European network is nationally adapted in order to legitimise HSR projects. While some HSR services have been named Eurostar, more local institutions present these projects as national or regional priorities. In this context, the territorial dimension in terms of national/regional identity and cohesion has played a very central role in the political discourses of HSR projects.

In the US, the HSR programme is regarded as the government's signature transportation initiative of the Obama presidency. The political discourse on HSR is directly linked to the 2008 electoral campaign rhetoric about *change* and contains at least two complementary significances. Firstly, the governmental initiative represents an attempt to involve the American society in a common strategy led by the federal administration. In so doing, the federal government affirms its role as central stakeholder shaping the American society, since the actions of Washington are traditionally questioned in the US. Secondly, the HSR initiative brings a significantly different vision of the US position in the world. The federal administration, considering that the US has 'lagged behind other countries in developing modern intercity passenger rail' (DOT 2009, 6), advocates learning from the experiences abroad. In this regard, the implementation of HSR should require a technological transfer, resulting in an unusual situation in the largest economy of the world.

Moreover, the HSR programme involves a cultural change. When scholars have attempted to examine the challenges of implementing HSR in the US (De Cerreño et al. 2005; Dobbin 1993; Perl 2002), they have frequently mentioned the cultural dimension in order to explain why HSR is not likely to be developed in the US. For example, Minn (2013) suggests that the debate over HSR in the US reveals a contradictory sentiment on HSR by the American public. While HSR may provide linkages to solve American spatial contradictions, the idea of HSR in the US may be futile given the unique characteristics of contemporary American urban form as reflected in an automobile society. Indeed, although the railway's role in shaping the culture of the US can be considered more deterministic than its European counterpart (Perl 2002), it is commonly assumed that the US developed a strong automobile culture during the second half of the 20th century. Thus, some of the core values of the American society such as individualism, anti-statism, populism and egalitarianism seem to be better materialised through private transportation (Chen 2012). During the presentation of the new programme, President Obama offered his own vision of change, pointing out the possible cultural resistances:

> Imagine boarding a train in the center of a city. No racing to an airport and across a terminal, no delays, no sitting on the tarmac, no lost luggage, no taking off your shoes. Imagine whisking through towns at speeds over 100 miles an hour, walking only a few steps to public transportation, and ending up just blocks from your destination. I know Americans love their cars, and nobody is talking about replacing the automobile and our highways as critical parts of our transportation system.
>
> (White House 2009, no page)

The HSR programme represents, in this regard, not just an attempt to transform the territorial and industrial infrastructure as a part of the economic recovery strategy; it is also an instrument to intervene in the opinions, attitudes or ways of life of the American public. It is especially this cultural transformation of the American society that the HSR programme evokes that is directly contested in some cases.

In contrast, the HSR policy in China symbolises the success of a distinctive model of modernisation. The HSR development in China represents one of the most notable achievements during the Jintao Hu's presidency. The Beijing-Shanghai line, for example, is regarded as a national pride, and its launching date coincides with the 90th anniversary of the Communist Party (Singh 2011). In addition, almost all Chinese HSR trains are branded as Harmony, which is actually the major political slogan during Hu's presidency. The rapid development of HSR in China demonstrates the endeavour of the Chinese political leadership in implementing a national strategy and promoting its achievements all over the world. Weiwei considers that the HSR policy reflects the Chinese development strategy over the last decades:

> China has adopted Tian Ji's strategy, i.e. in a situation where your overall strength is weaker, you should be aware of and make the best use of your comparative advantages, and create and build up your own asymmetric

strengths over your opponents and eventually win. This is what China has done with regard to shaping its own standards in HSR development.

(Weiwei 2012, 107)

Nevertheless, the development of HSR in China also reveals the limits of its modernisation model, since HSR development seems often to have been used by bureaucrats and governmental officials for individual benefits due to the non-transparent institutional structure and the centralised political characteristic of the Chinese railway system. Ma and Adams (2013) indicate that the Chinese HSR programme provides linkages among the growth strategy, technological ambition and political interests. The train accident that occurred in 2011 on the Yongtaiwen HSR line, for example, reveals the scandal of the former railway minister, Zhijun Liu, who was named as the father of China HSR and Great Leap Liu because of his strong efforts in pushing ahead with the ambitious plans of HSR development. As a railway minister, he promoted HSR projects in order to win political allies by awarding contracts and, during the crisis of 2008, convinced other leaders that HSR plans should be accelerated to boost economic growth.

Despite these limits, the development of HSR systems seems to play a relevant role in symbolising and legitimising the modernisation strategy led by the Chinese government. In this context, it is possible to affirm that the HSR projects have not only served to respond to the population's demands or desires of mobility induced by the economic growth, they have also been an opportunity to show the public the beneficial effects of such a strategy.

The people against HSR: disruptive and heterogeneous mobilisations

The analysis now focuses on the dynamics of contestation against the HSR systems led by the people. The people contest HSR systems as apparatuses oriented towards both the population and the public, presenting its desires as well as its opinions that are radically different from those of the population and the public.

HSR policies have encountered several oppositions in Europe over the last decades. The protests have primarily been organised in countries such as France, Spain and Italy where HSR policies have been more ambitious. Some of the major HSR-related protests have taken place in Val di Susa (Italy), the Basque area (Spain and France) and the Rhone Valley (France). These protests have usually involved local communities, environmental associations and left-wing radical groups.

Shared territorial identity is a common characteristic of HSR protests in Europe. Without a sense of 'solidarian community' (Bobbio 2007, 219), protests are not likely to survive. In some cases, such as in the French side of the Basque Country (Rui 2001) or, more recently, in Chiltern Hills in the United Kingdom (Marshall 2012), the territorial identity is notably based on the solidarity between house and land owners, while protesters in the Spanish Basque Country defend small towns, agricultural land and the 'motherland' (Audikana 2012). In Val di Susa, citizens' committees and squatted social centres participating in protests have also been territorially rooted (Della Porta and Piazza 2008).

In general, protesters have articulated a broader justification against HSR through a generalisation process (Lolive 1999). Firstly, they consider that HSR causes huge environmental damages without bringing an effective response to problems related to transportation, energy consumption and pollution. Secondly, HSR is considered as a wrong public spending decision, which diverts financial resources away from other local transportation investments or other social policies. Thirdly, HSR is viewed as an elitist transportation solution benefiting few people. Finally, protesters criticise the lack of participation during the decision-making process, which 'is seen as an expression of inefficiency and inadequacy in the mechanisms of representative democracy, against which protesters propose an alternative model of local democracy' (Della Porta and Piazza 2008, 111). In some cases, new decision procedures have been adopted in France (Lolive 1999) and several local consultations organised in the Basque Country (Barcena 2009).

Based on these arguments, the opposition to HSR systems represents an opportunity to elaborate broader political discourses. Opposing HSR becomes an opportunity, for example, to question the national political systems, the European integration model or neo-liberal development. Such political discourses were initially elaborated in France (APOTN 1991) and have been extensively developed during the protests in Val di Susa and the Spanish side of the Basque Country. In 2010, several associations from France, Spain and Italy elaborated a common document that summarises the claims expressed over the last decades:

> These projects constitute an ecological, socioeconomic and human disaster for the territories they cross . . . These projects are unable to lead to the participation of the population in decision processes . . . We oppose the aberrant expansion of transport provoked by the globalized capitalism, and which does not allow a uniform local development, but on the contrary supports abnormal concentration of the traffics and productions and a wild delocalization.
>
> (Charter of Hendaye 2010, no page)

Despite these efforts, the political consensus in favour of the HSR programmes remains strong. This situation has changed in Italy, where the Five Star Movement[4], led by the comic actor Beppe Grillo, has supported opposition to the HSR project in Val di Susa. The local opposition to the HSR project inspires this anti-establishment movement that opposes both the national political system and the European integration model. When Beppe Grillo stated that 'we are all *No TAV*' during the 2013 Italian general election campaign, he assumed that opposition to HSR policy also represented the opposition to the establishment. The local opposition against the HSR project symbolised the national wish for social change and new politics.

In the US, it is notably in California, where a project for a HSR line to connect the Bay area to the Los Angeles metro area is envisaged, that a strong local opposition has emerged. Although the HSR project in California was supported by the former Schwarzenegger administration, Democrat representatives at the state legislature have been the strongest proponents of it. The HSR project, which was backed by Californian voters in 2008, is currently being contested locally by several groups in the Bay Area and the Central Valley. In the Bay Area, several local groups, environmental associations and city councils have expressed their opposition to the project due to the concerns of environmental impacts, technological difficulties, the lack of transparency during the decision-making process and the negative impacts on properties. In general, the opponents in the Bay Area are located in the Peninsula and represent a highly qualified and well organised upper class.

In contrast to the liberal contestation in the Bay Area, opposition in the Central Valley and Southern California is more conservative and communitarian. Led by business and farmers organisations, the opposition in the Central Valley combines the economic concerns related to the agricultural industry and about environmental justice with the defence of a singular way of life including values such as territorial identity, 'hard work' or a sense of family. Local population has also expressed its opposition during the public review process, since the project is not considered to have benefits for local communities.

These local opposition campaigns have been directly influenced by the position that conservative think tanks and Republican representatives have adopted across the nation. Conservative think tanks, such as the Cato Institute and the Reason Foundation, have actively combated the federal initiative. By questioning the economic, environmental and transportation-related benefits of the HSR, these organisations consider that the success of HSR in the US is far less probable than in other countries. They point out that American taxpayers will have to bear the cost of a transportation system serving only a few states and benefiting a high-income population. Based on these criticisms, the opposition to the federal HSR programme has emerged in the political arena led by Republican representatives. The most obvious examples of such an adverse sentiment on HSR are the federal grant rejections in Florida, Wisconsin and Ohio by their new elected Republican governors in 2011 and 2012. Local Tea Party activists in some cases have played a decisive role in these decisions (APTA 2012).

In this situation, opposition to HSR in the US has been conducted principally by conservative and anti-statism groups that consider HSR as an example of interventionism into social life, a boondoggle and, to some extent, a cultural intrusion. Through their opposition to HSR projects, these groups seek to reaffirm and defend some fundamental values of the American society.

In China, the development of HSR encounters a variety of criticisms. Although they have not evolved into a system-wide movement, they have acquired visibility through media reports, Internet blogs and demonstrations. One of the major criticisms is concern about the potential impact on public health and environment. Nowadays, new proposed HSR plans are harder to implement than before because of the strong opposition from environmental groups and local communities. For example, the Beijing-Shenyang HSR project has been postponed for two years since its initial planning due to the heavy opposition from residents who live very close to the proposed line in Beijing.

A similar opposition occurred in Shanghai in 2008 when the local government announced the plan to extend the existing magnetic levitation (maglev) train service from its current terminal in downtown Shanghai to Hangzhou city. Because the system would run through a few residential areas in Shanghai, many residents protested and opposed the project, fearing that the maglev system might be too noisy and produce electromagnetic radiation. In order to avoid any direct conflict with the government, local residents expressed their opposition in a gentle way: 'they took a "stroll" (*sanbu*) rather than conducting a demonstration' in front of the local government buildings (He 2013, 129).

A major HSR-related protest campaign was held in reaction to the 2011 train accident that killed more than 40 people and injured at least 192. After the accident, the government responded extremely fast to bury the derailed carriages and restricted media coverage, which rapidly flamed public discontent via Internet and micro blogs nationwide (Bondes and Schucher 2014). In this situation, the government was obliged to back down. As observed by Saich (2013, 118), 'photos and comments critical of the response and suggesting a cover-up spread quickly' and 'even the official media criticised the Ministry of Railways and official account for the accident'.

HSR-related mobilisations have also arisen from a sense of patriotism. At the early stage of HSR train procurement in 2003, the government encountered huge public opposition when it decided to adopt the Japanese Shinkansen technology. Because Japan had built the Manchurian railroad in the 1930s and used it to invade China, a large number of citizens signed petitions to urge the government not to adopt the Japanese HSR technology (Reilly 2008). Consequently, the government had to consider the public sentiment and opinions, and a more open bidding process was implemented for rolling stock procurement.

Public discontent regarding HSR also comes after the completion of the projects. Problems of HSR quality and reliability have been reported periodically by social media, which further raises public concerns for HSR safety. For instance, the HSR pricing system has recently earned public criticism. HSR is normally designed as a premium travel service that targets upper-class travellers, like business people. Given the fact that the majority of the passengers in China who choose the train as their long-distance travel option are from middle- and low-income groups, this market orientation causes huge public discontent. The governmental web portal itself acknowledged this controversy.[5]

Although HSR-related mobilisations in China do not seem to have developed a general and structured political discourse frontally opposing the governmental HSR programme, HSR has been criticised by the people because of discontent regarding inappropriate arrangements during the implementation process. The mobilisation of the people around HSR projects has raised the issues of non-transparency, corruption and social justice. The issue of the HSR is an opportunity to address demands for internal transformation rather to propose completely alternative development models.

Conclusion

In order to further investigate the interplay between mobility and power, this chapter has explored how HSR, as a particular mobility infrastructure, is continuously (re)conceptualised in political discourses in Europe, the US and China in relation to three different political subjects: the population, the public and the people.

It suggests that a convergent political discourse on HSR has been constructed in relation to the population in the three cases analysed. HSR systems have been conceived as apparatuses or instruments aimed to provide a spatial arrangement to the demands and desires for mobility by the population, considered primarily as a biological and functional entity. In the three cases, HSR systems seek to ensure higher levels of mobility and to deal with problems related to increasing circulation. Such political discourse on HSR has been applied and adapted to different contexts. In Europe, HSR systems have been promoted as a way to ensure the integration of the European market and to improve the quality of mobility in terms of comfort, security and sustainability. In the US, the political discourse on HSR has been elaborated in the context of the recent economic crisis. In this context, HSR systems have essentially been presented as the mobility infrastructures by which an economic transition can be completed. In China, HSR systems have been elaborated in order to respond to the mobility desire and demands of the 'new population' that has emerged in parallel to the economic modernisation process. The Chinese HSR network structures the territorial platform to respond to the new mobility patterns.

Of course, these demands and desires for mobility have been not individually elaborated but socially constructed. The efficacy of the political discourses reside in the ability to promote these claims as a way to reach individual satisfaction and well-being, while presenting these infrastructures as necessary for the social system as a whole.

In contrast to the relative convergence of the political discourse on HSR in relation to the population, the public − considered as a territorially defined political subject characterised by its opinions − has been differently shaped by governmental authorities. In Europe, discourses on HSR have primarily targeted the publics at the national and local levels, especially in recent times. Based on HSR systems, national and regional authorities have envisioned the internal territorial integration in terms of social cohesion and national/regional identity. In the US, HSR represents a cultural transformation that directly challenges the American way of life. In China, the achievements in HSR development are a way to legitimise to the Chinese public the modernisation model implemented by governmental authorities.

Lastly, this chapter discusses how, in some cases, alternative political discourses have been elaborated by the people more or less directly contesting HSR programmes. These alternative political discourses on HSR vary considerably among the three contexts analysed. In Europe, opposition to the HSR is led by left-wing political parties, environmentalist and alternative political groups. HSR is often regarded by these groups as a symbol of neoliberalism, as an elitist's policy or as an imposition. The opposition presents the opportunity to advocate for alternative development models, social justice and more participation in decision-making. In contrast, in the US, the opposition has been conducted principally by conservative and anti-statism groups that consider HSR as an example of interventionism into social life, a boondoggle and, to some extent, a cultural intrusion. Through their opposition to HSR projects, these groups seek to reaffirm and defend some fundamental values of the American society. In China, the mobilisation around HSR projects has raised issues regarding non-transparency, corruption and social justice. Since Chinese mobilisations in general have not frontally challenged the government's HSR policy, these mobilisations can be placed in the context of internal democratisation and reform of the political system.

A study of the political discourses on HSR suggests that mobility infrastructures play a relevant role in shaping contemporary political subjects. In a context where much attention is focused on the way that Internet and information technology affect power distribution and foster the emergence of new political subjects, this chapter illustrates how mobility infrastructures are powerful apparatuses around which the dynamics of political domination and resistance are organised. Instead of considering that politics will simply disappear in a world of increasing mobilities, this chapter suggests that mobility remains a very critical and universal element shaping political life, and vice versa, beyond different political regimes and societies. In sum, mobility remains 'one of the arenas in which the struggle for control and power is fought' (Swyngedouw 1993, 324).

The question that must be raised is why and to what extent can mobility be considered a specific issue structuring power relationships? At first view, the political centrality of mobility could be directly linked to its functional centrality in contemporary societies, since we have presented HSR projects as concrete instruments oriented to the constitution of a biological object-subject (the population). Nevertheless, the functional centrality (in terms of mobility) of HSR systems is far from being proven. In general, these infrastructures should be considered complementary or accessory to the main transportation networks (road and air transportation). Indeed, many advanced countries have not defined HSR development as a priority, and the number of passengers transported by this mode is lower than those using other global or local transportation systems. In this view, despite the importance of the population-oriented functional discourse or environmental arguments, it must be admitted that the functional role of HSR systems in terms of mobility does not seem critical in contemporary societies.

Two additional elements make it possible to reconsider the functional centrality of HSR systems. The first element is in relation to their material visibility. High-speed trains are 'physical animals' (Flyvbjerg et al. 2003, 1) with notable territorial impact and attracting considerable media attention. The second element is in relation to its technical fascination. HSR systems are still commonly recognised as technological innovations in the field of transportation. The technological added value is a critical argument in understanding their political attraction. These two elements are certainly essential to understanding the complexity of the functional dimension of mobility infrastructures. Furthermore, both elements have strong economic consequences in terms of investment, industrial development and job creation. Thus, these two elements reinforce the functional justification of such projects and the political attention consecrated to them.

Nevertheless, it would be a mistake to conclude that HSR systems are *essentially conceived in order to* boost economic growth, create jobs or contribute to industrial development. These arguments strengthen the functional justification of HSR policies, but they cannot be considered as 'real ones'. Indeed, similar arguments can also be evoked in other circumstances to justify other types of investments in other activity sectors with completely different goals. Although the real effects of HSR systems in terms of mobility cannot be always considered relevant, their specificity is directly linked to the issue of mobility.

At this point, we could be tempted to advance an 'ideological' explanation that would place the political discourses of HSR within a general framework. HSR systems could be understood as part of an ideological orientation that could be defined as 'neoliberal', 'capitalist' or 'developmentist'. However, such articulation would be an oversimplification. Our study shows several elements of this inherent complexity: HSR was initially developed in France (after Japan) in a Fordist/corporatist economic model; some of the stronger opponents to HSR can be defined, especially in the US but also in the UK, as fervent neoliberalists; HSR systems have been justified as an environmental solution in opposition to 'developmentism'. A generalised monotopia across the world cannot be excluded, since convergent territorial trends have been observed when considering HSR systems in relation to the population. But the development of HSR is not a sine qua non to qualify an ideological framework as 'neoliberal', 'capitalist' or 'developmentist'. In sum, we accept the fact that HSR has the function of ensuring that 'things are always in movement' and that it adopts different significations locally (involving the public and the people), but it is not possible to provide a label or to identify a whole ideological programme within which their promotion must be understood.

On the contrary, by describing the elaboration of political discourses, our analysis shows HSR systems as malleable objects that can be adapted to different contexts. This malleability can be linked to a specificity that seems to characterise mobility issues, namely, their integrative or inclusive nature. In contrast to other areas (such as education, health or housing but, also to some extent, telecommunications or energy), mobility is commonly conceived as an issue *potentially* affecting every community and member of the community. In a narrow sense, mobility *potentially* involves and structures a whole territory (city, country, continent). In a large sense, mobility *potentially* affects the life framework of every individual. Equally, opponents to HSR projects root their criticisms on communitarian solidarity or individuality principles. This *potentially* generalised involvement around mobility issues can immediately produce real (desirable or undesirable) effects for everyone. Thus, the integrative or inclusive nature of mobility issues in relation to every community and each member of the community facilitates the continuous development of political discourses that seek 'to connect beings to others so that the collective holds together'. It is this specificity of mobility issues that seems to be exploited continuously by political discourses.

All of this leads to a paradox: while the functional centrality of HSR within transportation systems cannot be considered critical, their political visibility is huge. HSR services operate limited routes serving some metropolitan areas and are usually aimed at a relatively restrained group of travellers. On the contrary, as mobility infrastructures, their disposition to hold the collective together explains the large political fascination. In a context where common goods become a rarity, this quality becomes essential for political investment. And that is why it is possible to affirm that in some contexts 'making politics' and constructing (or opposing!) HSR systems are activities that are not only inseparable, but ultimately they are not even distinguishable.

Acknowledgements

The authors would like to thank Professors Kenneth Button (George Mason University), Vincent Kaufmann (Ecole Polytechnique Fédérale de Lausanne), Anthony Perl (Simon Fraser University), Beatriz Pérez de las Heras (University of Deusto), Blas Pérez Henríquez (University of California, Berkeley) and María Luz Suárez (University of Deusto) for their support. They also thank the editors for their many insightful comments. A Fulbright-Schuman fellowship during the 2012/2013 academic year provided the authors the opportunity to collaborate in this project.

Notes

1 *No-TAV* (No High-Speed Train) is a social movement against high-speed rail policy in Italy.
2 Ander Audikana has completed his PhD dissertation on the politics of HSR in Spain and has also investigated the evolution of the HSR programme in the United States. Zhenhua Chen has completed different analyses focused on HSR planning and policies in China and the US. Overall, these researches combine decision-making analysis, economic evaluation and the sociology of mobilisation.
3 They mentioned disciplines such as anthropology, cultural studies, geography, migration studies, science and technology studies, tourism and transport studies and sociology.
4 Created in 2009, this political movement is inspired by ideas related to anti-corruption, environmentalism or direct/digital democracy. The Five Star Movement won 25 per cent of the votes in Italy's general election in 2013.
5 'New High-Speed Railway Spurs Debate over Prices'. Accessed 10 December 2013. http://english.gov.cn/2012–09/26/content_2233494.htm.

References

Albalate, Daniel, and Germà Bel. 2012. *The Economics and Politics of High Speed Rail: Lessons from Experiences Abroad.* Lanham, MD: Lexington Books.
APOTN (Alliance pour l'opposition à toutes les nuisances). 1991. *Relevé provisoire de nos griefs contre le despotisme de la vitesse à l'occasion de l'extension des lignes du TGV.* N.p.: Author.
APTA (American Public Transportation Association). 2012. *An Inventory of the Criticisms of High-Speed Rail with Suggested Responses and Counterpoints.* Washington, DC: Author. www.apta.com/resources/reportsandpublications/Documents/HSR-Defense.pdf

Audikana, Ander. 2012. *La politisation de la grande vitesse espagnole (1986–2011): Construction d'un mythe, production d'un consensus, émergence d'une controverse.* PhD dissertation, Université Paris-Est. Accessed 18 January 2016. www.theses.fr/2012PEST1039.

Barcena, Iñaki. 2009. Democracia versus alta velocidad, participación, información y consultas. In *TAV: Las razones del NO*, edited by Iñaki Barcena and Josu Larrinaga, 261–288. Tafalla: Txalaparta.

Bærenholdt, Jørgen Ole. 2013. Governmobility: The powers of mobility. *Mobilities* 8(1): 20–34. doi:10.1080/17450101.2012.747754.

Bel, Germà. 2010. *España, capital Paris: Origen y apoteosis del Estado radial: Del Madrid sede cortesana a la 'capital total'.* Barcelona: Destino.

Berlusconi, Silvio. 2013. *Silvio Berlusconi – L'alta velocita` ha un genitore Silvio Berlusconi.* YouTube. Accessed 18 January 2016. www.youtube.com/watch?v=D77RG5tRGvk.

Bobbio, Luigi. 2007. L'alta velocità in valle di Susa: Troppo decisionismo o troppo poco? In *Politica in Italia*, edited by Jean Louis Briquet and Alfio Mastropaolo, 209–228. Bologna: Il Mulino.

Bondes, Maria, and Günter Schucher. 2014. Derailed emotions: The transformation of claims and targets during the Wenzhou online incident. *Information, Communication & Society* 17(1): 45–65. doi:10.1080/1369118X.2013.853819.

Button, Kenneth J. 2006. Transportation and infrastructure. In *Handbook of Public Policy*, edited by B. Guy Peters and Jon Pierre, 323–338. London: Sage.

CEC (Commission of the European Communities). 1990. *The European High-speed Train Network.* Brussels: CEC.

CER (Community of European Railways). 1989. *Proposition pour un réseau européen à grande vitesse.* Paris: Author.

Charter of Hendaye. 2010. *Charter of Hendaye: Joint Declaration of 23 January 2310.* Accessed 18 January 2016. www.voiesnouvellestgv.webou.net/document/strasbourg/jointdeclaration.pdf.

Chen, Zhenhua. 2012. *Cultural Constraints on High-Speed Rail in the US: Is American Exceptionalism an Explanation?* Accessed 18 January 2016. http://dx.doi.org/10.2139/ssrn.2240989.

Cresswell, Tim. 2010. Towards a politics of mobility. *Environment and Planning D: Society and Space* 28(1): 17–31. doi:10.1068/d11407.

De Cerreño, Allison L. C., Daniel M. Evans and Howard Permut. 2005. *High-Speed Rail Projects in the United States: Identifying the Elements for Success.* San José, CA: Mineta Transportation Institute. Accessed 18 January 2016. http://transweb.sjsu.edu/MTIportal/research/publications/summary/0501.html.

Deleuze, Gilles. 1988. *Foucault.* Minneapolis: University of Minnesota Press.

Della Porta, Donatella, and Gianni Piazza. 2008. *Voices of the Valley, Voices of the Straits: How Protest Creates Communities.* New York: Berghahn.

Dobbin, Frank. 1993. Public Policy and the Development of High Speed Trains in France and the United States. In *High Speed Trains: Fast Tracks to the Future*, edited by John Whitelegg, Staffan Hulten and Torbjorn Flink, 124–144. London: Leading Edge.

———. 2001. Rail and Transport Policy: National Paradigms and Supranational Structures. In *Making Policy in Europe*, edited by Svein S. Andersen and Kjell A. Eliassen, 63–85. London: Sage.

DOT (Department of Transportation). 2009. *Vision for High-Speed Rail in America.* Washington, DC: Author. Accessed 18 January 2016. www.fra.dot.gov/Elib/Document/1468.

EC (European Commission). 2010. *High-speed Europe: A Sustainable Link between Citizens.* Luxembourg: Publications Office of the European Union. Accessed 18 January 2016. http://ec.europa.eu/transport/themes/infrastructure/studies/doc/2010_high_speed_rail_en.pdf.

————. 2011. *White Paper on Transport: Roadmap to a Single European Transport Area—Towards a Competitive and Resource-Efficient Transport System*. Luxembourg: Publications Office of the European Union.

Favell, Adrian. 2008. *Eurostars and Eurocities: Free Movement and Mobility in an Integrating Europe: Studies in Urban and Social Change*. Malden, MA: Blackwell.

Flyvbjerg, Bent, Nils Bruzelius and Werner Rothengatter. 2003. *Megaprojects and Risk: An Anatomy of Ambition*. Cambridge: Cambridge University Press.

Foucault, Michel. 2001. *Dits et écrits III (1976–1979)*. Le Foucault électronique, Folio Editions.

————. 2007. *Security, Territory, Population: Lectures at the Colle`ge de France, 1977–78*. Basingstoke: Palgrave Macmillan.

Fourniau, Jean-Michel. 1995. Problèmes d'histoire des grandes vitesses ferroviaires. *Revue d'histoire des chemins de fer* (12–13): 14–51.

Fragola, Fleur. 2007. *Vers une politique ferroviaire européenne: L'Europe à toute vapeur?* Paris: L'Harmattan.

Graham, Stephen, and Simon Marvin. 2001. *Splintering Urbanism: Networked Infrastructures, Technological Mobilities and the Urban Condition*. London, New York: Routledge.

Hajer, Maarten A. 2000. Transnational Networks as Transnational Policy Discourse: Some Observations on the Politics of Spatial Development in Europe. In *The Revival of Strategic Spatial Planning*, edited by Willem Salet and Andreas Faludi, 135–142. Amsterdam: Royal Netherlands Academy of Arts and Sciences.

Halpern, Charlotte, Pierre Lascoumes and Patrick Le Galès. 2014. *L'Instrumentation de l'action Publique, Controverses, Résistance, Effets*. Paris: Presses de Sciences Po.

He, Baogang. 2013. Political participation. In *Handbook of China's Governance and Domestic Politics*, edited by Chris Ogden, 120–130. London: Routledge.

Hughes, Murray. 1988. *Rail 300, the World High Speed Train Race*. London: David & Charles.

Jensen, Anne. 2011. Mobility, space and power: On the multiplicities of seeing mobility. *Mobilities* 6(2): 255–271. doi:10.1080/17450101.2011.552903.

————. 2013. Mobility regimes and borderwork in the European community. *Mobilities* 8(1): 35–51. doi:10.1080/17450101.2012.747780.

Jensen, Anne, and Tim Richardson. 2007. New region, new story: Imagining mobile subjects in transnational space. *Space and Polity* 11(2): 137–150. doi:10.1080/13562570701722014.

Jensen, Ole B., and Tim Richardson. 2004. *Making European Space Mobility, Power and Territorial Identity*. London: Routledge.

Kaufmann, Vincent, Manfred Max Bergman and Dominique Joye. 2004. Motility: Mobility as capital. *International Journal of Urban and Regional Research* 28(4): 745–756. doi:10.1111/j.0309-1317.2004.00549.x.

Latour, Bruno. 2013. *Inquiry into Modes of Existence: An Anthropology of the Moderns*, translated by Catherine Porter. Cambridge: Harvard University Press.

LNO (Le Nouvel Observateur). 2007. *TGV: les réactions*. Accessed 18 January 2016. http://tempsreel.nouvelobs.com/societe/20070403.OBS0429/tgvles-reactions.html.

Lolive, Jacques. 1999. *Les contestations du TGV-Méditerranée*. Paris: L'Harmattan.

Ma, Damien, and William Adams. 2013. *In Line behind a Billion People: How Scarcity Will Define China's Ascent in the Next Decade*. Upper Saddle River, NJ: Financial Times Press.

Marshall, Tim. 2012. *Planning Major Infrastructure: A Critical Analysis*. London: Routledge.

Minn, Michael. 2013. The political economy of high speed rail in the United States. *Mobilities* 8(2): 185–200. doi:10.1080/17450101.2012.655973.

Ohnmacht, Timo, Hanja Maksim and Manfred Max Bergman. 2009. *Mobilities and Inequality: Transport and Society*. Farnham, Burlington, VT: Ashgate.

Oosterlynck, Stijn, and Erik Swyngedouw. 2010. Noise reduction: The postpolitical quandary of night flights at Brussels airport. *Environment and Planning A* 42(7): 1577–1594. doi:10.1068/a42269.

Perl, Anthony. 2002. *New Departures: Rethinking Rail Passenger Policy in the Twenty-first Century*. Lexington: University Press of Kentucky.

Reilly, James. 2008. Harmonious World and Public Opinion in China's Japan Policy. In *Harmonious World and China's New Foreign Policy*, edited by Sujian Guo and Jean-Marc F. Blanchard, 189–223. Lanham, MD: Lexington Books.

Ross, John F. L. 1994. High-speed rail: Catalyst for European integration? *Journal of Common Market Studies* 32(2): 191–214. doi:10.1111/j.1468-5965.1994.tb00493.x.

Rui, Sandrine. 2001. *L'expérience démocratique: Observation et analyse de l'implication des citoyens dans les procédures de concertation relatives à la mise en œuvre de projets d'infrastructure et d'aménagement*. PhD dissertation, Université de Bordeaux II.

Saich, Tony. 2013. Political Representation. In *Handbook of China's Governance and Domestic Politics*, edited by Chris Ogden, 109–119. London: Routledge.

Sheller, Mimi, and John Urry. 2006. The new mobilities paradigm. *Environment and Planning A* 38(2): 207–226. doi:10.1068/a37268.

Singh, Teshu. 2011. Beijing-Shanghai high speed railway: Strategic significance. *Inside China* July–September. Accessed 18 January 2016. www.ipcs.org/Inside_China_(July-Sep_2011).pdf.

Söderström, Ola, Didier Ruedin, Shalini Randeria, Gianni D'Amato and Francesco Panese. 2013. *Critical Mobilities*. Lausanne: EPFL Press.

Summerton, Jane. 1999. Power Plays: The Politics of Interlinking Systems. In *The Governance of Large Technical Systems*, edited by Olivier Coutard, 93–113. London: Routledge.

Swyngedouw, Erik. 1993. Communication, Mobility and the Struggle for Power over Space. In *Transport and Communications Innovation in Europe*, edited by G. A. Giannopoulos and A. E. Gillespie, 305–325. London: Belhaven Press.

VRT (Ville, Rail & Transports). 2011. *Nicolas Sarkozy: Le TGV, c'est la France*. Accessed 18 January 2016. www.ville-rail-transports.com/content/16373-nicolas-sarkozy-%C2%AB-le-tgv-c%E2%80%99est-la-france-%C2%BB.

Weiwei, Zhang. 2012. *The China Wave: Rise of a Civilizational State*. Hackensack, NJ: World Century.

Wen, Jiabao. 2011. *Premier Wen attends high-speed rail launch*. Accessed 18 January 2016. http://english.cntv.cn/program/newsupdate/20110630/108755.shtml.

White House. 2009. *Remarks by the president and the vice president on a vision for high-speed rail in America*. Accessed 18 January 2016. www.whitehouse.gov/the_press_office/Remarks-by-the-President-and-the-Vice-President-on-High-Speed-Rail.

9 Small technologies and big systems

Thomas Birtchnell and John Urry

This chapter is based on research under ESRC Project ES/J007455/1.

When you get to your car, you realise you have left your car keys (and the apartment keys) in the apartment. That's okay, because there is a spare apartment key hidden in the hallway for just such emergencies. (This is a safety device, a redundancy, incidentally). But then you remember that you gave a friend the key the other night because he had some books to pick up, and, planning ahead, you knew you would not be home when he came. (That finishes that redundant pathway, as engineers call it) (Perrow 1999, 8).

The role of the small

This chapter explores systems. Systems are what make the world go round. And much of the time systems work away without those whose actions presuppose such systems being aware that they are parts of such a system (or systems). It is often only when some event happens – the lost key, the broken spectacles, the mis-remembered password, the broken watch, the undelivered tickets, the uncharged battery, the credit card that suddenly no longer gives credit – that people realise just how dependent they are upon such systems and the array of diverse elements that comprise such systems in the contemporary world. This chapter is especially concerned with the history and future of so-called mobility systems and the disparate elements that make them up, especially the role played by what we call small technologies.

George Orwell nicely illustrates the importance of such small items within the experiences of everyday life. In *Down and Out in Paris and London*, he is surprised by a fellow homeless person who, despite having no access to facilities to wash, 'carried a razor and boot brush that he would not sell, though he had sold his "papers" and even his pocket-knife long since' (Orwell 1933, 131). For those outside of most systems – the homeless, poor or immobile – the ability of small technologies to be used across different systems makes these 'things' important. With Orwell's homeless friend, the razor not only allowed him to feel acceptable in society – being shaven meant that he did not attract attention – it linked him to emergency systems of welfare and work when life on the streets became too difficult.

Orwell also understood the importance of small technologies to personal freedom. In *Nineteen Eighty-Four*, Orwell interestingly describes a world where the ownership of personal items is forbidden, including items we take for granted, such as pens, paper, 'shoelaces and razor blades' (Orwell 1949, 9). Small technologies make effective life possible, and removing them from the population powerfully removes crucial elements of mundane citizenship. Their significance is also shown in Goffman's account of an individual's admission procedures into total institutions that remove and then process 'programme', 'trim', 'shape', and 'code' these small personal items (Goffman et al. 1997, 57).

Some systems are relatively simple since they are closed, with their conditions of functioning being rather like, or even literally, a 'laboratory'. Types of process engineering or wafer production form such a closed system. But social systems are not simple since they are comprised of many different and often contradictory elements. Systems that interpellate humans in some way or other possess various features that we will review, document and examine in this chapter.

Geels (2005b) has highlighted the importance of 'niches' within system transitions and plotted the different possible pathways across multiple levels as they move through so that they may develop into 'regimes' and ultimately whole new 'landscapes'. He suggests that some niches can be part of the existing landscape, 'incumbents', and still be involved in system transitions. Incumbent pre-existing technologies 'evade to other market niches' or 'hold on for a long time' but can also cross over into other systems and become central elements of them, not only as anachronistic technologies (Geels 2005a, 693). Mundane technologies that are already incumbent can be 'fitted' into existing practices as their users are practised and do not require much adjustment to apply them in different contexts. Thus incumbent elements of material cultures such as keys, shoes, spectacles and wallets can be elements of different systems through practitioners being unwilling to set aside well-accustomed small technologies and to adopt radical alternatives.

In this chapter, we discuss such 'incumbents' that map out new systems and suggest that, through them both being 'to hand' and also in combination with other new or incumbent 'elements', such technologies can cross systems and help to realise new systems. Disparate elements can be 'synchronized' into new systems (Urry 2011). A focus on these multiple large and small elements can inform research on new system transitions.

We show here that mobility systems presuppose very diverse elements that have to be contingently assembled and 'synced' (see Strogatz 2003). It is the diversity of elements that we emphasise, elements that often seem to have nothing to do with the 'system' as such. The significance of such diverse elements is under-examined in the literature on 'systems transitions' with regard to changing mobilities (see Schwanen 2007).

We show in particular that large-scale sociotechnical systems depend on small 'technologies' and that, when one plots the contours of sociotechnical change, it may be as much the small as well as the large scale that is relevant to how technologies develop. Thus more research needs to be undertaken on how significant small technologies pan out, combine, interconnect and transform different larger scale systems. We are concerned with various small technologies, some of which have nothing much to do with 'transport' per se, that then come to be part of what has been or can be 'assembled' into an existing or new mobility system. We now set out some features of these 'small technologies'. Subsequently, we demonstrate aspects of such technologies through the potential evolution of the small 'car key' into the equally small 'superfob'.

The first point to note is that there are often many varied elements within systems, both 'human' and 'non-human', which can get drawn into and become part of the system under investigation even though they may appear to have nothing to do with it and its environment. In particular, many 'non-transport technologies' come to be part of mobility systems. Examples include waterproof clothing and leisure walking, disposable cups and rail transport, combination locks and cycling, spurs and horse riding, car locks and keys and automobility, portable electrical devices (PEDs) and aeromobility and so on (see Urry 2007 on many of these). More generally, Arthur (2009) explains that new socio-technological systems generally involve 'combinations' of pre-existing elements. Novel mobility systems will involve the combining of many different and disparate elements, including some that appear to have little to do with mobility per se and that may seem insignificant.

Second, many elements or technologies are ambivalent in their nature and functioning, and they can be drawn into and become elements of quite different systems. The apparently same technology will vary in its effects when located within different systems. Some elements are thus ambivalent.

Third, such disparate and ambivalent elements do from time to time become combined with other systems. System-ness is a matter we might say of contingent assembly. Powerful effects follow, especially as these systems are not necessarily fixed in place but move about, transforming the material and social landscape.

Fourth, it is not just people, money or ideas that move, but so too do systems. Such systems can then exert powerful effects, as the automobility system has during the last century as it almost literally drove out all contenders to its powerful monopolisation of space and movement as it spread around the world (Dennis and Urry 2009, chapter 2).

Fifth, these small technologies are often embodied. They are carried on next to or close to the body and so acquire a kind of corporeality. They seem as important as bodily parts, or they are almost like organs of the body. So what appear as big, distant and overwhelming technologies often presuppose a wide and surprising array of small, intimate and embodied technologies, such as keys, bags, makeup, pads, phones, cards, pens, knives, purses, screwdrivers, wallets, sprays, receipts, books, paper and so on. These can be put to work because they enable many aspects of life to be routinely performed. This is especially important when people are on the go, away from 'home', and hence especially dependent upon mobility systems (see Watts and Urry 2008). To lose certain of these corporeal technologies can be viewed as being like losing an organ, as research on losing one's 'mobiles' or 'handies' shows in various contexts (Harper 2003; Mauer 2006; Ventä et al. 2008).

Sixth, small technologies do not always remain significant within a system since they may become mere 'ornaments'. The long-term life of a small technology does not mean that it continues to be functional within a system. Technologies can sometimes endure remarkably because they got there first and cannot be dislodged, even though they may be less functional and more ornamental.

Seventh, such closely coupled systems are only contingently secured since there can be what Perrow calls 'normal' accidents waiting to happen (1999). And in order to deal with such accidents, redundant pathways are developed as noted in the quote at the beginning of this chapter. And such redundancy is necessary because small events can potentially wreak damage upon closely coupled systems, as the Eyjafjallajökull ashcloud in April 2010 revealed. Minute particles of ash brought the aeromobility systems within Europe and North America to a standstill (Birtchnell and Büscher 2011). As the analysis of complex systems brings out, there are non-linear relations between causes and effects with no presumption that large changes presuppose large causes. Indeed, large technical systems often presuppose many small technologies; and these include the various techniques and systems of repair by both experts and users (Thrift 2005).

Finally, many of these small, intimate and embodied technologies are necessary for the system to spring to life and must not be forgotten, such as the car and apartment keys Perrow discusses (1999). So elements of large-scale systems are multiple small technologies. There are also various techniques by which people remember these small technologies, sometimes through mnemonics to make sure they are 'ready-to-hand'. Combinations of everyday objects are intrinsic to diverse routines and activities that need to be remembered in order that they are effectively deployed by systems over the course of the day. Thus certain routines that make up big systems (leave work, enter building, leave for basketball) could not be enacted without the small technologies (keys, wallet, phone, keycard) that are used for security, communication, identification and entertainment (see Davies et al. 2004, 42).

The different systems can be mobilised only if elements of material cultures are remembered and are present. Moreover, there can be redundancy, such as extra keys, spare spectacles, alternative credit cards and so on. But such redundancy may in turn generate complacency in one's remembering practices and lead to the crucial small technology being in fact forgotten. In the next section we look in more detail at the importance of remembering in enacting mobilities and also the processes involved in forgetting.

Remembering and forgetting

The book *After the Car* explores various intimations of a new system that might replace the car system in response to the intersections of changing climates, the peaking of oil supply a the proliferation of virtual worlds (Dennis and Urry 2009). As part of such a large-scale system change are many enduring, redundant and combining small technologies that link people with such systems. These small, embodied technologies can be taken for granted and make up the 'fine details' of human life.

A concern here is to establish their place in systems change in the past, present and future. People depend on embodied small technologies as elements of systems, so ambivalence can arise in how systems cope and standardise these diverse elements. These objects of keys, wallets, clothing, watches, credit cards and spectacles might seem simple, mundane and stable, but they can become crucial elements of systems, tied into habits of use and practice. Systems indeed form and reproduce habits, and these taken for granted habits are the stuff of social life and not easily changeable, certainly not by states, in which people have low trust, instructing people to change.

This dependency of big systems upon small, enduring and path-dependent technologies shows the power of mundane objects in promoting or hindering system change. The potential growth of a worldwide system of electric vehicles would seem to depend in part on generating the small technology of universal plugs that would fit all charging points in all countries and that could not be vandalised (The Royal Academy of Engineering 2010). Without such a small technology, which is more a matter of innovation and interoperability within the 'electricity industry', there is little prospect of the replacement of petrol-driven cars by a global fleet of electric vehicles.

The curiously named 'biscuit' can illustrate the importance of such small technologies. Colonel Robert Patterson revealed that US President Bill Clinton lost the 'biscuit' on two separate occasions, and Jimmy Carter sent his to the dry cleaners in a suit. The biscuit is a small disc containing the country's nuclear missile launch key codes, 'one of the most important symbols of military power' (Patterson 2003, 56). These systems that rely on remembering but are also prone to forgetting demonstrate that even those with system responsibilities can be prone to accidents at the level of the small technologies. Regardless of the importance to personal – and in the case of President Clinton global – welfare, the potential is there for anyone, including a US president, to forget or misplace the tiny items relied upon in complex systems. In this case, the tiny item was a necessary element in the most awesome of military systems ever devised. The likelihood of launching the country's warheads due to error was slight but above zero.

Small technologies like the 'biscuit' have the potential to wreak havoc in big systems. Even a simple shoe can be thrown as a weapon, as experienced by another US president, George W. Bush, at a press conference (Shoes Thrown at Bush on Iraq Trip 2008). Incidents such as these are reminders that the sophisticated practices of modern life depend on the taken for granted mundane objects often carried on the body and on the social practices, habits and routines associated with them. Such objects are combined and distributed on the body and often accessed as resources for various tasks as evidenced by the longevity of many taken-for-granted technologies.

The fact that important items can be forgotten, lost or discarded shows the taken for grantedness that occurs in people's relationships to the responsibilities and investments that bind them with the systems of which they are elements. It is an uneasy relationship that requires checks, borders, routines, reminders and interventions. Everyday taken for granted objects are in this sense 'high-risk technologies'. In the next section, we consider the disruptive power of the small.

Disruptions

The significance of small technologies is demonstrated in the BBC thriller *The Last Enemy*, first shown in 2008. This describes a near future world where a gifted mathematician is recruited as a consultant to develop a complex national identification system based upon identity cards, embedded bio-tags and the integration of multiple databases. The mathematician soon realises that this work is linked to the very systems that he takes for granted. When he becomes embroiled in a political intrigue involving his brother and using the side effects of tests of secret ethnic-specific chemical bio-tags, the small technologies and movements he takes for granted are closed down. In the final episode, he is frozen out of the systems and their integration that he helped to develop. His bankcards are frozen, his national identity card rejected, entry to his house refused and access to the rail system is blocked. His lack of access to digitised small technologies precludes the systems that underpin everyday life from operating. He is turned into a digital outcast through the disruptions of the small technologies.

Borgmann foresaw some dangers of depending upon such small digital devices. He says that they will have the advantage that 'we will be spared the possibility of losing the house key or of having it stolen' (1987, 115). But he was at the same time sceptical about the 'upgrading' of what he terms 'focal' things and practices by digital 'devices', warning that such change represents a major threat to the conditions of life. Thus losing an old-fashioned house key involves only a house key with no implications for many other small technologies unless they are all housed within the same bag. In *The Last Enemy*, the main character is not only rejected from his house when the key is lost but excluded from all systems when the digital device that consists of an RFID implant is blocked and meaningful movement and activity are entirely disrupted.

Borgmann's warnings about digital electronic devices are a reminder that small technologies can become compromised by the power of systems into which they are embedded. A copyright glitch in the Amazon copyright system meant that digital copies of Orwell's *Nineteen Eighty-Four* were automatically removed from personal Kindle e-readers without the owners' knowledge after they had been purchased (Striphas 2011, xvii). There is thus a more general dark side of the digitisation of these small technologies to which we return.

This in turn is related to the issue of standards. Standards allow the coordination of small technologies with larger systems. Designers and producers of new technologies seek to establish their product as the industry standard, or they try to shape it to an existing standard (Biggart and Beamish 2003). In light of this jockeying between design for compliance and design for exception, there is ambivalence in what is standardised at any time. The innovations that standards are set by occur not in a controlled, careful manner but often through 'tinkering' and experimentation, which can play a major role in system development (Dennis and Urry 2009, 108).

Such small technologies are relied upon for many different things that can be outside and across systems. For instance, in Kenya where many state and local finance systems are risky, 'mobile wallets' called M-Pesa, where M stands for mobile phones and *pesa* is Swahili for money, become 24-hour ATMs that allow safe, convenient and flexible transactions (Hughes and Lonie 2011). Intuitive uses of mobile phones allow leapfrogging over older currency formats such as bank-cards, coins and notes that are less secure to carry and exchange. The explosion of this use of phones has been through disruptive, grassroots innovation rather than top-down system change.

Science and technology writers describe this as the historical or contingent aspect of evolutionary change and term accumulations of these contingencies technological 'ecosystems' (Kelly 2010). In light of these 'natural' processes in the dynamics of large systems unforeseen consequences from minor accidents is part of the ambivalence in technologies that standardisation seeks to overcome but that it may actually enhance.

Indeed, different systems will presume different standards, but accidents may occur if systems happen to intersect. For instance, Perrow describes how the cabin of an aeroplane caught fire due to a failed circuit breaker and a bundle of wires that happened to pass behind a coffee maker on the plane (1999, 134). The different standards were adhered to, but no one had examined the possibility of a unique interface between the different systems.

Small technologies, then, form a set of personal resources that interface with all sorts of systems. The logistics of systems are set by common shared standards that are defined by social practices. Many redundant standards remain in common use, creating localised distinctions that engender ambivalence. Latour's example of the 'Berliner key' demonstrates this ambivalence (1992). This common key found in Berlin requires the user to remember to lock the door upon leaving and is frequently a source of confusion for those used to different standards in other regions. Travellers' abodes in Berlin are prone to burglaries due to this ambivalence as doors are often left unlocked by those used to the key standards of other places.

Norman highlights how personalisation occurs even in standardised, mass-produced technologies through individual acts of design. These have the effect of changing:

> the otherwise anonymous, commonplace things and spaces of everyday life into our own things and places. Through our designs, we transform houses into homes, spaces into places, things into belongings. While we may not have any control over the design of the many objects we purchase, we do control which we select and how, where, and when they are to be used.
>
> (Norman 2004, 224)

The designs of most mobility systems include complex safeguards. These safeguards are taken for granted and invisible when everything is running smoothly.

However, when they do not, significant disruptions arise. A report on an event on the London Underground stated, 'It is a difficult time in the control room. A suspect package has been found which requires a suspension of the service, and also a train captain has lost his keys which means that his vehicle cannot be operated manually' (Heath and Luff 2000, 148). Thus two small items, a package and a lost key, disrupt the otherwise smooth passages that the Underground system generally brings about.

In systems that require a very low tolerance of risk, small technologies are removed and replaced by those kept within the system's boundaries, such as hospital equipment or armaments. And often odd habits protect against normal accidents happening within different systems, such as sleeping with a 'gun under the pillow' as US President Franklin D. Roosevelt apparently did during his World War II presidency (MacMurray and Radford Jr. 2007, 327).

Certain kinds of small technologies can be particularly disruptive in aeromobility systems. The discomfort experienced at the airport scanner upon removing many small technologies (mobile, sprays, medicines, shampoos, keys, coins, shoes) is acute as the owner is 'denuded', exposed and made vulnerable to a 'digitised dissection' – now even a 'full body' scan (Marey et al. 2009). Items are screened and managed within strictly governed areas. And this is because small technologies have the power to disrupt and occasionally bring down aircraft. This was dramatically shown on 11 September 2001, when a particular network of objects and people caused monumental damage. Penknives, mobile phones, and pepper spray are simple objects but, combined, constituted a powerful 'actor-network' that, in the right place at the right time, could demolish the twin towers of the World Trade Center (Urry 2002). The 'shoe-bomber' also sought to mobilise a bomb housed in a humble shoe as a weapon of mass destruction but was caught when observed attempting to light a match on the tongue of his sneaker (Price and Forrest 2008, 72).

Small technologies empowered with digital connectivity present further complications to big systems. There are stringent international regulations on in-cabin use of what are termed PEDs (personal electronic devices). It is believed that in certain circumstances these can impact upon aircraft navigation systems. These PEDs include mobile phones, laptops, music players, small toys with RFID chips and wireless networking. The increasing presence of electronics within normal small technologies is the source of uncertainty in diagnosing the threat. While interference from common and known PEDs is reproducible in controlled conditions, it is the sheer range and possible combinations of small technologies, as well as the potential for people to regard them as essential to their lives and to breach regulations, that produces potential for significant disruption (Perry and Geppert 1996).

Thus the dangers posed by inadvertent small technologies such as disposable packaging and PEDs stem from their embodied taken for grantedness and also latent combinatory power. Such embedded and sometimes discarded objects are difficult to monitor, regulate and standardise without breaching privacy and the sanctity of the body. Thus most people now have on their person or in a small bag keys, wallets, spectacles and other items that are in some ways 'organs' of the body and improve movement through space and assist in daily activities. And when these wallets, keys or spectacles are lost, then people are suddenly vulnerable and suffer withdrawals not unlike the loss of an organ or limb.

We now consider the car key with regard to the automobility system and the potential development of the 'superfob' in a future 'Mobility Internet'. In past research, small technologies such as the pocket watch have been linked to the development of timekeeping and network capital (Larsen et al. 2006). As well, many small technologies have become 'embroiled' in driving and flying practices (Cresswell and Merriman 2011). In each case, a 'small' technology makes all the difference to the successful emergence of a potential mobility system.

From car keys to superfobs

In the UK, more than 250 hours per year are spent on 'small tasks' associated with cars, including looking for the car keys (Sloman 2006). The automobility system now dominant in most societies would not have developed into a widespread system without locks and car keys. Keys start the ignition and open lockable 'gloveboxes' in early designs and later enabled access to the enclosed locked interior. The idea of a secured mobility vehicle was unfamiliar before the so-called 'horseless age' (1903): horses could not be locked up! Early motor vehicles such as the Benz Velo and the Oldsmobile Curved Dash Runabout lacked an enclosed canopy, and in these and later early designs, motors were started by vigorously turning a crank.

While taken for granted now, social practices around remembering and setting up safeguards of spare or hidden keys, in cases of small technologies being lost, accompany the growth of personal automobile ownership and the reliance on automobiles for everyday tasks. Being able to leave automobiles unattended was crucial to developing systems of shopping, entertainment and commuting. The small technology of the lock and key played a pivotal role in constructing these emergent systems.

Routines for remembering keys were common in motoring lifestyle and popular interest magazines as the automobile became integrated into modern living. In the transition to cars with locks, custom fittings were available to attach a padlock to the door, a solution that would look strange today. At this time enclosed cars were generally 'not provided with door locks' (Locking the Closed Car 1924, 154). *Popular Mechanics* magazine included guides to many social practices around keys at the beginning of the automobile system, which created a new level of confusion when applied to multiple systems with which many people were unfamiliar. Such magazines offered much advice on how to install padlocks on car bodies, practices to store and remember keys and processes to enact when losing keys on a journey:

> Lost keys occasionally bring calls for help. The service manager advises having three keys, one at home, one on the key ring for the car, and the third on

the regular key ring in your pocket. The key at home is insurance against losing both the others, and, if you have a closed car, the one in your pocket guards against shutting yourself out of your own car by leaving the other in the ignition lock. One motorist, for example, had to hunt through the dark on a lonely country road for a rock to break a $12.50 plate-glass window of his car because he carried both keys on one ring, and left the bunch in the lock.

(Adventures of an Auto Trouble Shooter 1924, 1011)

The organising of security around keys allowed cars to be developed as storage facilities for other belongings and even as temporary homes. The success of the Model T Ford was partly due to its closed body and superior security, including an ignition key.

As dependencies grew around locked cars and keys, new potential normal accidents emerged. As Nye notes:

When faced with an inadvertently locked automobile with the keys inside, for example, one has a problem with several possible solutions – in effect, a story with several potential endings. One could call a locksmith, or one could use a rock to break one of the car's windows. Neither is as elegant a solution as passing a twisted coat hanger through a slightly open window and lifting the door handle from inside.

(2006, 3)

Thus automobiles have now been embedded in complex systems of shopping, for example, combinations of small technologies underlying these large transport technologies and play equally important roles in sustaining path dependencies. Yet it is at this level that disruptions to such systems can occur as crises outside the boundaries and standards set by supermarkets or system designers:

Let's take for instance the problem situation that occurs when you accidentally lock your car keys inside the car after a trip to the supermarket. Clearly this situation involves a problem that requires a solution . . . Clearly, you are posed with a problem that you will have to overcome, but what is your goal? Is it to regain access to the car keys in the car? Not if you have access to a spare set of keys that a friend can readily bring over. Is it to be able to drive the car again? Not necessarily if your greatest need is to return home as rapidly as possible. The search for a solution is not directed toward a single, unique goal, but involves a continuous weighing of different needs, including the estimated damage to the automobile, the cost of lost time, returning home or making appointments promptly, and so on.

(Brey 2001, 47)

Systems with many complex parts in effect gamble against these normal accidents becoming cumulative crises. The potential for these sorts of everyday 'normal' accidents to undermine systems is a matter of probability: a supermarket car park full of people locked out of their cars by accident is a highly unlikely – or abnormal – accident that can render a system immobilised, as well as a cascade into other systems. Much recent innovation has concentrated on making small technologies that combine various functions into an all-in-one device to manage security, banking, communications and identification. In this drive for an all-in-one device, the small car key looks set to undergo radical transformation.

Mitchell and his MIT collaborators mobilise the notion of the superfob as a central element of their programme to 'reinvent' the automobile through what they term a 'Mobility Internet'. They argue that people will be able to save time and money by deploying the superfob to integrate connectivity inside and outside the vehicle. It 'will dock into the vehicle's interior and provide all the navigation, music, radio, movie, and Internet content the driver needs' (Mitchell et al. 2010, 48). So, for them, part of the shift to a post-car system would involve a superfob as the basis of digital communications.

There are various ways of developing a superfob, a 'fob' being an attachment to a car key that combines many small technologies for convenience. One example of this is the *eierlegendewollmilchsau*, which is a combined bank card, transit ticket and car-sharing access key (Dennis and Urry 2009). These all-in-one devices seek to combine the functions of many taken for granted small technologies. The combination into one small technology represents an uncluttering of taken for granted objects. These new composite devices are 'personal servers' that can link to various digitally enhanced built environments. In this idea, users interact with common locations to establish routines and set off reminders and safeguards at specific points of the day through embedded RFID chips and readers.

Developing this further is BMW's prototype 'superfobs' and Apple Computer's recent patents for future iPhone devices, the iKey and iWallet, combining a mobile phone with sensors and chips. This would eliminate coins, keys and cards in the way that mobile phones have replaced wristwatches for many users. The idea of a 'superfob' clusters all embodied technologies into one device that can lock a car, pay for a ticket, make a purchase from a store and unlock one's front door.

An article in *The Guardian*, sponsored by LG, describes 'the World of the Future: How Technology is Transforming Our Lives'. It provides the examples of spoons with sensors, lamp posts that connect to mobiles and networked cars 'more like a shopping cart' that can be summoned wirelessly and stacked (Jha 2011). However, with these uncluttered futures, there is more at stake when items are lost as they are no longer taken for granted. Thus cascading failures can occur with such 'uncluttered' small technologies:

> The term 'cascading failure' refers to when the failure of one element of a network is able to bring the entire network to its knees. If you lose your house keys today it's a problem but hardly the end of the world. In the future, though, you won't have house keys: you'll have smartcard or biometric entry, and if your card gets lost or the fingerprint reader breaks down it really will be a headache because it will all be linked to all the other devices inside your house.
>
> (Watson 2008, 28)

Material and technological networks are likely to be connected to systems of mobility, creating network paradoxes of global connections and local disconnection (Graham and Marvin 2001). As Gershenfield points out, an extended reliance on digital possessions enhances the consequences arising from accidents:

> There is a disconnect between the breathless pronouncements of cyber-gurus and the experience of ordinary people left perpetually upgrading hardware to meet the demands of software, or wondering where their files have gone.
>
> (1999, 8)

In GM's Mobility Internet concept, small networked cars called EN-Vs are dependent on personal 'servers', or digital storage and communications technologies, in a superfob, a combined device including keyfob, music player, cell phone and map (Mitchell et al. 2010). The future projection of a ubiquitous 'superfob' as a concept device allows connectivity to a networked society of small cars. While cutting out many issues with redundant pathways, the superfob presents different types of risks in combining a range of devices. Cybercrime and ID theft, digital terrorism and hacking would play out in the physical world amidst the entire breadth of society, possibly excluding individuals from their homes or causing major traffic network accidents.

Combinations of networked, automated and digital infrastructures of smart vehicles controlled through superfobs raises the spectre of complex and covert user heresies, such as hacking, presenting new unforeseen circumstances and precipitating 'abnormal accidents' that might cascade into different systems. These types of connected combined devices are even more 'locked in' than the small technologies that make up the usual repertoire of everyday life.

The changing material cultures of objects such as wallets, keys, and shoes are due to their resilience and independence across many different systems. Modelling future systems of transport on a Mobility Internet has scope for minimising accidents and increasing efficiencies in traffic flows; however, while digitisation offers many efficiencies and the possibility of automating personal routines, a new class of possible accidents is generated from code-based [invisible] small innovations.

Different companies offering various versions of superfobs also challenge the notion of an uncluttered future free from accidents. The idea of uncluttering involves 'removing things [small technologies] that do not matter' so that loss, misuse and negligence are limited by standards set by oneself:

> [C]ar keys will end up in the same place when you walk through the door of your home, your paperwork on your job will always end up in the proper file folders, and your car will render a more pleasant driving experience because your car seats (and possibly the floor of your car) won't carry a lot of excess items that aren't needed as you travel from day to day.
>
> (Sanders 2008, 44)

Historically, transportation and communications have been based upon differ-ent systems. A post-car reinvention of the automobile would entail integrating the two, and it seems for many current innovators it is the superfob that would affect the apparently seamless integration of movement and communications. This small technology of the superfob is viewed by Mitchell and his team as key to a post-car new mobility system. Looking back at how the material cultures of objects such as wallets, keys, shoes and other small technologies have become elements of some systems (automobility) but also have disrupted other systems (aeromobility), there is a heightened likelihood in combining them together for generating more normal accidents.

Conclusion

Mobilities are thus not just about horses, planes, trains, boats and automobiles. Many of the taken for granted possessions carried on or close to the body are imbued with agency when combined with others and applied within sets of social practices in order to make systems work. Accompanying bearers in movement, they act as important interfaces to big mobility systems. Movement thus depends on 'non-transport' technologies; otherwise the car would not start without keys; the horse would not go faster without spurs; the train ticket could not be pur-chased without credit cards; the border could not be crossed without ID cards and passports; public spaces would not be traversable without shoes, clothes, and spectacles; the post-car system would not develop without the superfob and so on.

Small technologies, often taken for granted and unnoticed, can thus affect big systems. Small technologies can be part of the identities of users allowing people to do their jobs and defining their status, self-worth and capabilities. Such embod-ied agency makes small technologies difficult to standardise and regulate. They are often ambivalent. These small technologies and associated practices vital in managing and remembering them have many unintended consequences in daily life. These include precipitating accidents for individuals (through losing their keys), normal accidents in systems (horse and car accidents) and powerful disrup-tions of the system (for example on September 11).

Thus in tracking and tracing mobilities, bodies are important, and so too are the transport technologies and the big systems of which they are a part; however, the myriad of small technologies that sit between these act to link them, particu-larly when future scenarios present unique changes to their composition and roles. These transitions will necessitate new social practices and engender social values and change that might be deeply resisted when considered as part of the social 'fabric'.

Further, small technologies can become obsolete (planned or naturally), or they can endure as function or ornament. People and the small technologies they carry – as consumers, travellers and citizens – are central elements of systems rather than external to them. Their social practices are shaped by and facilitated through various small technologies. In transport planning and policy, understand-ings of sociotechnical change have predominantly focused on the direct impacts of specific 'transport' technologies and not upon the small, often hidden and taken for granted technologies that engender system development. Future system changes may come about through initiating a 'small technology' that has a big system change effect. Innovation may come from unexpected sources or directions – leftfield – but sometimes are incumbent; many small technologies may come to be combined unpredictably because they are in effect already within the existing 'landscape' but get relocated within a different system. This may even come to make a different large sociotechnical system. If there is sociotechnical change, then small technologies will surely be a crucial element of any new such system.

References

Adventures of an Auto Trouble Shooter: How to Prevent Breakdowns on the Road. 1924. *Popular Mechanics* 42(6): 1005–1011.

Arthur, W. B. 2009. *The Nature of Technology: What It Is and How It Evolves.* New York: Free Press.

Biggart, N. W., and T. D. Beamish. 2003. The economic sociology of conventions: Habit, custom, practice, and routine in market order. *Annual Review of Sociology* 29: 443–464.

Birtchnell, Thomas, and Monika Büscher. 2011. Stranded: An eruption of disruption. *Mobilities* 6(2): 1–9.

Borgmann, A. 1987. *Technology and the Character of Contemporary Life: A Philosophical Inquiry.* Chicago: University of Chicago Press.

Brey, P. 2001. Herbert Dreyfus: Humans versus Computers. In *American Philosophy of Technology: The Empirical Turn*, edited by Hans Achterhuis, translated by Robert P. Crease, 37–63. Bloomington: Indiana University Press.

Cresswell, T., and P. Merriman. Ed. 2011. *Geographies of Mobilities: Practices, Spaces, Subjects.* Farnham: Ashgate.

Davies, N., E. D. Mynatt and I. Siio. 2004. *'UbiComp 2004: Ubiquitous Computing' 6th International Conference., Proceedings, Nottingham, UK, September 7–10*, Berlin, Heidelberg: Springer.

Dennis, K., and J. Urry. 2009. *After the Car.* Cambridge: Polity.

Geels, F. 2005a. Processes and patterns in transitions and system innovations: Refining the co-evolutionary multi-level perspective. *Technological Forecasting and Social Change* 72(6): 681–696.

———. 2005b. The dynamics of transitions in socio-technical systems: A multi-level analysis of the transition pathway from horse-drawn carriages to automobiles (1860–1930). *Technology Analysis & Strategic Management* 17(4): 445–476.

Gershenfeld, N.A. 1999. *When Things Start to Think.* New York: Henry Holt.

Goffman, E., C. C. Lemert and A. Branaman. 1997. *The Goffman Reader.* Malden, MA: Wiley-Blackwell.

Graham, S., and S. Marvin. 2001. *Splintering Urbanism: Networked Infrastructures, Technological Mobilities and the Urban Condition.* London: Routledge.

Harper, R. 2003. People versus Information the Evolution of Mobile Technology. In *Human-Computer Interaction with Mobile Devices and Services: 5th International Symposium, Mobile HCI 2003, Udine, Italy, September 2003 Proceedings*, edited by L. Chittaro, 1–14. Berlin, Heidelberg: Springer.

Heath, C., and P. Luff. 2000. *Technology in Action.* Cambridge: Cambridge University Press.

The Horseless Age. 1903. New York: Horseless Age.

Hughes, N., and S. Lonie. 2011. M-PESA: Mobile money for the "unbanked" turning cellphones into 24-hour tellers in Kenya. *Innovations: Technology, Governance, Globalization* 2(1–2): 63–81.

Jha, A. 2011. Get ready for Robocar. *The Guardian Unlimited.* Accessed February 1, 2011. www.theguardian.com/guardianweekly/story/0,12674,1677888,00.html.

Kelly, K. 2010. *What Technology Wants.* New York: Penguin.

Larsen, J., J. Urry, and K. W. Axhausen. 2006. *Mobilities, Networks, Geographies.* Aldershot: Ashgate.

The Last Enemy. 2008. TV series. Accessed October 2, 2012. http://en.wikipedia.org/wiki/The_Last_Enemy.

Latour, B. 1992. Where Are the Missing Masses? The Sociology of a Few Mundane Artifacts. In *Shaping Technology/Building Society: Studies in Sociotechnical Change*, edited by W. E. Bijker and J. Law, 225–258. Cambridge, MA: MIT Press.

Locking the Closed Car. 1924. *Popular Mechanics* 41(1): 154.

MacMurray, R. L., and K. R. Radford Jr. 2007. *Everything You Always Wanted to Know about America's Presidents* (*But Were Afraid to Ask).* Glendale, CA: Burbank Press.

Marey, E. J., L. Amoore and A. Hall. 2009. Taking people apart: Digitised dissection and the body at the border. *Environment and Planning D: Society and Space* 27: 444–464.

Mauer, B. 2006. Proposal for a Monument to Lost Data. In *Writing and Digital Media*, edited by L. Waes, M. Leijten and C. M. Neuwirth, 287–310. Kidlington: Emerald.

Mitchell, W. J., C. Borroni-Bird, and L. D. Burns. 2010. *Reinventing the Automobile: Personal Urban Mobility for the 21st Century.* Cambridge, MA: MIT Press.

Norman, D. 2004. *Emotional Design.* New York: Basic Books.

Nye, D. 2006. *Technology Matters: Questions to Live with.* Cambridge, MA: MIT Press.

Orwell, G. 1933. *Down and Out in Paris and London.* London: Victor Gollancz.

———. 1949. *Nineteen Eighty-Four.* London: Secker and Warburg.

Patterson, R. 2003. *Dereliction of Duty: Eyewitness Account of How Bill Clinton Compromised America's National Security.* Washington, DC: Regnery Publishing.

Perrow, C. 1999. *Normal Accidents: Living with High-Risk Technologies.* New York: Basic Books.

Perry, T. S., and L. Geppert. 1996. Do portable electronics endanger flight? The evidence mounts. *Spectrum, IEEE* 33(9): 26–33.

Price, J. C., and J. S. Forrest. 2008. *Practical Aviation Security: Predicting and Preventing Future Threats.* Waltham, MA: Butterworth-Heinemann.

The Royal Academy of Engineering. 2010. *Electric Vehicles: Charged with Potential.* London: Royal Academy of Engineering.

Sanders, C. L. 2008. *Keys to Manifesting Your Destiny.* Longwood: Xulon Press.

Schwanen, T. 2007. Matter(s) of interest: Artefacts, spacing and timing. *Geografiska Annaler: Series B, Human Geography*, 89(1): 9–22.

Shoes Thrown at Bush on Iraq Trip. 2008. *BBC News.* Accessed 19 January 2016. http://news.bbc.co.uk/1/hi/7782422.stm.

Sloman, L. 2006. *Car Sick: Solutions for Our Car-Addicted Culture.* London: Green Books.

Striphas, T. 2011. *The Late Age of Print: Everyday Book Culture from Consumerism to Control.* New York: Columbia University Press.

Strogatz, S. 2003. *Sync: The Emerging Science of Spontaneous Order.* Harmondsworth: Penguin.

Thrift, N. 2005. *Knowing Capitalism.* London: Sage.

Urry, J. 2002. The Global Complexities of September 11th. *Theory, Culture & Society* 19(4): 57–69.

———. 2007. *Mobilities*. Cambridge: Polity.

———. 2011. *Climate Change and Society*. Cambridge: Polity.

Ventä, L., M. Isomursu, A. Ahtinen and S. Ramiah. 2008. My Phone Is a Part of My Soul; How People Bond with Their Mobile Phones. At *The Second International Conference on Mobile Ubiquitous Computing, Systems, Services and Technologies* (UBICOMM), Valencia, Spain. http://ieeexplore.ieee.org/xpl/abstractAuthors.jsp?tp=&arnumber=46 41353&url=http%3A%2F%2Fieeexplore.ieee.org%2Fiel5%2F4641295%2F4641296 %2F04641353.pdf%3Farnumber%3D4641353.

Watson, R. 2008. *Future Files*. London: Nicholas Brealey Publishing.

Watts, L., and J. Urry. 2008. Moving methods, travelling times. *Environment and Planning D: Society and Space* 26(5): 860–874.

10 From the urban planning discourse to a circulation *dispositif*

An epistemological approach to the mobility turn

Pauline Wolff

Introduction

As of now, the mobility turn has become essential to the social sciences; it is thoroughly transforming their conceptual frameworks and offers a new perspective on their research objects and world views. An abundant literature illustrates this turn. It is no surprise that disciplines focusing on spatial issues have adopted it (Canzler et al. 2008). Indeed, the mobility turn actually offers a new way to explore our understanding of spatial elements and to go beyond their mere physical aspects, while taking representations, habits, practices, norms and values into account. In doing so, it questions the deep-seated motivations behind spatial planning and decision-making in spatial development.

It is tempting to explain what some call a new paradigm (Sheller and Urry 2006) in terms of changes in everyday life: globalisation, new technologies and engineering advances have definitely shaped behaviours and the ways we understand and make sense of the world. The assertion that it would be reductive to think that the mobility turn could be 'justified as a mere reflection "in the field of theory" of a set of transformations taking place in the field of reality' has already been made (Franquesa 2011, 1014). In fact, mobility is not a new phenomenon (Cresswell 2010, 2011), but our current view of it is. It is then unquestionably an epistemological change because it refers to an altered relationship to reality. How should this change be understood, and to which historical structure is it connected? How can this moment be reinserted into a broader epistemological framework when it comes to the creation and change of meaning? In other words, why are we talking about mobility today?

These questions arose as part of my research on the epistemology of urban planning[1] through its connection with transport planning. I initially examined the emergence of the mobility turn in the field of urban planning. Why now? From a historical point of view, what is the significance of this epistemological transformation for this discipline? From a practical perspective, it is tempting to reduce this turn to a new stage of transport theory, a sort of 'transport 2.0'.[2] So, should we simply move from transport planning to mobility planning the way that historians suggested a transition from the history of transport to the history of mobility (Flonneau and Guigueno 2009)? This linearity deserves to be examined.

For the purpose of this task, I suggest regarding the mobility turn from a different perspective, my field of research, rather than determining the extent to which the mobility turn influences urban planning practices and theories. Starting from the definition of urban planning as a discourse in the broader epistemological sense [i.e. Foucault thought it is more than a simple statement and rather a means of providing information about its conditions of possibility [Foucault (1971) 1981], I examine its relationship to the issue of mobility in a long-term perspective.

Therefore, I propose to introduce the concept of circulation. If mobility is movement being made meaningful (Cresswell 2006), I suggest adding an intentional dimension and thus considering circulation as movement with intention added to meaning. This intentional dimension, through choices and representations, is fundamental in spatial development as a social construction (Gottdiener 1985) and remains central to spatial planners in the process of making and materially implementing decisions. My research uses Michel Foucault's theoretical framework [Foucault (2004) 2007] and shows a circulation *dispositif*[3] emerging through the history of urban planning as explanatory for the various meanings and validations of mobility issues over time. From this perspective, I examine whether the mobility turn might be a current step in this *dispositif* within the field of urban planning, which may lead to the study of this turn within other social sciences in the longer term.

To develop this argument, this chapter begins with a reminder of the current debate over the mobility turn as a new epistemological framework for the social sciences and, more specifically, for sciences interested in spatial development. Then I review the historical construction of urban planning and how its own identity is linked to transport and movement issues. I later develop the idea of circulation as a key concept in the development of representations that shape the way cities are organised. Using Michel Foucault's theories, I return to the issue of how the meanings of transport and movement-related elements have changed in history and therefore have influenced intentions behind spatial planning, suggesting that these changes should be regarded through the logic of a circulation *dispositif.*

From the mobility turn to its adoption in urban planning

The mobility turn and its adoption by spatial development practitioners

The field of social studies took a major turn over a decade ago by developing the conceptual framework known as 'mobility'. Marc Augé and John Urry are often cited as the major initiators of this turn [Augé (1992) 1995; Urry 2000]. In the early 2000s, Urry undertook the large task of explaining sociology-related issues in light of modern realities, whose prevalence he affirmed (globalisation, new technologies, new practices, new objects, etc.), proposing a redefinition of the methods and world views of sociology and the social sciences (Urry 2008).

Transport historians also began to use the term in the 2000s, as illustrated by the creation of the International Association for the History of Transport, Traffic and Mobility (T^2M). Their work revisits the history of transport, which has long been built upon division by modes and has thereby limited its own potential for understanding the world (Flonneau 2004; Mom 2003; Mom et al. 2009; Sparke 2008). They argue that a cross-disciplinary view should now be used to study the representations associated with transport (Divall and Revill 2005) and to observe 'the practices of agents, the controversies and the conflicts in the use of public space'[4] (Flonneau and Guigueno 2009, 19).

These theoretical changes and conceptual overtures are now currently known as the mobility turn (Cresswell 2010). Some feel that they constitute a new paradigm (Amar 2010; Sheller and Urry 2006; Urry 2008) or even a new epistemological foundation for the social sciences (Flonneau and Guigueno 2009; Sheller 2011). Spatial theorists and practitioners are directly concerned by the mobility turn (Canzler et al. 2008): the concept of mobility actually allows geographers, engineers, urban planners, architects, sociologists and others to examine the complex connections among spaces, territories, cities and phenomena associated with movement in a broader sense (Cresswell 2010, 2011; Graham and Marvin 2001). These connections are therefore freshly observed in light of the new theoretical framework: from the materialisation of space (infrastructure, urban form etc.) and the management of transport modes with their associated physical and social dynamics, to individual relationships to urban life and its representations (Allemand et al. 2004; Amar 2010; Bonnet and Aubertel 2006; Canzler et al. 2008; Jensen 2009; Kaufmann 2008, 2011; Kaufmann et al. 2004; Lannoy and Ramadier 2007; Wiel 2005). All these authors show that the concept of mobility is broader than that of transport: it refers to practices and world views and not just means of movement (modes and their infrastructure).

It seems logical that these fields have adopted the new theoretical framework of mobility: there is a fairly clear connection between movement (of individuals, goods, information etc.), form and spatial practices, but this connection also includes representations and experiences (Cresswell 2006; Desportes 2005). Furthermore, given the potential pull exerted by the other social sciences, it is understandable why spatial theorists have made the conceptual jump from transport to mobility.

Urban planning makes a sudden jump to mobility...

I will now take a detour and share my own experience in order to show that the connection between urban planning[5] and the mobility turn is not the result of linear evolution. After earning a bachelor's degree in geography and land use planning, I began a master's programme in urban planning at the University of Montreal. There were no transport courses offered in the master's programme in 2005; the course that came closest was Management of Urban Services, which addressed the management of transport infrastructure, public transport, municipal libraries and waste collection. The only transport courses offered at the university were given by other faculties, such as the Polytechnique (Engineering School) or the Geography Department, and could be taken as non-programme courses. The first transport course at the Institute of Urban Planning appeared later in 2010, and I was a part of its development. At first the title of the course was Urban Planning, Transport and Mobility, but after the reform in 2013, it changed to Urban Planning and Mobility. Notice, however, that the term transport had disappeared from the course title.

This may seem incidental, but the fact remains that while urban planners seem to have collectively adopted the term mobility today, as illustrated by the abundant literature on mobility written by urban planners in the last decade, they did not seem to talk much about transport just nine years ago. At best, they barely taught about it. This anecdote underscores the fact that the transition to mobility was fairly direct, as if the mobility turn was not an epistemological development of the concept of transport within this discipline. Clearly, I am taking a few shortcuts; for instance, some famous works address transport and urban planning issues prior to the 2000s. For example, Dupuy's work (1991), which is still of reference in this area, deals with networks in the broader sense and not just transport. Nevertheless, there is something worth investigating here, not only in terms of the connection between transport and urban planning but also the spontaneous appearance of the theoretical framework of the mobility turn and its significance in this context.

... Where the origins of urban planning are concerned

In fact, this is all surprising at different levels. The connection between spaces (their configuration and their meaning) and mobility issues (from transport to movement in general) indeed seems fairly evident from a strictly material point of view. And beyond that, the broader sense of transport is historically embedded in the genetic code of the urban phenomenon. The origin and purpose of the city actually depend directly upon the issue of trade and movement. At its origins, the city probably developed in response to the need to come together and trade, or the choice between nomadism and sedentariness [Braudel (1967) 1981; Mumford 1961; Pinol 2003]. Thus, a city could be a stopover on a journey, along a natural or artificial path, a place of trade, a bastion of intellectual activity, a place of physical protection, a meeting place, a point of tension or a haven.

Furthermore, the historical emergence of urban planning as a discipline in the 19th century coincides with concerns about transport and movement. Ildefons Cerdà,[6] a Catalan civil engineer, coined the term 'urbanism'[7] in his 1867 *Teoría General de la Urbanización* (*General Theory of Urbanisation*) [Cerdà (1867) 2005]. The purpose of his work was to propose an extension plan for the city of Barcelona that was akin to a new urban development model, which was largely supported with technical arguments related to transportation concerns. Cerdà rejected the old city because he considered it obsolete for the modern man and the needs of 'the new civilization, whose characteristics are movement and communication' [Cerdà (1867) 2005, 71 (9)]. He proposed a new development model for the city, the *Eixample*, whose form was largely dictated by the technical requirements of rail transportation. Thus, the famous angled intersections[8] of his project came from an idea he had about the bend radius of the railway tracks that should cross the city. Moreover, the design of the urban structure that he proposed reflected his idea of progress, which he believed should be fully in step with the development of electricity and steam [Aibar and Bijker 1997; Cerdà (1867) 1999, (1867) 2005].

The 19th century was actually a period of major urban works. Large networks (water, public transport and electricity) were developed. Roads were extended and urban networks were aligned. Glacis were redeveloped, and the last of the city walls were removed. All of these activities were related to concerns about transport and movement. Baron Haussmann's renovation of Paris is one of the most famous examples of this, but all large Western cities would eventually undergo massive transformations (Benevolo 1980). Often, these were brought about by public health principles, which required cities to be reorganised based on the way air, water, goods and people circulated. At the same time, these major works were necessary due to the emergence and acceptance of new modes of transportation (rail transport and bicycles) and communication (the telegraph but also, on an entirely different scale, the world expositions), which were also related to new practices and representations.[9]

Beyond the period in which urban planning was born, a summary review of the history of the discipline after the 19th century is more than sufficient to understand that urban planning theorists have primarily had to study problems resulting from transport and movement in cities, which were key issues for most of them. Aside from Cerdà and Haussmann, other examples include Eugène Hénard with his intersections and traffic circles (Hénard 1903), William Phelps Eno with his traffic regulation methods (Eno 1909), Le Corbusier with his condemnation of the side street [Le Corbusier (1930) 1960] and his proposal of the 7V principle (Le Corbusier 1957), Frank Lloyd Wright with Broadacre City (Wright 1958) and Colin Buchanan with his management of the automobile invasion [Buchanan (1963) 1964]. Others have addressed these issues more indirectly: Raymond Unwin's Garden City (Unwin 1909), Camillo Sitte's aesthetic studies on squares [Sitte (1889) 1965], Kevin Lynch's issue of reference points in spaces (Appleyard et al. 1964; Lynch 1960) and Lawrence Halprin's studies on motation (Halprin 1965), to name a few.

A quick review of history shows that there is a specific connection between transport and movement issues and urban planning and that this connection was restored with the emergence of the new conceptual framework of mobility. It should come as no surprise that urban planning, a social science that deals with space, adopted the mobility turn as other disciplines have done. But how do we explain the re-emergence of these issues within this discipline, and their earlier momentary disappearance, when they are the very issues that formed it to begin with? To answer this question, we should look at it from a different perspective.

From urban planning as a discourse to mobility and circulation

Like all other disciplines, urban planning as a practice and theory has no significance in isolation. It is a discourse that depends on a historical and epistemological context. Its intentional aspect, represented by the goal of improving the urban living environment when it became a discipline, encourages a strategic interpretation of mobility issues throughout history. I propose here that this interpretation should be considered through the concept of circulation in a broader sense (circulation of people, goods, ideas etc.), thereby adding an intentional dimension to mobility as movement being made meaningful within the framework of power.

Urban planning as a discursive formation

Urban planning became a discipline in the 19th century in order to diagnose the industrial city, which was perceived to be a sick organism that needed to be healed (Choay 1965; Frey 2000). At the same time, Darwin was writing his theories of evolution and German idealism, English utilitarianism and the positivist philosophy of Auguste Comte were widespread (López de Aberasturi 2005). Given the context, the discipline could only claim a scientific status. Without this status, it would have served a strictly aesthetic purpose and would have been reduced to an urban art form, whereas it endeavoured to find useful solutions that were validated at the time. Following this logic, the new discipline asserted 'a scientific universality' (Choay 1965): Cerdà claimed that he offered 'a new world to science' (López de Aberasturi 2005, 41) while he started using new tools such as statistics and surveying. Later, Le Corbusier would call for 'the true point of view' (Choay 1965, 8–9).

It was the birth of this epistemologically representative discourse in the 19th century that makes it possible to consider it the birth of urban planning as a discipline. According to López de Aberastruri, it was Cerdà who:

> brought about the definitive change in the way that the urban transformation was viewed by developing knowledge that was purportedly based on science. Before Cerdà, the city was a tool whose nature was not understood insofar as it was essentially perceived as an image. With urban planning, the city became a "machine that operates" according to a program of human needs and desires; it seems to be the instrument that can be used to conceive a comprehensive social project.

> (López de Aberasturi 2005, 42)

Thus, urban planning is in fact a discursive formation (Choay 1965; López de Aberasturi 2005), it formally and theoretically translates ways of seeing the world. Moreover, these ways of seeing the world change over time, thereby influencing discourses. Here a 'discourse' should be understood according to Foucault's meaning [Foucault (1971) 1981, (1969) 2002], that is neither a simple statement nor an exclusion from operational urban planning in opposition to theoretical urban planning. The operationalisation could itself be a form of discourse, as a trace of what can be said (or done) or what must be said (or done) at a given moment in time. For Foucault, it is an account that essentially serves to make its context visible:

> We must not go from discourse towards its interior, hidden nucleus, towards the heart of a thought or a signification supposed to be manifested in it; but,

on the basis of discourse itself, its appearance and its regularity, go towards its external conditions of possibility, towards what gives rise to the aleatory series of these events, and fixes its limits.

[Foucault (1971) 1981, 67]

According to this logic, when considered over a longer time scale, urban planning is a lens through which the evolution of the history of ideas can be observed. Through this discursive formation, it is possible to observe the changes in what is considered 'true' and 'valid' from one era to another, as it is not enough to simply 'say the truth but to be in the truth'[10] [Foucault (1971) 1981]. Since the purpose is to put these discourses into perspective, they are the 'node within a network' [Foucault (1969) 2002, 26], and it is the network that interests us.

From mobility to circulation in the city

From mobility to circulation

Kaufmann attempts to 'define and analyse the city based on the movements and mobilities that traverse it' (Kaufmann 2011, ix) and, for that purpose, 'to conceptualize mobility based on three analytical dimensions': field of possibilities, aptitude for movement (i.e. motility) and movement (Kaufmann 2011, 37). The view that I propose in my research is the opposite of this perspective: I examine the external conditions that create, make possible and give meaning to these three dimensions. In other words, I look at the epistemological context that created them and gives them meaning, as well as the way in which this context changes over the long term. Naturally, these dimensions are relative on many levels and relate to issues of representation and perception, which is precisely what the mobility turn has been advancing for several years. However, in the context of spatial development, there is reason to question the types of justifications and representations that underlie choices and decisions, as well as individual practices and experiences.

Over time, it seems that priorities and changes of epistemological nature have caused variations in the spatial injunctions or at least in the justification of urban development choices. As Cresswell develops throughout his work, 'movement is rarely just movement; it carries with it the burden of meaning' (Cresswell 2006, 10–11). And since the meaning of mobility changes over time, the injunctions prohibiting, encouraging and governing it change as well, that is going from the fear of mobility in the feudal period (Cresswell 2006; Mumford 1961) and the creation of ghettos to supervise behaviours (Cresswell 2006; Sennett 1994) to the use of the famous 'circulate!' in the 18th century (Barles 2006; Rousseau 2008). What is the reason for these injunctions and what justifies them? This remains a central question, as Jensen (2011) and Salter (2013) remind us, in relation to the exercise of power and its materialisation on a space considered a social and cultural production.

To explore this issue in urban planning, I introduce the concept of circulation. Indeed, if mobility is movement being made meaningful (Cresswell 2006),

I suggest adding an intentional dimension, considering circulation as movement with intention added to meaning. Circulation as the result of knowledge-based formations of mobility systems and spatial practices has been discussed by Cresswell in a way (Cresswell and Merriman 2011).[11] My point here is to emphasise that this intentional aspect, through choices and representations that are relative to the period, is in fact fundamental to urban development and remains central to spatial planners in the process of making and materially implementing decisions. Through intention, I look at the origins of spatial choices, meaning the conditions of possibility for different planning choices to exist. Thus, I examine not what is done but what is epistemologically legitimised as an opportunity for urban planners to act on, think about and organise space.

In his courses on security, territory and population at the Collège de France, Foucault broadly examined the connection between the issue of circulation and the exercise of power within a territory. Likewise, he provided a definition that is adopted here: 'circulation in the very broad sense of movement, exchange, and contact, as form of dispersion, and also as form of distribution, the problem being: How should things circulate or not circulate?' [Foucault (2004) 2007, 64]. He later wrote:

> By "circulation" we should understand not only this material network [of roads, rivers, and canals etc] that allows the circulation of goods and possibly of men, but also the circulation itself, that is to say, the set of regulations, constraints, and limits, or the facilities and encouragements that will allow the circulation of men and things in the kingdom and possible beyond its borders.
> [Foucault (2004) 2007, 325]

Salter argues that the concept of circulation can be viewed as 'a new frame for describing and explaining the mobility turn' (Salter 2013, 9) and suggests that ' "[c]irculation" then is another way for Foucault to make one of his main points about power, and its analysis: it must be considered both in its repressive and its productive guise' (Salter 2013, 11). According to this concept, it is possible to clarify certain aspects of the purpose, the creation and the organisation of the city throughout history while using the intention associated with mobility. This constitutes a framework for explaining how 'spatial rationalities' (Huxley 2006) and therefore planning rationalities have evolved over time.

Circulation: origin and identity of the city

Foucault's courses remind us that issues related to limiting or stimulating circulation are fundamental to the origin and identity of the city. He illustrated this by placing the city back in its environment as a defined entity and/or not only in opposition to rural areas but also to the central state. Before the 17th and 18th centuries, the city's isolation within a territory and its self-confinement imposed a logic that was prohibitive to circulation (Foucault 2004, 14). At the same time, trade and commerce with communities near the city required the exchange and circulation not only of goods but also of people and ideas. After which, the self-imposed isolation of the city began to cause problems, as economic trade on several scales became necessary, demographics changed and mentalities modified. As a result, this would 'resituat[e] the town in a space of circulation', and Foucault refers to Jean-Claude Perrot to show 'that the problem of the town was essentially and fundamentally a problem of circulation' [Foucault (2004) 2007, 13]. Cresswell also illustrates the phenomenon when he considers 'the early modern sense of mobility' (Cresswell 2006, 12). Through new dynamics of exchange (the circulation of goods, people, capital and ideas), which was encouraged by the rise of mercantile capitalism, the identity of the city began to change, often in opposition to the central state.

Circulation: power, norms and security in the city

Later, Foucault emphasised the importance of circulation as part of the exercise of power and sovereignty over a territory:

> A good sovereign . . . is someone well placed within a territory, and a territory that is well policed in terms of its obedience to the sovereign is a territory that has a good spatial layout. . . . this idea of the political effectiveness of sovereignty, is linked to the idea of an intensity of circulations: circulation of ideas, of wills, and of orders, and also commercial circulation.
> [Foucault (2004) 2007, 14–15]

He also highlighted the extent to which control and surveillance would directly depend upon proper circulation management according to clearly defined goals. Some of these goals were economic (Salter 2013), which is why the collection of duties would partially justify the reorganisation of road networks and the gradual separation of different types of circulation at the end of the 17th century: goods had to circulate for the tax system to function, and to achieve this, it was necessary to remove the things that were not circulating (beggars, street entertainers etc.) (Barles 2006).

But the strategic perspective does not stop here. There is in fact a clear normative dimension to these issues. 'New types of mobility called for new forms of social surveillance and control', wrote Cresswell (2006) in reference to Foucault. While the purpose of the street was in fact to organise the different flows, its function was defined and carried out based on what was considered desirable or undesirable, dangerous or safe. This explains why the police were created during the same period. 'It is simply a matter of maximizing the positive elements, for which one provides the best possible circulation, and of minimizing what is risky and inconvenient, like theft and disease, while knowing that they will never be completely suppressed' [Foucault (2004) 2007, 19].

The problem is therefore twofold: there is a qualitative definition of what should circulate on one hand and what should not circulate on the other, from putrid odours that need to dissipate [Corbin (1982) 1986] to waste that needs to be removed (Barles 2005). What is desirable to see or smell, and what is not? What do we tolerate or ignore? Although these issues have evolved over time, they have nevertheless served as the impetus for many spatial development projects, from the Haussmannian building with its back staircases for servants, to the Jewish ghetto in Venice during the Renaissance. In today's cities, similar issues may be found in logistical strategies, such as removing garbage or delivering goods at night in urban centres, for example.

Circulation: health and vitality of the city

The form of the city is directly defined by the alternation of constructions and spaces for circulating (which cannot be reduced to road networks, as shown in Giambattista Nolli's famous plan). This issue is behind the most common analogy in urban planning: the analogy of the body. The city is in fact often compared to a body or an organism. It is presented as a complex, ever-changing or adapting system, compared to a living thing. Cerdà illustrated this by using medical terminology throughout his 1867 *Teoría*, to include 'body, anatomical dissection, intimate, scalpel, remedy, disease, tumour' and more [Cerdà (1867) 2005]. However, this analogy had been used for several centuries, as illustrated by Alberti [Alberti (1452) 1988]. Cresswell uses this as his starting point (2006), and Sennett refers directly to it:

> John of Salisbury in turn connected the shape of a human body and the shape of a city: the city's palace or cathedral he thought of as its head, the central market as its stomach, the city's hands and feet as its houses. People should therefore move slowly in a cathedral because the brain is a reflective organ, rapidly in a market because digestion occurs like a quick-burning fire in the stomach.
>
> (Sennett 1994, 23)

Following this analogy, the health and vitality of the urban body clearly depend upon its irrigation: if the streets are arteries and circulation has a vital function, circulation problems are therefore indicators of poor health. This analogy is made in relation to sanitary issues and miasmas but also in relation to economic issues, as Adam Smith did when he 'imagined the free market of labor and goods operating much like freely circulating blood within the body and with similar life-giving consequences' (Sennett 1994, 256).

The association between streets and arteries or veins started in the 17th century with the blood circulation discoveries of William Harvey and Thomas Willis. These discoveries, which were then applied to air and skin, would contribute to changing the ways urban spaces were developed:

> The desire to put into practice the healthy virtues of respiration and circulation transformed the look of cities as well as the bodily practices in them. . . . Enlightened planners wanted the city in its very design to function like a

healthy body, freely flowing as well as possessed of clean skin.[12] . . . The medical imagery of life-giving circulation gave a new meaning to the Baroque emphasis on motion. Instead of planning streets for the sake of ceremonies or movement toward an object, as did the Baroque planner, the Enlightenment planner made motion an end in itself.

(Sennett 1994, 263–264)

Sennett (1994) partially explains why the transfer from one field to another was historically possible: as the new paradigm of motion/circulation emerged as an explanans for life itself through Harvey's work, it seemed relevant to apply it to every complex living thing. With its own elaborated logic of growth and organisation and its whole being greater than the sum of its parts, the city was then considered a complex organism to which the same rules could be applied.

Circulation as an epistemological issue

In the same order of ideas, even though the issue of circulation is central to the city, both in concrete ways and through certain underlying analogies of urban development, it can in fact be examined even more substantively at the epistemological level. It should be understood at first as a framework for interpreting the world. Sennett's argument shows this; movement, along with a qualitative selection of types of circulation, became a goal in itself starting in the 18th century because medical discoveries proved that movement is healthier and more natural than inactivity. From that point onwards, everything had to circulate. Prior to this specific point in time, too much circulation was considered a bad thing; dirty skin was soothing and thought to be protective, which is why it was better not to remove dirt and allow the air to circulate over the skin (Sennett 1994). Thus, the world became mobile as circulation was associated with life.

Beyond the interpretation and comprehension of the world, the issue of circulation was also thought of as a means of acting on the world and therefore an empirical truth. In the context of the city, circulation was an element that could be acted upon, and traffic (vehicles, people, sludge, water etc.) the component that was physically possible to understand, which made it 'true' according to the rules of knowledge at the time. This logic can be directly linked to the emergence of statistics as a new relationship to reality in the 18th century. Foucault demonstrated this with smallpox, where the mathematical support was 'a sort of agent of . . . integration within the currently acceptable and accepted fields of rationality' [Foucault (2004) 2007, 59]. Circulation could be validated and formally coded, and it would comply with the rules of the emerging positivism in the early 19th century. It was empirically observable and expressed through mathematics [Comte (1830) 2007].

Accordingly, codes and rules for circulation appeared at the end of the 18th century, at the same time as counting vehicles and accidents (Barles 2006), and certain logical connections were defined. For instance, in Paris in 1838, 'Partiot, a bridge and road engineer, points out that the width of the road should be a multiple of the number of cars that need to travel on it' (Barles 2006, 133). In the context of urban planning, Cerdà, for whom the three languages of the urban planner were design, text and numbers, would later claim the key role of statistics (López de Aberasturi 2005). He was in fact searching for scientifically valid tools for urban planners. The statistical tool would encourage reliance upon the materiality of vehicles and people: their standardised size and number make it possible to set criteria validated by mathematics, which justifies the decisions made in development projects (size, flow and bend radius). In theory, it was the age of common sense, which is admirably illustrated by the prophetic novels of the time. In this regard, Edward Relph recalls that Edward Bellamy, visionary author of the 19th century, imagined futuristic 'electrical cars travelling swiftly on roads half the width of the roads of 1890 (impeccable logic – if the same number of vehicles travel at twice the speed, only half as much space is needed for them)' (Relph 1987, 18).

Starting in the 20th century, the engineer's growing role in managing automobile traffic contributed significantly to continuing the association of positivist solutions to transport problems in the city. In the 1920s, some suggested that it would be wiser to 'create a science of road traffic' that, for savings purposes and from a positivist desire to rationalise, would become 'a hydraulic equation with one unknown, the traffic jam; this equation being based on one single constant: the road' (Barles and Guillerme 2000, 11).

Therefore, certain historical arguments draw attention to a fundamental connection between the issues of mobility and the city. By incorporating an intentional dimension in these issues, we can observe them from the angle of circulation. This dimension is central to the framework for spatial intervention and includes normative dimensions as well as an important strategic perspective. The idea of circulation seems to have epistemologically marked the discipline of urban planning, offering an acceptable lens within the framework of the theory of knowledge to view reality, as well as the tools to act on this reality.

Towards a circulation *dispositif*

Meaning and its evolution within spatial planning

Cresswell illustrates the relative meaning of movement when he states that 'the idea of mobility and freedom would have made little sense in feudal society' (Cresswell 2006, 15). This observation can also be made with regard to spatial development, and it is surprising to observe the frequency of changes in meaning given to certain modes or practices and their physical manifestations in space. Although the tramway was the pride of the 19th century, it had become obsolete by the mid-20th century and then came back around 1990 as a mode associated with contemporary progress.[13] Regarding the bicycle, at the end of the 19th century, '[t]he multiplication of velocipedes was . . . problematic. These machines looked nothing like other vehicles; they appeared suddenly without a noise, scaring horses and passers-by: their use was prohibited in many streets of Paris starting in 1874' (Barles 2006, 135–136). Similarly, in Germany and England, cyclists were regularly disparaged, insulted and even beaten by coach drivers because they were considered a nuisance. The velocipede was increasingly criticised for moral reasons and deemed an affront to decency, particularly when women used it (Bijker 1995). Crossing different frameworks of meaning depending on relevant social groups, as demonstrated by Bijker (1995), the bicycle is now a popular mode of transport, associated with hipsters and valued in the urban space. Schivelbush (1986) and Desportes (2005) illustrate the inconsistency in the different meanings also given to the train; it was at first feared and blamed for all types of problems, then gradually became the familiar means of transport that we know today. Following the same logic, the meaning of walking has also changed a great deal through the centuries. First the mode of transport of the poor, it became a upper-middle-class activity at the turn of the 17th century (Loir and Turcot 2011; Turcot 2007; Vaillancourt 2009) and continued to transition into the ordinary urban activity it is today, where it is now valued within the paradigm of sustainable development.

The different meanings given to these practices and modes shaped urban development, as illustrated by the creation of the sidewalk as a space for strolling, which participated in the emergence and definition of an upper-middle class and not simply as the result of a mere division of flows in the public space (Vaillancourt 2009). In the same order of ideas, the view of the automobile as a futuristic, modern mode of transportation and the promotion of the concept of speed resulted in extensive urban adaptations during the 20th century. From Hénard to Bel Geddes and Buchanan, positive and futurist representations of road transportation were considered irrefutable arguments for carrying out drastic developments, as the city's adaptation to the automobile was perceived as necessary, non-negotiable and obvious at the time.

But while it is common nowadays to hear criticism of modernist conceptions of the city and the way circulation has been organised, how should these changes in meaning be understood over the long term? In other words, in which context of historical development can they be understood? These questions are even more important within a discipline that intervenes in reality and thus necessarily sets criteria to justify actions. According to this logic, if the meanings and values attributed to mobility issues vary over time, the types of answers given also vary, and this poses the fundamental problem of defending choices. While urban planning was founded on positivist grounds, it is now acknowledged that it is not a hard science: there is not one true answer in urban development. Nevertheless, it is necessary to make a distinction between doxa and scientific knowledge to justify choices in the public interest. But on what bases is this possible in this context?

Foucault's theories on the evolution of meaning over time

Michel Foucault's thinking was largely influenced by the search for meaning on a long historical scale where power is conceived as a series of 'relations' [Foucault

(2004) 2007]. This is generally developed in *The Archaeology of Knowledge* [Foucault (1969) 2002] and illustrated as part of his work on sexuality:

> [I]t is a question of forming a different grid of historical decipherment by starting from a different theory of power; and, at the same time, of advancing little by little toward a different conception of power through a closer examination of an entire historical material. We must at the same time conceive of sex without the law, and power without the king.
>
> [Foucault (1976) 1990, 90–91]

His thoughts and the conceptual tools he proposed provide a framework for thinking about the changes just discussed.

Changes in the fields of rationality

When considering the emergence of the dynamics associated with security, at the heart of which he also placed the city, Foucault distinguished two different systems: one specific to the implementation of disciplinary mechanisms and the other specific to what he called a security *dispositif* [Foucault (2004) 2007]. His logic and the distinction he made between these two systems allow for an examination of the process of historical reconstruction and construction of meaning.

The distinction between the two systems (disciplinary mechanisms and security *dispositif*) is fundamental to Foucault's thought. He examined the order of steps that enabled new practices to be accepted within specific fields of rationality in one period when they did not meet the criteria defining fields of rationality in another. In other words, he questioned changes in meaning through time. The order of steps of the integration process in these fields of rationality is central. When discussing smallpox and the use of inoculation in the 18th century, he questioned the factors 'of importation, of the immigration of these practices, into accepted medical practices' [Foucault (2004) 2007, 59], while this method seemed 'unthinkable in the terms of medical rationality of this time' [Foucault (2004) 2007, 58].

He proposed the precedence of the so-called security *dispositif* system as a step that changes what is normal and then influences norms. In the second system, the disciplinary mechanism, the changed norms will participate in defining a new normal in the long term. 'The normal comes first and the norm is deduced from it, or the norm is fixed and plays its operational role on the basis of this study of normalities' [Foucault (2004) 2007, 63]. Following this logic, not only is there a transition from one normal to another and the 'new normal' is crystallised by the disciplinary mechanism, but the 'old normal' is also forgotten, because it no longer has any reason to exist as knowledge within the new framework that has been created.

The concept of the dispositif

The *dispositif* was both a conceptual and methodological tool for Foucault. The term appears at a specific point in Foucault's work to meet the need to invent a new conceptual tool to explain a series of findings associated with the way sex has been handled in societies through time, while developing a theory of power.[14] It first served Foucault as an interpretative key (Bussolini 2010) to explain the treatment of phenomena or ideas through time (e.g. the issue of how sex is dealt with). Then, it allowed him to re-examine the objects that interested him in light of the concept. Alongside this re-examination, the *dispositif* tool was explained and completed by a consideration of various *dispositifs* as Foucault's thinking evolved, thereby gradually demonstrating the theoretical and methodological contributions of the concept (Bussolini 2010).

The most thorough definition that Foucault provided for a *dispositif* is the one he gave in 1977 (*in the following excerpt, Foucault uses the word *dispositif* for 'apparatus'):

> What I'm trying to pick out with this term is firstly, a thoroughly heterogeneous ensemble consisting of discourses, institutions, architectural forms, regulatory decisions, laws, administrative measures, scientific statements, philosophical, moral, and philanthropic propositions – in short, the said as much as the unsaid. Such are the elements of the apparatus.[15] The apparatus* itself is the system of relations that can be established between these elements.
>
> Secondly, what I'm trying to identify in this apparatus* is precisely the nature of the connection that can exist between these heterogeneous elements. Thus, a particular discourse can figure at one time as the program of an institution, and at another it can function as a means of justifying or masking a practice which itself remains silent, or as a secondary re-interpretation of this practice, opening out for it a new field of rationality. In short, between these elements, whether discursive or non-discursive, there is a sort of interplay of shifts of position and modifications of function which can also vary very widely.
>
> Thirdly, I understand by the term "apparatus"* a sort of – shall we say – formation which has as its major function at a given historical moment that of responding to an urgent need. The apparatus* thus has a dominant strategic function.
>
> [Foucault (1977) 1980, 194–195]

A number of Foucault's expressions throughout his work can help to clarify what he meant by this term, which continues to be an attempt to name, conceptualise and summarise something extremely complicated. While these expressions do not systematically refer to the *dispositif* as such, they make it possible to clarify his view of reality and the way in which he tries to explain it: 'relations . . . fields of forces . . . mechanisms . . . coordinations . . . subordination . . . analogies . . . series . . . system of correlation . . .' [Foucault (2004) 2007].

Towards a circulation dispositif in urban planning

Foucault's work does not often address the question of the city (with the exception of his 1977–1978 lecture at the Collège de France), and his references to spatial planning are mainly about geography [Foucault (1976) 2001], architecture [Foucault (1982) 1984] or space itself [Foucault (1967) 1984]. However, some authors have used his theories to think about the city itself [Pløger 2008; Rabinow (1989) 1995] and how the concept of *dispositif* could be useful for doing so. Pløger argues that Foucault's 'term *dispositif*, in relation to space, relies on a social, discursive, "reading" meaning into space, and this is what makes plausible a certain relation between "forms and norms" [Rabinow (1989) 1995, 53]' (Pløger 2008). He later states that:

> Urban planning concerns several *dispositif* problematics: first urban planning concerns the relationship between the articulated and the visible; the discourse and the material. Second, urban planning is predetermined on relations and connections between the said (plans, texts, communications) and the unsaid (strategies, intentions with regard to effect and affect, prejudices and so on).

> (Pløger 2008, 52)

In this context and concerning the issue of circulation, the use of the conceptual tool of the *dispositif* seems particularly relevant (Salter 2013). Indeed, a circulation *dispositif* seems to deploy over time: a formation that slowly modifies its own structure and elements (i.e. discourses, institutions, architectural forms etc.) to make sense of certain components or to condemn others that do not fit within the bigger picture of meaning. By evolving, this *dispositif* changes the fields of rationality and therefore comes to progressively validate behaviours or ideas that would not have found an appropriate context before. Thus, specific crises in time, such as the rapid adoption of the automobile in the early 20th century or even the events of 9/11, call for specific configuration of that *dispositif* to rationalise spatial choices and to accordingly modify views of the world to validate those choices. In the end, the strategic role of the circulation *dispositif* is to draw out actions and choices that are justified and legitimatised according to specific purposes. These actions and choices are validated and physically inscribed in spaces based on the specific relationship to the 'truth' of these periods, and that is to resolve and satisfy the priorities and crises of different historical moments. The very configuration of the elements that form the *dispositif* will then be reorganised and create a new logic, a new normal. In a way, by being a discourse within that *dispositif*, urban planning, like other disciplines, bears the burden of materialising specific elements. Therefore, having coped with this materialisation for many years, the discipline must permanently question its conceptual basis but still find ways to rationalise past choices.

The different historical steps are made visible in periods of latency, which are later left out of the historical narratives often presented in 'glossed over' versions of history (Wolff, 2015).[16] In fact, no mode of transportation has been adopted and no change has been made without first being subjected to mistrust, criticism and even rejection. Examples include the harsh reactions of horse-drawn carriage drivers to the electrification of transportation (Mom and Kirsch 2001; Rousseau

1961), distrust of the first bicycles (Barles 2006; Bijker 1995), complete disinterest in the steamboat for almost a century (Rousseau 1961) and so on. A similar argument could be made regarding examples that did not turn out the way society thought they would: telecommuting did not enjoy the success that many expected in the 1970s, nor are the mechanical moving sidewalks.

Looking at urban planning in this way aids understanding of what could be called inconsistencies, delays or paradoxes in spatial planning. For instance, how do we explain discrepancies between what is generally said about density and public transit and the continuously growing economically based discourse that promotes individual automobile ownership? Changes in relationships to the truth are not immediately implemented, and this is precisely why the two-step explanation of the rationality change is meaningful. We see this now in the debate over the issue of induced travel demand: it was acknowledged several decades ago that there is a connection between the increased supply of road space and increased demand (Cervero 2003), yet this has not resulted in changing practices on a broader scale. It seems that it is still difficult to justify a reduction in the supply of road space based on currently 'valid' conditions. However, the contemporary argument for sustainable development would go along these lines on several levels. Are we witnessing an epistemological change before our very eyes?[17] Although the question is still open, it shows the possibility for analysis offered by Foucault's methodological tool of the *dispositif*.

Conclusion

As we have seen throughout this chapter, there is a strong ongoing connection between urban planning and issues of transport and movement. These are constituent elements of the discipline they influence its world view and its tools through time. Nevertheless, it is a complex task to understand what connects these different historical elements. I propose to consider circulation as a *dispositif* following the meaning of Foucault, that is an underlying structure, a network for strategic purposes, that generates changes in 'meaning' over time. Observing this *dispositif* could shed new light on the way 'meaning' and 'truth' evolve through the materialisation legitimated by the urban planning discourse. It also offers a broader framework for thinking about the mobility turn in urban planning as one step in a circulation *dispositif*, rather than just jumping on the bandwagon of the mobility turn. This could help to outline a different way to think about the link between spatial planning and movement in the city.

The task is to successfully draw the boundaries of the *dispositif* in question, which is what I am currently working on. However, this research ultimately suggests revisiting the epistemological context of the mobility turn and its materialisation in space, as well as its theorisation by the social sciences that focus on spatial development. Intentional and strategic dimensions are in fact important at several levels, and a theoretical framework that makes it possible to contemplate their materialisation is useful.

Acknowledgements

This chapter would not have been possible without funding from the Ivanhoé Cambridge Observatory of Urban and Real Estate Development. I also want to thank Gérard Beaudet and Michel Max Raynaud from the University of Montreal, as well as the reviewers, whose comments and advice were extremely useful.

Notes

1 For the purposes of this text, I have decided to use the expression urban planning to translate the French term *urbanisme*, which designates a specific field of spatial development practitioners.

2 Current vocabulary shows that we have often literally transitioned from transport to mobility: decision-making bodies like governments or city administrations stopped developing 'transport plans' a few years ago and now issue 'mobility plans'.

3 I will use *dispositif* and not *apparatus* to keep the French term. I do so in reference to Jeffrey Bussolini (2010), whose text in 2010 discusses an ambiguous translation that seems to sum up important theoretical points. Bussolini explains that the classic translation of the French term *dispositif* is *apparatus* in English. However, contrary to French and Italian, there is no difference in English between the French terms *appareil* and *dispositif*: the word *apparatus* is used to translate both terms. The risk here is that the meaning of two different, even opposite, concepts may be confused and cause some texts to be interpreted differently depending on the language.

An *appareil* in French refers to something technical, such as an *appareil photo* (camera), or something tangible, even if it refers to a larger system, such as *l'appareil judiciaire* (the judicial system) or *l'appareil digestif* (the digestive system). A *dispositif* is more theoretical and abstract, such as *un dispositif policier* (a police force or even police operation). While this distinction is fundamental in the translation process, it also aids understanding of Foucault's concept; when he talks about the *dispositif (de) prison*, he is of course referring to a system made of tangible things but also to what gives prisons meaning and justifies their existence.

4 All French translations are the author's own.

5 Urban planning is considered a social science here and is understood to be practiced as well as theorised.

6 Ildefons Cerdà (1815–1876) was a Catalan civil engineer known for his extension of Barcelona (the *Eixample*). Though ignored for a long time by city historians because his work had not been translated, he was 'rediscovered' by French urban planner Françoise Choay in the 1960s and is now considered one of the first theorists of urban planning [Aibar and Bijker 1997; Cerdà (1867) 1999].

7 In French and some other languages, *urbanisme* means urban planning.

8 Visiting Barcelona, it is striking how different the layout of the city looks outside of the old centre. The gigantic and geometric grid of square city blocks with angled intersections form a very unique urban form.

9 The way in which movement shapes perception of spaces and landscapes has been developed brilliantly by Desportes (2005). As far as modes of transport are individually concerned, some good examples include the train (Perriault 1981; Schivelbusch 1986), walking (Cresswell and Merriman 2011; Loir and Turcot 2011; Turcot 2007), the bicycle (Bijker 1995) and of course the automobile, which has been extensively discussed (Gartman 2004; Sheller and Urry 2000).

10 As Foucault reminds us by explaining that Gregor Mendel, with his theories on plant reproduction in the 19th century, 'spoke the truth, but he was not "within the true" of the biological discourse of his time. . . . Whereas about thirty years earlier, at the height of the 19th century, Scheiden [sic], for example, who denied plant sexuality, but in

accordance with the rules of biological discourse, was merely formulating a disciplined error' [Foucault (1971) 1981, 61].

11　Thanks to my reviewers for pointing that out.

12　Sennett refers here to new practices in cleaning streets and houses.

13　Georges Amar, former director of the forecasting department of the public transport operator of Paris (RATP), points out that 'in 1937, Paris boasted that it was the "first capital without a tramway!"' (Amar 2010, 176).

14　Foucault explains. 'Sexuality must not be thought of as a kind of natural given which power tries to hold in check, or as an obscure domain which knowledge tries gradually to uncover. It is the name that can be given to a historical construct: not a furtive reality that is difficult to grasp, but a great surface network in which the stimulation of bodies, the intensification of pleasures, the incitement to discourse, the formation of special knowledges, the strengthening of controls and resistances, are linked to one another, in accordance with a few major strategies of knowledge and power' [Foucault (1976) 1990, 105–106].

15　See note 3 for an explanation about the translation of *dispositif* and *apparatus*.

16　Smith and Marx (1995) refer to this process in the *context of technological determinism*, where an account and a narrative are gradually invented to gloss over reality.

17　Some authors claim that in the future, automobiles could be treated similarly to the way cigarettes are today and insist on the fact that their rejection by the majority might be no more than a question of time (Blanchard and Nadeau 2007).

References

Aibar, Eduardo, and Wiebe E. Bijker. 1997. Constructing a city: The Cerdà Plan for the extension of Barcelona. *Science, Technology, & Human Values* 22(1): 3–30.

Alberti, Leon Batista. (1452) 1988. *De re aedificatoria: On the Art of Building in Ten Books*. Cambridge, MA: MIT Press.

Allemand, Sylvain, François Ascher and Jacques Lévy. 2004. *Les sens du mouvement*. Paris: Belin.

Amar, Georges. 2010. *Homo mobilis, le nouvel âge de la mobilité*. Paris: Éditions FYP.

Appleyard, Donald, Kevin Lynch and John R. Myer. 1964. *The View from the Road*. Cambridge, MA: MIT Press.

Augé, Marc. (1992) 1995. *Non-Places – An Introduction to Supermodernity*. New York: Verso.

Barles, Sabine. 2005. *L'invention des déchets urbains – France: 1790–1970*. Seyssel: Éditions Champ Vallon.

———. 2006. De l'encombrement à la congestion ou la récurrence des problèmes de circulation: Le cas de Paris (1790–1970). In *La ville durable au risque de l'histoire*, edited by S. Descat, É. Monin and D. Siret, 129–143. Lille: Éditions de l'École nationale supérieure d'architecture et de paysage de Lille.

Barles, Sabine, and André Guillerme. 2000. Gestion des congestions: Seculum miserabile. *Annales des Ponts et Chaussées* 94: 4–12.

Benevolo, Leonardo. 1980. *The History of the City*. Cambridge, MA: MIT Press.

Bijker, Wiebe E. 1995. *Of Bicycles, Bakelites, and Bulbs: Toward a Theory of Sociotechnical Change, Inside Technology*. Cambridge, MA: MIT Press.

Blanchard, Martin, and Christian Nadeau. 2007. *Cul-de-sac: L'impasse de la voiture en milieu urbain*. Montreal: Héliotrope.

Bonnet, Michel, and Patrice Aubertel. 2006. *La ville aux limites de la mobilité*. Paris: Presses universitaires de France.

Braudel, Fernand. (1967) 1981. *Civilization and Capitalism, 15th–18th Century, Vol. I: The Structure of Everyday Life*, translated by S. Reynolds. New York: Harper & Row.

Buchanan, Colin. (1963) 1964. *Traffic in Towns – The Specially Shortened Edition of the Buchanan Report*. London: Penguin.

Bussolini, Jeffrey. 2010. What is a dispositive? *Foucault Studies* 10: 85–107.

Canzler, Weert, Vincent Kaufmann and Sven Kesselring. Eds. 2008. *Tracing Mobilities: Towards a Cosmopolitan Perspective*. Burlington, VT: Ashgate.

Cerdà, Ildefons. (1867) 1999. *Cerda – The Five Bases of the General Theory of Urbanization*, edited by A. Soria y Puigt, translated by B. Miller and M. F. i. Fleming. Barcelona: Electa.

———. (1867) 2005. *La théorie générale de l'urbanisation*, edited by A. L. d. Aberasturi, translated by A. L. d. Aberasturi. Paris: Éditions de l'Imprimeur.

Cervero, Robert. 2003. Road expansion, urban growth, and induced travel: A path analysis. *Journal of the American Planning Association* 69(2): 145–163.

Choay, Françoise. 1965. *L'urbanisme, utopies et réalités – Une anthologie*. Paris: Éditions du Seuil.

Comte, Auguste. (1830) 2007. *Premiers cours de philosophie positive*. Paris: PUF.

Corbin, Alain. (1982) 1986. *The Foul and the Fragrant: Odor and the French Social Imagination*. Cambridge, MA: Harvard University Press. [Originally published as *Le miasme et la jonquille*.]

Cresswell, Tim. 2006. *On the Move: Mobility in the Modern Western World*. New York: Routledge.

———. 2010. Mobilities 1: Catching up. *Progress in Human Geography* 35(4): 550–558.

———. 2011. Mobilities 2: Still. *Progress in Human Geography* 36(5): 645–653.

Cresswell, Tim, and Peter Merriman. Ed. 2011. *Geographies of Mobilities: Practices, Spaces, Subjects*. Farnham: Ashgate.

Desportes, Marc. 2005. *Paysages en mouvement: Transports et perception de l'espace XVIIIè–XXè siècle*. Paris: Éditions Gallimard.

Divall, Colin, and George Revill. 2005. Cultures of transport: Representation, practice and technology. *The Journal of Transport History* 26(1): 99–111.

Dupuy, Gabriel. 1991. *L'urbanisme des réseaux*. Paris: Armand Colin.

Eno, William Phelps. 1909. *Street Traffic Regulation*. New York: Rider and Driver.

Flonneau, Mathieu. 2004. Pour une juste place des transports dans l'histoire urbaine. *Histoire urbaine* 3(11): 5–8.

Flonneau, Mathieu, and Vincent Guigueno. 2009. *De l'histoire des transports à l'histoire de la mobilité*. Rennes: Presses universitaires de Rennes.

Foucault, Michel. (1977) 1980. *The Confession of the Flesh: In Power/Knowledge – Selected Interviews and Other Writings 1972–1977*, edited by C. Gordon, translated by C. Gordon, L. Marshall, J. Mepham and K. Soper. Brighton: Harvester Press. [Originally published as 'Le jeu de Michel Foucault'.]

———. (1971) 1981. *The Order of Discourse: In Untying the Text: A Post-Structuralist Reader*, edited by R. Young, translated by permission. Boston: Routledge. [Originally published as *L'ordre du discours*.]

———. (1967) 1984. Of Other Spaces, Heterotopias. *Architecture, Mouvement, Continuité* 5: 46-49. [Originally published as Des espaces autres, 1967.]

———. (1982) 1984. *Space, Knowledge and Power: In The Foucault Reader*, edited by P. Rabinow. London: Penguin.

———. (1976) 1990. *The History of Sexuality – Volume 1: An Introduction*, translated by R. Hurley. New York: Random House. [Originally published as *Histoire de la sexualité 1 – La volonté de savoir*.]

———. (1976) 2001. 169 — Questions à Michel Foucault sur la géographie. In *Dits et écrits Tome 2–1976–1988*, edited by Daniel Defert and François Lagrange, 28–40. Paris: Quatro, Gallimard.

———. (1969) 2002. *The Archaeology of Knowledge*, translated by A. M. S. Smith. Abingdon: Routledge. [Originally published as *L'archéologie du savoir*.]

———. (2004) 2007. *Security, Territory, Population: Lectures at the Collège de France, 1977–78*, edited by M. Senellart, translated by G. Burchell. Houndmills: Palgrave Macmillan. [Originally published as *Sécurité, territoire, population. Cours au Collège de France, 1977–1978.*]

Franquesa, Jaume. 2011. 'We've lost our bearings': Place, tourism, and the limits of the 'mobility turn'. *Antipode* 43(4): 1012–1033.

Frey, Jean-Pierre. 2000. La ville des architectes et des urbanistes. In *La ville et l'urbain: l'état des savoirs*, edited by T. Paquot, M. Lussault and S. Body-Gendrot, 106–114. Paris: Éditions de la découverte.

Gartman, David. 2004. Three ages of the automobile: The cultural logics of the car. *Theory Culture Society* 21: 169–195.

Gottdiener, Marc. 1985. *The Social Production of Urban Space*. Austin: University of Texas Press.

Graham, Stephen, and Simon Marvin. 2001. *Splintering Urbanism: Networked Infrastructures, Technological Mobilities and the Urban Condition*. London: Routledge.

Halprin, Lawrence. 1965. Motation. *Progessive Architecture* 46: 126–133.

Hénard, Eugène. 1903. *Études sur les transformations de Paris*. Paris: Librairies-imprimeries réunies.

Huxley, Margo. 2006. Spatial rationalities: Order, environment, evolution and government. *Social & Cultural Geography* 7(5): 771–787.

Jensen, Anne. 2011. Mobility, space and power: On the multiplicities of seeing mobility. *Mobilities* 6(2): 255–271.

Jensen, Ole B. 2009. Flows of meaning, cultures of movements – Urban mobility as meaningful everyday life practice. *Mobilities* 4(1): 139–158.

Kaufmann, Vincent. 2008. *Les paradoxes de la mobilité: Bouger, s'enraciner*. Lausanne: Presses polytechniques et universitaires romandes.

———. 2011. *Rethinking the City*. Lausanne: Routledge–EPFL Press.

Kaufmann, Vincent, Manfred Max Bergman and Joye Dominique. 2004. Motility: Mobility as capital. *International Journal of Urban and Regional Research* 28(4): 745–756.

Lannoy, Pierre, and Thierry Ramadier. 2007. *La mobilité généralisée: Formes et valeurs de la mobilité quotidienne*. Belgium: Academia Bruylant.

Le Corbusier. 1957. *La Charte d'Athènes*. Paris: Les Éditions de Minuit.

———. (1930) 1960. *Précisions sur un état présent de l'architecture et de l'urbanisme*. Paris: Vincent Fréal.

Loir, Christophe, and Laurent Turcot. 2011. *La promenade au tournant des XVIIIè et XIXè siècles*. Bruxelles: Éditions de l'Université de Bruxelles.

López de Aberasturi, Antonio. 2005. Pour une lecture de Cerdà – Le discours et ses histoires. In *La théorie générale de l'urbanisation*, edited by A. López de Aberasturi, translated by A. López de Aberasturi, 15–63. Paris: Éditions de l'Imprimeur.

Lynch, Kevin. 1960. *The Image of the City*. Cambridge, MA: MIT Press.

Mom, Gijs. 2003. What kind of transport history did we get? Half a century of JTH and the future of the field. *The Journal of Transport History* 24(2): 121–138.

Mom, Gijs, and David A. Kirsch. 2001. Technologies in tension: Horses, electric trucks, and the motorization of American cities, 1900–1925. *Technology and Culture* 42(3): 489–518.

Mom, Gijs, Gordon Pirie and Laurent Tissot. 2009. *Mobility in History – The State of the Art in the History of Transport, Traffic and Mobility.* Neuchatel: Éditions Alphil–Presses universitaires suisses.

Mumford, Lewis. 1961. *The City in History: Its Origins, Its Transformations, and Its Prospects.* New York: Harcourt, Brace & World.

Perriault, Jacques. 1981. La machine à vapeur. *Culture Technique* 2: 124–137.

Pinol, Jean-Luc. 2003. *Histoire de l'Europe urbaine: Volume 1: De l'Antiquité au XVIIIè siècle.* Paris: Éditions du Seuil.

Pløger, John. 2008. Foucault's *dispositif* and the city. *Planning Theory* 7(1): 51–70.

Rabinow, Paul. (1989) 1995. *French Modern: Norms and Forms of the Social Environment.* Chicago: University of Chicago Press.

Relph, Edward. 1987. *The Modern Urban Landscape.* Baltimore, MD: Johns Hopkins University Press.

Rousseau, Max. 2008. La ville comme machine à mobilité: Capitalisme, urbanisme et gouvernement des corps. *Métropoles* 3: 181–206.

Rousseau, Pierre. 1961. *Histoire des transports.* Paris: Fayard.

Salter, Mark B. 2013. To make move and let stop: Mobility and the assemblage of circulation. *Mobilities* 8(1): 7–19.

Schivelbusch, Wolfgang. 1986. *The Railway Journey: The Industrialization of Time and Space in the 19th Century.* Berkeley: University of California Press.

Sennett, Richard. 1994. *Flesh and Stone: The Body and the City in Western Civilization.* New York: Norton.

Sheller, Mimi. 2011. Mobility. *Sociopedia* 1–12.

Sheller, Mimi, and John Urry. 2000. The city and the car. *International Journal of Urban and Regional Research* 24: 737–757.

———. 2006. The new mobilities paradigm. *Environment and Planning A* 38(2): 207–226.

Sitte, Camillo. (1889) 1965. *City Planning According to Artistic Principles*, translated by G. R. Collins and C. C. Collins. New York: Random House.

Smith, Merritt Roe, and Leo Marx. 1995. *Does Technology Drive History? The Dilemma of Technological Determinism.* Cambridge: MIT Press.

Sparke, Penny. 2008. Mobility history from a design historian's perspective: The T^{2}M Conference, 2007. *The Journal of Transport History* 29(1): 131–135.

Turcot, Laurent. 2007. *Le promeneur à Paris au XVIIIè siècle.* Paris: Gallimard–Le promeneur.

Unwin, Raymond. 1909. *Town Planning in Practice: An Introduction to the Art of Designing Cities and Suburbs.* London: T. F. Unwin.

Urry, John. 2000. *Sociology beyond Societies: Mobilities for the Twenty First Century.* London: Routledge.

———. 2008. Moving on the Mobility Turn. In *Tracing Mobilities: Towards a Cosmopolitan Perspective*, edited by W. Canzler, V. Kaufmann and S. Kesselring, 13–24. Burlington, VT: Ashgate.

Vaillancourt, Daniel. 2009. *Les urbanités parisiennes au XVIIè siècle – Le livre du trottoir.* Quebec: Les Presses de l'Université Laval.

Wiel, Marc. 2005. *Ville et mobilité: Un couple infernal?* Paris: Éditions de l'Aube.

Wolff, Pauline. 2015. Du transport à la mobilité: Pour une remise en question épistémologique. In *Mobilité et exclusion, quelles relations?*, edited by S. Lord, P. Negron and J. Torres, 21–48. Quebec: Presses de l'Université de Laval.

Wright, Frank Lloyd. 1958. *The Living City.* New York: Horizon Press.

Index

For Product Safety Concerns and Information please contact our EU
representative GPSR@taylorandfrancis.com Taylor & Francis Verlag GmbH,
Kaufingerstraße 24, 80331 München, Germany

Printed and bound by CPI Group (UK) Ltd, Croydon, CR0 4YY
08/05/2025
01864522-0003